KT-583-797

HUTCHINSON POCKET

Dictionary of
Classical Music

Other titles in the Hutchinson Pocket series:

Pocket Chronology of World Events
Pocket Dictionary of Biology
Pocket Dictionary of Chemistry
Pocket Dictionary of Computing
Pocket Dictionary of First Names
Pocket Dictionary of Geography
Pocket Dictionary of Mathematics
Pocket Dictionary – On This Day
Pocket Dictionary of Physics
Pocket Dictionary of Quotations
Pocket Dictionary of Science
Pocket Dictionary of 20th Century World History
Pocket Guide to Countries of the World
Pocket Quiz Book

HUTCHINSON POCKET

Dictionary of
Classical Music

Helicon

Copyright © Helicon Publishing Ltd 1994

Helicon Publishing Ltd
42 Hythe Bridge Street
Oxford OX1 2EP

Printed and bound in Great Britain by
Unwin Brothers Ltd, Old Woking, Surrey

ISBN 0 09 178652 5

British Cataloguing in Publication Data

A catalogue record for this book is available
from the British Library

Introduction

This book is an invaluable pocket reference for anyone who appreciates or creates classical music.

The main aim is to reveal the facts and techniques of Western classical music as comprehensively and as clearly as possible. The book includes entries on composers, musicians, types of classical music, dynamics, theory, terminology, instruments, and techniques. But because music around the world is often interrelated, this Pocket dictionary gives a broader picture by also including general entries on: other forms of music such as jazz, opera, pop, country and western, rhythm and blues, and soul; dance such as polka, waltz, siciliano, and ballet; and non-Western instruments such as the sitar, tambura, and koto.

To complete the picture, cross-references are used when further, relevant information can be found at another entry, but where the reader may not otherwise think of looking.

Editorial director
Michael Upshall

Contributor
Tallis Barker

Project editor
Sheila Dallas

Text editor
Helen Maxey

Page make-up
Taurus Graphics

Production
Tony Ballsdon

A

ABA form in musical analysis, a compositional structure comprising three basic parts, in which the first section (A) is followed by a second, often contrasting section (B), before the original section (A) returns in the same or a varied state. A simple kind of ◊ternary form.

Abbado Claudio 1933– . Italian conductor. He became principal director of the Vienna State Opera 1986 and the Berlin Philharmonic Orchestra 1989. Associated early in his career with the La Scala Opera, Milan, his wide-ranging repertoire includes a significant number of 20th-century composers, among them Schoenberg, Prokofiev, Janáček, Bartók, and Stockhausen. He has conducted the European Youth Orchestra from its inception 1977.

absolute pitch or *perfect pitch* the ability to sing or to recognize by sound the pitch of a note, without any prior reference point with which to determine the particular note.

a cappella (Italian 'in the style of the chapel') choral music sung without instrumental accompaniment. It is characteristic of medieval and Renaissance church music, and in more recent years, gospel music and the evangelical Christian church movement.

accelerando (Italian 'quickening') gradual increase in speed.

accent an emphasis on individual notes or passages. Accents are of three types: ◊dynamic, adding loudness; ◊agogic, enlarging the beat; and rhythmic, placing an emphasized note on a weak beat, as in ◊syncopation.

acciaccatura (Italian 'crushed') an ornamental ◊grace note played simultaneously with, or just before a normal note. Notated as a quaver in small type with a line through the stem, it is released almost instantaneously.

accidental a sharp, flat, or natural sign preceding a note which changes the pitch of the note by a semitone up (sharp), down (flat), or back to a note of the original key (natural).

Music written in 'black-note' keys may require the rarer double sharp and double flat signs, indicating a change in pitch of a full tone.

accompaniment music and musicians providing a bass line, chord structure, and beat in support of the melody. Accompaniment may be written out in full or in a shorthand version known as ◊figured bass, and is usually played on the piano, harpsichord, or organ, or by an orchestra.

accordion musical instrument, held in the arms and sounded by arm-operated bellows that cause metal reeds to vibrate. It is a type of ◊free-reed instrument. The right hand plays the melody on a piano-style key-board of 26–34 keys while the left hand has a system of push buttons for selecting single notes or chord harmonies.

Invented by Cyrill Damien (1772–1847) in Vienna 1829, the accordion spread throughout the world and can be heard in the popular music of Germany, France, China, Russia, and the USA.

acoustic played without electrical amplification or assistance (acoustic guitar or acoustic piano, for example); also used non-technically to describe room response to an instrument, an important factor in performance. For example, a so-called 'bright' acoustic provides a lively reverberation, a 'dry' acoustic lacks response, and a 'muddy' acoustic is one where response is excessive.

acoustics the science of sound generation and propagation. Sound is the ear's perception of a body that vibrates between 16 and 20,000 times per second. The components of sound are ◊pitch, which is dependent on the frequency of the vibration; loudness, which is dependent on the amplitude (strength) of the vibration; and timbre (tone quality), which depends on the complex structure of the vibration and its harmonics. In music, vibrations are generated by hitting an object, bowing a string, vibrating the lips, and forcing air past a reed or flue. Hence the percussion, string, brass, and woodwind families, respectively. Sound may also be generated by electronic synthesis.

action the internal mechanism of a keyboard instrument, such as the piano, harpsichord or organ, which links the keys to the strings or pipes when the keys are depressed. On a string instrument, it refers to the space between the strings and the ◊fingerboard.

adagio (Italian 'at ease', 'leisurely') a slow pace, slightly faster than or approximately the same as ◊lento, depending on the historical period in which the music was written.

Adam Adolphe Charles 1803–1856. French composer of light operas and founder of the Théâtre National, Paris, 1847. His stage works include *Le Postillion de Longjumeau/The Postillion of Longjumeau* 1836 and *Si j'étais roi/If I Were King* 1852, but he is best remembered for his ballet score for *Giselle* 1841. Some 80 of his works were staged.

Adam de la Halle *c.* 1240–*c.* 1290. French poet and composer. His *Jeu de Robin et Marion*, written in Italy about 1282, is a theatrical work with dialogue and songs set to what were apparently popular tunes of the day. It is sometimes called the forerunner of comic opera.

Adams John Coolidge 1947– . US composer and conductor. Adams was director of the New Music Ensemble 1972–81 and artistic adviser to the San Francisco Symphony Orchestra from 1978. His minimalist techniques are displayed in *Electric Wake* 1968, *Heavy Metal* 1971, *Bridge of Dreams* 1982, and the operas *Nixon in China* 1988 and *The Death of Klinghoffer* 1990.

Adler Larry 1914– . US musician. A virtuoso performer on the harmonica, he commissioned the English composer Vaughan Williams's *Romanza in D flat* 1951.

ad lib(itum) (Latin 'at liberty') allowing a musician free interpretation of tempo or rhythm, or of the notes themselves, as in an improvized ◊cadenza. Alternatively, it allows freedom to omit a passage or an instrument.

Aeolian harp wind-blown instrument consisting of a shallow soundbox supporting gut strings at low tension and tuned to the same pitch. It produces an eerie harmony that rises and falls with the changing pressure of the wind. It is mentioned in Greek legend, but was not developed until the 17th century and not popularized in parts of Europe until the 19th century. Variants of it exist in the Far East.

aeolian mode mode or scale A–G, centred around and beginning on A, which uses only the notes of the C major scale.

agitato (Italian 'agitated') energetic, excited expression. If not part of the initial tempo designation (for example, *allegro agitato*), it implies a faster tempo than the preceding material.

agogic a musical accent, affecting pulse and rhythm rather than dynamics, increasing the duration of a particular note. 'Agogic' also applies more broadly to other types of rhythm-related expression, such as ◊rubato.

agréments ◊ornamentation of 17th-century French music, adopted as standard notation throughout Europe later in the Baroque period.

air a melody or song. Alternative spelling of ◊ayre.

Albéniz Isaac 1860–1909. Spanish composer and pianist. Born in Catalonia, he was a nationalist. His works include numerous ◊zarzuelas and operas, the orchestral suites *Española* 1886 and *Catalonia* 1908 (with the assistance of Paul Dukas), and some 250 piano works including the *Iberia* suite. Much of his work reflects the folk rhythms and melodies of his native country.

Albinoni Tomaso 1671–1751. Italian Baroque composer. He wrote over 40 operas and numerous sonatas and *concerti à cinque* (concertos in five parts) for oboe, trumpet, bassoon, violin, organ, and strings, which helped to establish Baroque orchestral style. His work was studied and adapted by J S Bach.

The popular *Adagio*, often described as being by Albinoni, was actually composed from a fragment of original manuscript by his biographer, the Italian musicologist Remo Giazotto (1910–).

Aldeburgh Festival annual festival of operas and other concerts, established in 1948 at Aldeburgh, Suffolk. The events have centred on the works of Benjamin Britten, who lived at Aldeburgh, and take place at *The Maltings*, a concert hall at nearby Snape. First performances of Britten's works to be given here include the operas *A Midsummer Night's Dream* 1960 and *Death in Venice* 1973.

aleatory music or *mobile form* (from Latin *alea* 'dice') a style of composition practised by certain postwar avant-garde composers, in which the performer or conductor chooses the order of succession of the composed pieces. Examples of aleatory music include Pierre Boulez's *Piano Sonata No 3* 1957, Earle Brown's *Available Forms I* 1961, and Stockhausen's *Momente/Moments* 1972.

Aleatory music is distantly related to the 18th-century 'musical dice game' and to the freely assembled music for silent movies using theme catalogues by Giuseppe Becce and others. The use by John Cage of dice and the I Ching differs in that chance procedures are used during the stage of composition rather than that of performance.

Alkan pseudonym of Charles Valentin Morhange 1813–1888. French composer and piano virtuoso. His formidably difficult piano pieces were neglected until the 1970s. Works include *Grande Sonate: les quatre âges* 1848 and 12 *Etudes* 1857 in every minor key, of which numbers 4–7 constitute a symphony for piano solo and numbers 8–10 a concert for piano solo.

alla breve or *cut time* of tempo, indicating that the minim rather than the crotchet is the basic unit of the beat in a bar of two beats.

allargando (Italian 'broadening') gradual slowing down, maintaining a full tone quality.

allegretto moderately quick, but not as fast as ◊allegro.

Allegri Gregorio 1582–1652. Italian Baroque composer. Allegri was *maestro di cappella* (chapel master) of the Sistine Chapel, Rome 1610–29. His output of sacred music includes Magnificats, motets, and the celebrated *Miserere mei* (Psalm 51) for nine voices, written for the exclusive use of the Chapel until it was transcribed from memory by Mozart 1770, when he was 14.

allegro (Italian 'merry', 'lively') a lively or quick tempo for a passage, movement, or composition of music. It may be used as a title to a work of this character.

allemande (from French '*danse allemande*' meaning 'German dance') a medium-paced dance with four beats in a bar, originating in Germany in the 16th century, which became established as the opening movement of the Baroque suite.

alphorn wind instrument consisting of a straight wooden tube terminating in a conical endpiece with an upturned bell, up to 4 m/12 ft in length. It has a mouthpiece similar to a ♭cornet. It is used to summon cattle and to serenade tourists in Switzerland, Scandinavia, and the highlands of central Europe. It has no valves and therefore can only play a restricted range of notes rather than the full ♭chromatic scale.

altered chord a chord in which one of the notes is raised or lowered a semitone. The chord then includes augmented (enlarged) or diminished (contracted) intervals. Altered chords are often used in the ♭modulation of keys.

alto (Italian 'high') voice or instrument between soprano and tenor (approximate range G3– D5). The traditional male alto voice of early opera, as revived by English singer James Bowman (1941–   ), also known as *countertenor*, is trumpetlike and penetrating; the low-register female *contralto* ('contra-alto'), exemplified by Kathleen Ferrier, is rich and mellow in tone. Alto instruments, playing at a lower register than the standard, or soprano, instrument of the same family, include the flute, clarinet, and saxophone.

alto clef C clef in which middle C is represented by the 3rd line of a 5-line stave. It was used by musicians and singers until the 18th century and is now used most commonly by viola players.

Alwyn William 1905–1985. English composer. Professor of composition at the Royal Academy of Music 1926–55, he wrote film music (*Desert Victory, The Way Ahead*) and composed symphonies and chamber music.

Amati Italian family of violinmakers working in Cremona about 1550–1700. Nicolò Amati (1596–1684) taught Andrea ♭Guarneri and Antonio ♭Stradivari. Nicolò's grandfather Andrea Amati (*c.*1520–*c.*1580) brought the violin to its classic form.

Ambrosian chant in Christian church music, a reformed chant or ♭plainsong introduced by St Ambrose in the 4th century. The number of available modes (scales) was reduced to four; the interval of the fifth was established as the basis of tonal music: a higher ♭dominant was established at the fifth, around which the chant was elaborated. Ambrosian chant retains many features of Middle Eastern religious chant.

anacrusis alternative term for ◊upbeat.

Anda Geza 1921–1976. Hungarian-born Swiss pianist and conductor. He excelled at Brahms, Bartók, and Mozart, whose piano concertos he conducted from the keyboard, inserting his own ◊cadenzas. His playing was noted for its clarity and subtle nuances.

andante (Italian 'going', 'walking') walking pace; that is, a moderate tempo. It is sometimes used as a title to a work of this tempo.

andantino a modification of ◊andante. Interpretation of the term has varied; it is not clear whether it denotes a faster or slower tempo than andante. Beethoven himself was unsure as to the meaning. Most recent composers intend a faster tempo.

Anderson Marian 1902–1993. US contralto. Her voice was remarkable for its range and richness. She toured Europe 1930, but in 1939 she was barred from singing at Constitution Hall, Washington DC, because she was black. In 1955 she sang at the Metropolitan Opera, the first black singer to appear there. In 1958 she was appointed an alternate (deputizing) delegate to the United Nations.

Anglican chant a form of ◊plainsong used by the Anglican church to set psalms, canticles (when they are not sung in a more elaborate setting), or other religious texts to music. It is usually sung in unison and with a free rhythm, based upon the inherent rhythm of the language. It may be accompanied by an organ, establishing a harmonic framework.

anima Italian 'soul'; as in *con anima*, meaning that the music should be played 'with soul'. It is often confused with ◊animato, which is concerned primarily with a faster tempo.

animando (Italian 'animating') gradual increase of tempo, in the manner of accelerando.

animato (Italian 'animated') immediate increase of tempo, not a gradual one as in ◊animando.

Ansermet Ernest 1883–1969. Swiss conductor. Ansermet performed with Diaghilev's Russian Ballet 1915–23. In 1918 he founded the Swiss

Romande Orchestra, conducting many first performances of works by Stravinsky.

antecedent in musical analysis, a phrase or passage which is followed by a complementary ◊consequent phrase. Antecedent/consequent phrases are also known as 'question/answer' phrases. Compositions favouring this technique are associated most closely with the Classical period.

Antheil George 1900–1959. US composer and pianist. He is known for his *Ballet mécanique* 1926, scored for anvils, aeroplane propellers, electric bells, car horns, and pianos. His later works, which became more conservative, include symphonies, ballets, and operas.

anthem a short, usually elaborate, composition sung by the choir in Protestant church services, generally with organ accompaniment. The Tudor composers developed it from the Catholic motet and it was given more complex forms by later composers, such as Purcell and Handel. Anthems continued to be composed during the 19th and 20th centuries and it remains a living musical form.

antiphon choral music in Greek or Roman liturgy, often chanted, involving the exchange of responses between solo voice and choir, or between choral groups, hence ◊antiphony.

antiphony music using widely spaced choirs or groups of instruments to create perspectives in sound. The form was developed in 16th-century Venice by Giovanni Gabrieli and in Germany by his pupil Heinrich Schütz and Roland de Lassus; an example is the double choir motet *Alma Redemptoris Mater* 1604. The practice was revived in the 20th century by Bartók, Stockhausen, and Berio.

appoggiatura or *leaning note* a type of ◊grace note, of varying length, occurring on a strong beat, which creates a ◊dissonance which is resolved by the melody moving a note lower. It was a form of ◊ornamention used in the 17th and 18th centuries, and to a more limited extent in the 19th century.

arabesque title of a piece characterized by florid or ornamental melody. Debussy and Schumann wrote famous arabesques.

arco (Italian 'with the bow') a direction to play with the bow, or to resume playing with the bow after playing ◊pizzicato (plucked string).

aria (Italian 'air') melodic solo song, often of reflective character, usually in ◊ternary form, expressing a moment of truth in the action of an opera or oratorio. Pioneered by Giacomo Carissimi, it became a set piece for virtuoso opera singers, for example Handel's aria 'Where'er you walk' from the secular oratorio *Semele* 1744 to words by William Congreve (1670–1729). As an instrumental character piece, it is melodious and imitative of a vocal line.

arioso a type of ◊recitative (sung narration), of more lyrical than speech-like quality. Some composers use the arioso to initiate or conclude a recitative, such as Bach in his cantata *Ein feste Burg/A Safe Stronghold* 1724. It can also refer to a section or passage in an instrumental work, which imitates recitative, as in Beethoven's Piano Sonata No. 31 1821.

armonica alternative name for the glass ◊harmonica.

Arne Thomas Augustus 1710–1778. English composer. Arne composed incidental music for theatre, and introduced opera in the Italian manner to the London stage with works such as *Artaxerxes* 1762 (revised 1777). He is remembered for the songs 'Where the bee sucks' from *The Tempest* 1746, 'Blow, blow thou winter wind' from *As You Like It* 1740, and 'Rule Britannia!' from the masque *Alfred* 1740.

Arnold Malcolm (Henry) 1921– . English composer. His work is tonal and includes a large amount of orchestral, chamber, ballet, and vocal music. His overtures *Beckus the Dandipratt* 1948, *A Sussex Overture* 1951, and *Tam O'Shanter* 1955 are well known. His operas include *The Dancing Master* 1951, and he has written music for more than 80 films, including *The Bridge on the River Kwai* 1957, for which he won an Academy Award.

arpeggio (Italian 'like a harp') the spreading of a chord to sound like a rapid succession of notes, usually from low to high.

It is a technique frequently used in keyboard and guitar playing. The term 'arpeggio' is found in early keyboard music, for example in J S Bach's *Chromatic Fantasia and Fugue* 1720 (revised 1730).

arranger one who adapts, transcribes, or assists in orchestrating the music of another composer. The use of an arranger became established in Hollywood; Rachmaninov, George Gershwin, and Leonard Bernstein, among others, composed concert works employing such assistance.

Notable arrangements include those by J S Bach (of Vivaldi), Mozart (Handel's *Messiah*), and Stravinsky (Tchaikovsky and Pergolesi).

Arrau Claudio 1903–1991. Chilean-born US pianist. A concert performer from the age of five, he specialized in 19th-century music and was known for his magisterial interpretations of Chopin, Beethoven, and Brahms.

ars antiqua (Latin 'old art') music of the Middle Ages, generally lacking ◊counterpoint. It includes ◊plainsong and ◊organum composed in France during the 12th and 13th centuries.

arsis (Greek 'lifting') alternative term, borrowed from Greek poetry, for ◊upbeat. The opposite of *thesis* (Greek 'lowering') or ◊downbeat. In German usage, however, *arsis* and *thesis* have opposite meanings to the original Greek and English words.

ars nova (Latin 'new art') music composed in France and Italy during the 14th century. Originally introduced by Philippe de Vitry, it is distinguished by rhythmic and harmonic variety, and the increased importance of duple time (two beats in a bar) and independent voice parts. Guillaume Machaut mastered the style in France. In Italy the ◊madrigal grew out of ars nova.

Ashkenazy Vladimir 1937– . Russian- born pianist and conductor. Ashkenazy was music director of the Royal Philharmonic, London, from 1987 and of the Berlin Radio Symphony Orchestra from 1989. He excels in Rachmaninov, Prokofiev, and Liszt.

After studying in Moscow, he toured the USA 1958. In 1962 he was joint winner (with English pianist John Ogdon) of the Tchaikovsky Competition.

a tempo (Italian 'in time') directing a return to the original tempo. It is often found after ◊accelerando or ◊ritardando.

atonality music in which the sense of ◊tonality is obscured; music of no apparent key. Atonality is often used by film and television composers for situations of mystery or horror; they exploit dissonance for its power to disturb.

For Schoenberg, pioneer of atonal music from 1908, the intention was to liberate tonal expression and not primarily to disturb, and he rejected the term 'atonality' as misleading, preferring 'pantonality' instead. Exponents of atonality include Berg, Webern, Stockhausen, and Boulez.

Auber Daniel François Esprit 1782–1871. French opera composer. Auber studied under the Italian composer and teacher Luigi Cherubini. He wrote about 50 operas, including *La Muette de Portici/The Mute Girl of Portici* 1828 and the comic opera *Fra Diavolo* 1830.

augmentation the enlarging of time values of a musical figure, or melodic idea, so that it recurs in a slower, more dignified form; used especially in ◊counterpoint in order to combine the figure with others of smaller time values. Opposite of ◊diminution.

Auric Georges 1899–1983. French composer. His works include a comic opera, several ballets, and incidental music to films including Jean Cocteau's *Orphée/Orpheus* 1950. He was one of the musical group called Les Six, who were influenced by Erik Satie.

authentic cadence or *perfect cadence* or *full close* harmonic progression or modulation ending with a ◊dominant harmony followed by ◊tonic.

authenticity a trend, beginning with the ◊Dolmetsch family in the early years of this century and gaining momentum in the postwar period, which aims to reproduce the performance of ◊early music, using original instruments or copies. It has stimulated important practical research in manuscript editing and transcription, instrumentmaking, dance, architectural acoustics, and vocal techniques.

ayre antiquated spelling of *air*, 16th-century verse song with lute or guitar accompaniment, as in *It was a lover and his lass* 1600 by Thomas Morley.

B

Babbitt Milton 1916–   . US composer and mathematics theorist. Babbitt pioneered the application of information theory to music in the 1950s, introducing set theory to ◊series manipulations and the term 'pitch class' to define every octave identity of a note name. His works include four string quartets, works for orchestra, *Philomel* for soprano and electronic tape 1964, and *Ensembles for Synthesizer* 1967, both composed using the 1960 ◊RCA Mark II synthesizer, which he helped to design.

Bach Carl Philip Emmanuel 1714–1788. German composer, second son of J S Bach. He was among the first composers to introduce a new homophonic style, and he helped to develop ◊sonata form, influencing Mozart, Haydn, and Beethoven.

In the service of Frederick the Great 1740–67, he left to become master of church music at Hamburg 1768. He wrote over 200 pieces for keyboard instruments, and published an important treatise on playing the piano. Through his music and concert performances he helped to establish a leading solo role for the piano in Western music.

Bach Johann Christian 1735–1782. German composer, the 11th son of J S Bach. J C Bach became celebrated in Italy as a composer of operas. In 1762 he was invited to London, where he became music master to the royal family. He remained in England until his death, enjoying great popularity both as composer and performer.

Bach Johann Sebastian 1685–1750. German composer. He is the most impressive of the distinguished Bach family. A master of ◊counterpoint, his music epitomizes the Baroque polyphonic style. His orchestral music includes the six *Brandenburg Concertos* 1721 and other concertos for keyboard instrument and violin, four orchestral suites, sonatas for various instruments, six violin partitas and six unaccompanied cello suites. Bach's keyboard music, for clavier and organ, his fugues, and his choral music are of equal importance. He also wrote chamber music and songs.

Born at Eisenach, Bach became a chorister at Lüneburg when he was 15, and at 19 he was organist at Arnstadt. His appointments included positions at the courts of Weimar and Anhalt-Köthen, and from 1723 until his death he was musical director at St Thomas's choir school in Leipzig. He married twice and had over 20 children (although several died in infancy). His second wife, Anna Magdalena Wülkens, was a soprano; she also worked for him when his sight failed in later years.

Bach's sacred music includes 200 church cantatas; the Easter and Christmas oratorios 1735; the two great Passions, of St Matthew and St John, first performed 1723 and 1729, and the Mass in B minor 1749. His keyboard music includes a collectio of 48 preludes and fugues known as *Das wohltemperierte Clavier/The Well-Tempered Clavier* 1742, the *Goldberg Variations* 1742, and the *Italian Concerto* 1735. Of his organ music the finest examples are the chorale preludes. Two works written in his later years illustrate the principles and potential of his polyphonic art – *Das Musikalische Opfer/The Musical Offering* 1747 and *Die Kunst der Fuge/The Art of Fugue*, published posthumously 1751.

Bach Wilhelm Friedemann 1710–1784. German composer, the eldest son of J S Bach. He was also an organist, improviser, and master of ◊counterpoint.

background music accompanying music for a stage or film production which serves to establish a mood or stimulate appropriate audience responses. It differs from ◊incidental music in not being part of the action, and in working on the listener subliminally, as in the use of piped music in today's shopping malls.

Badura-Skoda Paul 1927–   . Austrian pianist. He has recorded on both the ◊fortepiano and the modern piano, particularly the work of Mozart, and his playing is noted for its concern with authentic interpretation (see ◊authenticity).

bagatelle (French 'trifle') a short character piece, often for piano, of a light or humorous character. Examples include pieces by Couperin, Beethoven, and Dvořák.

bagpipes any of an ancient family of double-reed folk woodwind instruments employing a bladder or bellows as an air reservoir to a 'chanter' or melody pipe, and optional 'drones' providing a continuous accompanying harmony.

Examples include the old French ◊musette, Scottish and Irish pipes, smaller Northumbrian pipes, Breton *biniou*, Spanish *gaita*, and numerous variants in Eastern Europe, the Middle East, and North Africa. The Highland bagpipes are the national instrument of Scotland. Bagpipes are known to have existed for at least 3,000 years.

Baillie Isobel 1895–1983. Scottish soprano. Born in Hawick, Scotland, she became celebrated for her work in oratorio. She was professor of singing at Cornell University in New York 1960–61.

Baker Janet 1933– . English mezzo-soprano. She is noted for the emotional strength and richness of her interpretations of songs, oratorio, and opera from Purcell to Britten, including a notable Dido in Purcell's *Dido and Aeneas* 1689. She retired from the stage 1981.

Balakirev Mily Alexeyevich 1837–1910. Russian composer. He wrote orchestral works including the fantasy *Islamey* 1869, piano music, songs, and a ◊symphonic poem *Tamara* 1882, all imbued with the Russian national character and spirit. He was leader of the group known as The ◊Five and taught its members, Mussorgsky, Cui, Rimsky-Korsakov, and Borodin.

Balakirev was born at Nizhni Novgorod. At St Petersburg he worked with Mikhail Glinka, established the Free School of Music 1862, which stressed the national element, and was director of the Imperial Chapel 1883–95.

balalaika Russian musical instrument, resembling a guitar. It has a triangular soundbox, frets, and two, three, or four strings, and is played by strumming the strings with the fingers.

Balfe Michael William 1808–1870. Irish composer and singer. He was a violinist and baritone at Drury Lane, London, when only 16. In 1825 he went to Italy, where he sang in Palermo and at La Scala, and in 1846 he was appointed conductor at Her Majesty's Theatre, London. His operas include *The Bohemian Girl* 1843.

ballad originally the title or music of a dancing song. By the 14th century it had lost its connection to dance and by the 16th century it designated a simple, narrative song. In the 19th century a ballad described a popular song, often of romantic nature.

ballet dramatic performance consisting of dancers (usually in costume and with scenery) and a musical accompaniment (usually orchestral) which does not normally include singing or spoken narration. The dancers (through their actions) and the music (through appropriate orchestration) combine to relate a story.

The ballet tradition can be traced to 15th-century France and Italy, when dance performances were held at special occasions and festivals. During the 16th and 17th centuries there was not always a clear distinction between opera and ballet, since ballet during this period often included singing, and operas often included dance. Ballet was developed significantly in the French court of Louis XIV (1638–1715), especially under the influence of Lully, the court composer (who was a dancer himself, as was the king). During this period many courtly dances originated, including the ◊gavotte, ◊passepied, ◊bourrée, and ◊minuet. During the 18th century, Vienna became an important centre of ballet and was instrumental in developing the dramatic aspect of the art, as opposed to only the athletic qualities, which also evolved considerably during this century. During the 19th century, public interest in ballet increased and Russia cultivated its own school. Composers of international reputation, such as Tchaikovsky wrote ballets, including *Swan Lake* 1889 and *The Nutcracker* 1891.

The modern era of ballet began 1909 with the founding of the touring dance company of Sergei Diaghilev (1872–1929), the Ballets Russes (Russian Ballet). Innovative choreography transformed the visual aspects of ballet, and striking new compositions by Debussy, Ravel, and especially Stravinsky (in, for example, *Le Sacre du Printemps/The Rite of Spring* 1913) left their mark not only on following ballet composers, but on the course of music history itself. Later in the century, the formal tradition of ballet was upset by the influence of jazz, jazz rhythms, and modern dance originating in the USA, which introduced greater freedom of bodily expression.

Today there exists a wide range of musical and choreographic styles, ranging from the classical to the popular. Many full ballet scores have been reduced by composers to ballet ◊suites or purely orchestral works, which incorporate the essential musical elements, tending to omit musically non-thematic and transitional passages which may be, nevertheless, essential to the choreography and visual narration. Examples include Stravinsky's *Firebird Suite* 1910 and Ravel's *Boléro* 1928.

band music group, usually falling into a special category: for example, *military*, comprising woodwind, brass, and percussion; *brass*, solely brass and percussion; *marching*, a variant of brass; *dance* and *swing*, often like a small orchestra; *jazz*, with no fixed instrumentation; *rock* and *pop*, generally electric guitar, bass, and drums, variously augmented; and *steel*, from the West Indies, in which percussion instruments made from oil drums sound like marimbas.

In earlier times, 'band' could denote any combination of instruments, especially of highly skilled musicians. For example, Lully's *La Grande Bande*, and the 24 fiddles of Charles II, known as 'The King's Private Band'.

banjo resonant stringed musical instrument, with five strings, a long fretted neck, and circular drum-type ◊soundbox covered on the topside only by stretched skin (now usually plastic). It is played with either the fingers or a plectrum.

The banjo originated in the American South among black slaves (based on a similar instrument of African origin), and is today associated most strongly with American folk music.

It was introduced to Britain 1846, and greatly popularized by George Formby (1904–1961) using the ukelele-banjo.

Bantock Granville 1868–1946. English composer and conductor; professor of music at the University of Birmingham 1908–34. His works include the oratorio *Omar Khayyám* 1909, *Hebridean Symphony* 1915, and *Pagan Symphony* 1928. As a conductor, he was one of the first to introduce the music of Sibelius to the UK.

bar (US *measure*) segment of music incorporating usually a fixed number of beats, as in the phrase 'two/three/four beats to the bar'. Bars are shown in notation by the presence of vertical lines dividing the horizontal musical continuum.

Barber Samuel 1910–1981. US composer. Associated with a lyric, romantic, or sometimes astringent style, his works include *Adagio for Strings* 1936 and the opera *Vanessa* 1958, which won one of his two Pulitzer prizes. Another Barber opera, *Antony and Cleopatra* 1966, was commissioned for the opening of the new Metropolitan Opera House at Lincoln Center, New York City. His later works include *The Lovers* 1971.

Barbirolli John 1899–1970. English conductor. Noted for his interpretation of Vaughan Williams and Sibelius symphonies, Barbirolli trained as a cellist, and succeeded Toscanini as conductor of the New York Philharmonic Orchestra 1937–43. He was conductor of the Hallé Orchestra, Manchester, England, 1943–70.

barcarolle a song of the type sung by Venetian gondoliers. The barcarolle is always in moderate duple time (6/8 or 12/8), with a swaying rhythm. Instrumental barcarolles also exist, for example Chopin's *Barcarolle* 1846.

bard a Celtic minstrel who, in addition to composing songs usually at a court, often held important political posts. Originating in the pre-Christian era, bards were persecuted in Wales during the 13th century on political grounds. Since the 19th century annual meetings and competitions in Wales have attempted to revive the musical tradition of the bard.

Barenboim Daniel 1942– . Argentinian-born Israeli pianist and conductor. Pianist-conductor with the English Chamber Orchestra from 1964, he became conductor of the New York Philharmonic Orchestra 1970 and musical director of the Orchestre de Paris 1975. As a pianist he specializes in the solo works of Beethoven and chamber music; as a conductor he has extended into 19th- and 20th-century French music, including Boulez.

He was married to the cellist Jacqueline Du Pré.

baritone male voice pitched between bass and tenor (approximate range G2–F4), well-suited to lieder. The name is also applied to certain instruments playing at a higher register than the bass instrument within the same family. The baritone horn or saxophone are examples.

Dietrich Fischer-Dieskau and Hermann Prey (1929–) are well-known baritone singers.

Baroque music of the period following the Renaissance and preceding the Classical periods, lasting from about 1600 to the deaths of Bach and Handel in the 1750s. Baroque music is characterized by contrapuntal independence of voices and instrumental parts, as epitomized by the ◊fugue, which flourished during these years; the development of ◊continuo writing, specifically the ◊figured bass, as an accompaniment to a melody line or orchestral parts; the ◊concertante style of contrasting effects, both instrumental (as in the ◊concerto grosso) and dynamic (for example, from forte (loud) to piano (soft), in the manner of an echo); the importance of melodic ◊ornamentation; the grounding of ◊tonic and ◊dominant as primary harmonies; and the establishment of four-bar phrases as a compositional norm. Baroque Composers include Pachelbel, Bach, Handel, Vivaldi, Frescobaldi, and Monteverdi (in his later works).

barrel organ portable pipe organ, played by turning a handle. The handle works a pump and drives a replaceable cylinder upon which music is embossed as a pattern of ridges controlling the passage of air to the pipes.

It is often confused with the barrel or street piano used by buskers, which employed a barrel-and-pin mechanism to control a piano hammer action.

The barrel organ was a common entertainment and parish church instrument in England during the 18th and 19th centuries.

Bartók Béla 1881–1945. Hungarian composer and pianist. His musical works are influenced by folk music (a subject he spent his life researching) and often involve mathematical concepts of tonal and rhythmic proportion. He combines a Baroque rigour regarding ◊counterpoint with often harsh dissonances. His large output includes six string quartets, a *Divertimento* for string orchestra 1939, concertos for piano, violin, and viola, and the *Concerto for Orchestra* 1945, a one- act opera *Duke Bluebeard's Castle* 1918, and graded teaching pieces for piano *Mikrokosmos* 1939.

A child prodigy, Bartók studied music at the Budapest Conservatory, later working with Zoltan Kodály in recording and transcribing folk music of Hungary and adjoining countries. He was a virtuoso pianist, and his first two piano concertos, which are technically difficult, were written for himself to play. His ballet *The Miraculous Mandarin* 1919 was banned because of its subject matter (it was set in a brothel). Bartók died in the USA, having fled from Hungary 1940.

baryton complex bowed stringed instrument producing an intense singing tone. It is based on an 18th-century viol and modified by the addition of ♭sympathetic strings, which add resonance.

The baryton was a favourite instrument of Prince Nicholas Esterházy, the patron of Haydn, who, to please him, wrote many trios for violin, baryton, and cello.

bass the lowest male voice (approximate range C2–D4). The best-known bass singers have been the Russians Fyodor Chaliapin and Boris Christoff. The term also covers the bass instrument of a consort or family, for example bass clarinet, bass tuba, and bassoon, having a similar range. An instrument an octave lower than bass is a ***contrabass***.

bass clef F clef in which the F below middle C is represented as the second line from the top of the 5-line stave. Instruments with a range below middle C use bass clef, including double bass, tuba, and piano (left hand).

bass drum the largest drum of the orchestra or military band, with notes of indeterminate pitch, consisting of a cylindrical wooden body with two drumming surfaces (of hide or plastic). It is usually placed upright and drummed from the side.

bass drum

basset horn musical woodwind instrument, a wide-bore alto clarinet pitched in F, invented about 1765 and used by Mozart in his *Masonic Funeral Music* 1785, for example, and by Richard Strauss. It was revived 1981 by Stockhausen and features prominently as a solo in the opera cycle *LICHT/LIGHT*. Performers include Alan Hacker (1938–   ).

basso continuo (Italian 'continuous bass')   bassoon
full term for ◊continuo.

bassoon double-reed woodwind instrument
in B flat, the bass of the oboe family. It doubles
back on itself in a tube about 2.5 m/7.5 ft long
and has a rich and deep tone. The bassoon concert repertoire extends from the early Baroque,
from Vivaldi and Mozart, to the 20th century,
including Paul Dukas and Stockhausen.

The bassoon was developed from the
Renaissance ◊curtal about 1660 as a continuo
instrument for providing bassline support.
Further development in the 18th century led to
the *double bassoon* or *contrabassoon*, an
octave lower. Both instruments demonstrate an
agility humorously at variance with their low
pitch range and rich, glowing tone, but are also
capable of dignified solos at high register,
famously in the eerie opening bars of
Stravinsky's ballet *The Rite of Spring* 1913.

baton stick used by a conductor to control the
orchestra. Typically, the baton is held in the
right hand and is used in order to make the
conductor's signals more apparent. Generally,
conductors do not use a baton when working
with choirs or small instrumental ensembles.
Earliest records of the baton date to the Sistine
Chapel during the 15th century, when the conductor used a roll of paper to beat time. Lully
used a large cane. During the 19th century the
first violinist waved his bow to conduct. The
modern baton seems to have originated in the early 19th century, with its
use by Beethoven and Mendelssohn.

Bax Arnold Edward Trevor 1883–1953. English composer. His works,
often influenced by the literature and landscape of Ireland, include seven

symphonies and *The Garden of Fand* 1916 and *Tintagel* 1919 (both ◊symphonic poems). He was ◊Master of the King's Musick 1942–53.

Bayreuth town in Bavaria, S Germany, where opera festivals are held every summer. It was the home of composer Richard Wagner, and the Festspielhaus was established 1876 as a performing centre for his operas.

The Festspielhaus introduced new concepts of opera house design, including provision of an enlarged orchestra pit extending below the stage and projecting the sound outwards and upwards.

beat a pulsation giving the tempo, for example a conductor's beat, or a unit of tempo, as in 'four beats to the bar'.

beat frequency in ◊acoustics, a periodic fluctuation of tone intensity, produced when two notes of nearly equal pitch are heard together. Beats result from the interactions between the sound waves of the notes. The frequency of the beats equals the difference in frequency of the notes. Musicians use the effect when tuning their instruments.

bebung (German 'trembling') musical vibrato achieved on the clavichord by a rapid fluctuation of finger pressure on a depressed key.

Bechstein Friedrich Wilhelm Carl 1826-1900. German piano maker. He founded his own firm 1856, after having worked as an employee of several other companies. It expanded rapidly, taking advantage of new technological developments, some of which were invented by ◊Steinway. The company was bankrupt 1993, but was saved by the intervention of the German government. Bechstein pianos are noted for their smooth but not particularly brilliant tone.

Beecham Thomas 1879–1961. English conductor and impresario. He established the London Philharmonic Orchestra 1932 and Royal Philharmonic Orchestra 1946, and fostered the works of such composers as Delius, Sibelius, and Richard Strauss.

Beethoven Ludwig van 1770–1827. German composer and pianist. His mastery of musical expression in every genre made him the dominant influence on 19th-century music. Beethoven's repertoire includes concert overtures; the opera *Fidelio* 1814; five piano concertos and two for violin (one unfinished); 32 piano sonatas; 17 string quartets, and other chamber music; the Mass in D (*Missa solemnis*) 1824; and nine symphonies, as well as many youthful works. He usually played his own piano pieces and conducted his orchestral works, until he became deaf 1801.

Of his symphonies the best known are the Third (*Eroica*) 1804, originally intended to be dedicated to Napoleon with whom Beethoven became disillusioned, the Fifth 1808, the Sixth (*Pastoral*) 1808, and Ninth (*Choral*) 1824, which includes the passage from Schiller's *Ode to Joy* chosen as the national anthem of Europe.

Born in Bonn, the son and grandson of musicians, Beethoven became deputy organist at the court of the Elector of Cologne at Bonn before he was 12; later he studied under Haydn and possibly Mozart, whose influence dominated his early work. From 1809, he received a small allowance from aristocratic patrons.

Beethoven's career spanned the transition from Classicism to Romanticism. His early works are influenced by Haydn, but he soon established his own style, relying on motivic development and rhythmic vitality. The works of his so-called 'middle period' became increasingly lengthy and harmonically complex. Some of his late works, especially the string quartets, were virtually incomprehensible to his early-19th-century audience.

bel canto (Italian 'beautiful song') an 18th-century Italian style of singing with emphasis on elaborate technique, beautiful tone, and legato phrasing. The style reached its peak in the operas of Rossini, Donizetti, and Bellini. Instrumentalists strove to capture this quality of playing, starting in the 19th century.

bell musical instrument, of many sizes, comprising a suspended resonating vessel swung by a handle or from a pivoted frame to make contact with a beater which hangs inside the bell. *Church bells* are among the most massive structures to be cast in bronze in one piece; from high up in a steeple they can be heard for many miles (see ◊bell ringing). Their shape, a flared bowl with a thickened rim, is engineered to produce a mixture of clanging tones. Miniature ◊hand bells are tuned to resonate harmoniously. Orchestral *tubular bells*, of brass or steel, are tuned to a chromatic scale of pitches and are played by striking with a wooden mallet. A set of steeple bells played from a keyboard is called a ▷*carillon*.

bell in a woodwind or brass instrument, the enlarged opening at the opposite end of the tube from the mouthpiece.

Bellini Vincenzo 1801–1835. Italian composer. Known for his operas (he wrote little else), Bellini employs long, legato melodic lines, which are constructed from shorter symmetrical phrases. He collaborated with the tenor Giovanni Battista Rubini (1794–1854) in romantic evocations of classic themes, as in *La Sonnambula/The Sleepwalker* and *Norma*, both 1831. In *I Puritani/The Puritans* 1835, his last work, he discovered a new boldness and vigour of orchestral effect.

bell ringing or *campanology* the art of ringing church bells individually or in sequence by rhythmically drawing on a rope fastened to a wheel rotating the bell, so that it falls back and strikes in time. *Change ringing* is an English art, dating from the 17th century, of ringing a patterned sequence of permutations of 5–12 church bells, using one player to each bell.

Benjamin Arthur 1893–1960. Australian pianist and composer. He taught composition at the Royal College of Music in London from 1925, where Benjamin Britten was one of his pupils. His works include *Jamaican Rumba*, inspired by a visit to the West Indies 1937.

Benjamin George (William John) 1960– . British composer, conductor, and pianist. A pupil of Messiaen, his colourful and sonorous works include *Ringed by the Flat Horizon* 1980, *At First Light* 1982, *Antara* 1987, and *Cascade* 1990.

Bennett Richard Rodney 1936– . English composer. He has written jazz, film music, symphonies, and operas. His film scores for *Far from the Madding Crowd* 1967, *Nicholas and Alexandra* 1971, and *Murder on the Orient Express* 1974 all received Oscar nominations. His operas include *The Mines of Sulphur* 1963 and *Victory* 1970.

berceuse a lullaby, usually in the form of an instrumental piece in moderately relaxed duple time (6/8). The most famous example is Chopin's *Berceuse* 1844.

Berg Alban 1885–1935. Austrian composer. He studied under Arnold Schoenberg and developed a personal ◊twelve-tone idiom of great emotional and stylistic versatility, generally less severe than those of Schoenberg and Webern. For example, his lyrical Violin Concerto 1935 contains numerous references to a tonal underlay. His relatively small output includes two operas – *Wozzeck* 1925, a grim story of working-class life, and the unfinished *Lulu* 1935 – and chamber music incorporating coded references to friends and family.

Berio Luciano 1925– . Italian composer. His work combines ◊serialism and ◊indeterminacy with commedia dell'arte (16th- to 18th-century Italian comic theatre) and ◊antiphony, as in *Alleluiah II* 1958 for five instrumental groups. His prolific output includes nine *Sequenzas/Sequences* 1975 for various solo instruments or voice, *Sinfonia* 1969 for voices and orchestra, *Formazioni/Formations* 1987 for orchestra, and the opera *Un re in ascolto/A King Listens* 1984.

Berkeley Lennox (Randal Francis) 1903–1989. English composer. His works for the voice include *The Hill of the Graces* 1975, verses from Spenser's *Fairie Queene* set for eight-part unaccompanied chorus; and his operas *Nelson* 1953 and *Ruth* 1956.

Berlioz (Louis) Hector 1803–1869. French composer, conductor, and critic. One of the first great Romantic composers, much of his music was inspired by drama and literature and has a theatrical quality. His symphonic works reveal innovative techniques of orchestration, such as *Symphonie fantastique* 1831 and *Roméo et Juliette* 1839. He also wrote dramatic cantatas, including *La Damnation de Faust* 1846 and *L'Enfance du Christ* 1854; sacred music; and three operas.

Berlioz studied music at the Paris Conservatoire. He won the Prix de Rome 1830, and spent two years in Italy. In 1833 he married Harriet Smithson, an Irish actress working in Paris, but they separated 1842. After some years of poverty and public neglect, he went to Germany 1842 and conducted his own works. He subsequently visited Russia and England. In 1854 he married Marie Recio, a singer. His operas are *Benvenuto Cellini* 1838, *Les Troyens* 1858, and *Béatrice et Bénédict* 1862.

Bernstein Leonard 1918–1990. US composer, conductor, and pianist. He was one of the most energetic and versatile of US musicians in the

20th century. His works, which established a vogue for realistic, contemporary themes, often influenced by jazz harmonies and rhythms, include symphonies such as *The Age of Anxiety* 1949, ballets such as *Fancy Free* 1944, and scores for musicals, including *Wonderful Town* 1953, *West Side Story* 1957, and *Mass* 1971 in memory of President J F Kennedy.

From 1958 to 1970 he was musical director of the New York Philharmonic, where, as conductor, he revived the works of Mahler. Among his other works are the symphony *Jeremiah* 1944, the ballet *Facsimile* 1946, the musicals *Candide* 1956 and the *Chichester Psalms* 1965.

Biber Heinrich von 1644–1704. Bohemian composer and violinist. He was ◊kapellmeister (chapel master) at the archbishop of Salzburg's court. He composed a wide variety of music including 16 *Mystery Sonatas c.*1676 for violin; church music; the opera *Chi la dura la vince* 1687; and various pieces, for example the *Nightwatchman Serenade*.

binary form a composition in two, often symmetrical, sections. First common in Baroque music, the first section often modulates, usually to the ◊dominant. The second, which may or may not contrast with the first, returns to the ◊tonic.

Birtwistle Harrison 1934–   . English composer. A writer of avant-garde music, he has specialized in chamber music, for example, his chamber opera *Punch and Judy* 1967 and *Down by the Greenwood Side* 1969.

Birtwistle's early music was influenced by Stravinsky and by the medieval and Renaissance masters, and for many years he worked alongside Peter Maxwell Davies. Orchestral works include *The Triumph of Time* 1972 and *Silbury Air* 1977; he has also written operas including *The Mask of Orpheus* 1986 (with electronic music by *Barry Anderson* (1935–1987)) and *Gawain* 1991 a reworking of the medieval English poem 'Sir Gawain and the Green Knight'. His tape composition *Chronometer* 1972 (assisted by *Peter Zinovieff* (1934–   )) is based on clock sounds.

bitonality the simultaneous sounding of music in two different keys, as in Stravinsky's *Duo Concertante* 1932 for violin and piano, and much other 20th-century composition. Music of two or more simultaneous keys employs ◊polytonality.

Bizet Georges (Alexandre César Léopold) 1838–1875. French composer. His style is marked by distinctive melody and instrumental colour. He is best known for his operas, among them *Les Pêcheurs de perles/The Pearl Fishers* 1863 and *La Jolie Fille de Perth/The Fair Maid of Perth* 1866. He also wrote the concert overture *Patrie* and incidental music to *L'Arlésienne/The Woman of Arle* by novelist Alphonse Daudet (1840–1897). His operatic masterpiece *Carmen* was produced a few months before his death 1875.

Bliss Arthur (Drummond) 1891–1975. English composer and conductor. He became Master of the Queen's Musick 1953. Among his works, which show an influence of Stravinsky and other contemporaries working in France, are *A Colour Symphony* 1922; music for the ballets *Checkmate* 1937, *Miracle in the Gorbals* 1944, and *Adam Zero* 1946; an opera *The Olympians* 1949; and dramatic film music, including *Things to Come* 1935. In 1918 he conducted the first performance of Stravinsky's *Ragtime* 1918.

Blitzstein Marc 1905–1964. US composer. Born in Philadelphia, he was a child prodigy as a pianist at the age of six. He served with the US Army 8th Air Force 1942–45, for which he wrote *The Airborne* 1946, a choral symphony. His operas include *The Cradle Will Rock* 1937. He used Neo-Classicism and jazz in his compositions.

Bloch Ernest 1880–1959. Swiss-born US composer. Among his works are the lyrical drama *Macbeth* 1910, *Schelomo* 1916 for cello and orchestra, five string quartets, and *Suite Hébraique* 1953 for viola and orchestra. He often used themes based on Jewish liturgical music and folk song.

Blomdahl Karl-Birger 1916–1968. Swedish composer. He was influenced by Hindemith and ◊serialism. His opera *Aniara* 1959 incorporates electronic music and is set in a spaceship fleeing Earth after nuclear war.

Blow John 1648–1708. British composer. He taught Purcell and wrote church music, for example the anthem 'I Was Glad when They Said unto Me' 1697. His masque *Venus and Adonis* 1685 is sometimes called the first English opera.

blues jazz form consisting of 12 or occasionally 16 bars to each section. When sung it usually relates tales of woe or unhappy love. Classical composers such as Ravel, Copland, and Michael Tippett have used the term loosely to refer to mood rather than a strict musical form.

Boccherini (Ridolfo) Luigi 1743–1805. Italian composer and cellist. He studied in Rome, made his mark in Paris 1768, and was court composer in Prussia and Spain. Boccherini composed some 350 instrumental works, an opera, and oratorios.

Boehm Theobald 1794–1881. German flautist and composer, inventor of the Boehm System of improvements to the flute 1832. Using metalworking skills, he applied a series of levers and keypads to the instrument which improved performance and enabled the pitch holes to be drilled at optimum acoustical positions instead of, as formerly, to suit the player's fingers. His system was later applied to other woodwind instruments.

Böhm Karl 1894–1981. Austrian conductor. He is remembered for his stately interpretation of Beethoven and of Mozart and Strauss operas.

bolero a Spanish dance in moderate triple time (3/4), invented in the late 18th century. Ravel's *Boléro* 1928 is the most famous example, consisting of a theme which is constantly repeated and varied instrumentally, building to a powerful climax. The bolero is still a contemporary form in Caribbean countries.

bongos small Cuban drums played in pairs by the fingers and thumbs. They consist of hollowed-out pieces of wood with animal skin stretched over one end.

bore term describing the internal diameter of tubing of a brass or woodwind instrument, as in 'wide bore', 'narrow bore'.

Borodin Alexander Porfir'yevich 1833–1887. Russian composer. Born in St Petersburg, the illegitimate son of a Russian prince, he became by profession an expert in medical chemistry, but in his spare time devoted himself to writing music. He was one of The ◊Five group of composers. His principal work is the opera *Prince Igor*, left unfinished; it was completed by Rimsky-Korsakov and Glazunov, and includes the Polovtsian Dances.

Boulanger Lili (Juliette Marie Olga) 1893–1918. French composer. She was the younger sister of Nadia Boulanger. At the age of 19, she became the first woman to win the Prix de Rome with the cantata *Faust et Hélène* for voices and orchestra.

Boulanger Nadia (Juliette) 1887–1979. French music teacher and conductor. A pupil of Fauré, and an admirer of Stravinsky, she included among her composition pupils at the American Conservatory in Fontainebleau, France, (from 1921) Aaron Copland, Roy Harris, Walter Piston, and Philip Glass.

Boulez Pierre 1925– . French composer and conductor. He is founder and director of ◊IRCAM, a music research studio in Paris opened 1977. His avant-garde music has involved ◊indeterminacy, ◊integral serialism and electronic techniques, and includes the cantatas *Le Visage nuptial* 1952 and *Le Marteau sans maître* 1955; *Pli selon pli* 1962 for soprano and orchestra; and *Répons* 1981 for soloists, orchestra, tapes, and computer-generated sounds.

Boult Adrian (Cedric) 1889–1983. English conductor. He conducted the BBC Symphony Orchestra 1930–50 and the London Philharmonic 1950–57. He promoted the work of Holst and Vaughan Williams, and was a celebrated interpreter of Elgar.

bourdon French term for the drone of a ◊hurdy-gurdy or bagpipes, or for a piece of music imitating a ◊drone accompaniment, for example in a ◊musette; also an organ stop of dull tone.

bourrée French dance form originating in the 17th century, it starts on the upbeat in fast ◊duple time. It forms a movement of the Classical suite.

bow a stick, holding lengths of stretched horsehair, which is drawn across the string of a member of the violin or viol family in order to produce sound. Before the 17th century bows were convex, but changes in violin technique prompted the development of concave bows, perfected by *François Tourte* (1747–1835) at the end of the 18th century.

Unusual instruments that have been played with a bow include the ◊glass harmonica and ◊musical saw.

Bowles Paul 1910– . US writer and composer. Born in New York City, he studied music composition with Aaron Copland and Virgil

Thomson, writing scores for ballets, films, and an opera. A collector of N African folk music, he settled in Morocco, where he has been successful as a novelist.

Boyce William 1711–1779. English composer and organist. He was one of the most respected English composers of his time. He composed church music, symphonies, and chamber music. He is most famous for his song *Heart of Oak* 1759. Much of his music exhibits a fresh liveliness, particularly his many dance movements.

braccio, da (Italian 'on the arm') suffix originally used to distinguish violins, played resting on the arm, from viols, played 'da gamba' (on the leg). The term 'viola da braccio' in 17th-century music signifies a violin or viola; today only the viola (German *bratsche*) is so called.

Bradley Scott 1914– . US composer of animation-film music. Working for the US film-production company Metro-Goldwyn-Mayer (MGM), with Carl Stalling he developed the ♭click-track, which enables a composer to write a music track to any desired tempo for a given length of film. He also introduced classical music to *Tom and Jerry* cartoons, arranging Liszt's *Hungarian Rhapsody No 2* for *Cat Concerto* 1947.

Brahms Johannes 1833–1897. German composer, pianist, and conductor. Considered one of the greatest composers of symphonic music and of songs, his works include symphonies (four), lieder, concertos for piano and for violin, chamber music, sonatas, and the choral *Ein Deutsches Requiem/A German Requiem* 1868. He performed and conducted his own works.

In 1853 he was introduced to Liszt and Schumann. Although Schumann encouraged and promoted him, Liszt, and later Wagner, became ideologically opposed to Brahms. Brahms continued the classical tradition of lucid form while achieving a romantic profundity of emotion, as opposed to Wagner, who strove for romantic sensuality without a strong formal underpinning.

Brain Dennis 1921–1957. English horn player. The greatest virtuoso of his day, he inspired composers including Britten and Hindemith to write pieces for him, such as Britten's *Serenade* 1943 for tenor, horn, and strings.

brass band instrumental ensemble consisting of ◊brass instruments and sometimes ◊percussion instruments. The brass usually comprises (in descending order of pitch) the cornet, flügelhorn, tenor horn, B-flat baritone, euphonium, trombone, and bombardon (bass tuba). The brass band developed during the 19th century from the military band, and was particularly associated with the manufacturing towns of Lancashire and Yorkshire. Classical composers have written for the medium, including Elgar in his *Severn Suite* 1930.

brass instrument any of a class of musical instruments made of brass or other metal, including trumpets, bugles, trombones, and horns. Sound is generated by vibrating the lips, shaped and tensed by the mouthpiece, acting as a valve releasing periodic pulses of pressurized air into the tube. Orchestral brass instruments are derived from signalling and hunting instruments, such as the bugle, which, in their natural or valve-less form, produce a directionally focused range of tones from the ◊harmonic series.

In the symphony orchestra the brass instruments are the French horn, trumpet, trombone, and tuba. The brass band comprises (in descending order of pitch) the cornet, flugelhorn, tenor horn, B-flat baritone, eupho-nium, trombone, and bombardon (bass tuba).

bravura (Italian 'bravery' indicating a passage demanding brilliant ◊virtuoso standards. It is associated especially with Romantic 19th-cen-tury music, such as many of Liszt's piano works.

Bream Julian (Alexander) 1933– . British virtuoso of the guitar and lute. He has revived much Elizabethan lute music and encouraged com-position by contemporaries for the guitar. Benjamin Britten, William Walton, and Hans Henze have written for him.

Brendel Alfred 1931– . Austrian pianist. He is known for his fastidi-ous and searching interpretations of Beethoven, Schubert, and Liszt. He is the author of *Musical Thoughts and Afterthoughts* 1976 and *Music Sounded Out* 1990.

breve (Latin 'short') the shortest note of 13th-century music. Since the subsequent addition of many other shorter notes, it is now the longest, equal in duration to eight crotchets. It is rarely used and is notated by an unfilled, white note-head (often in the shape of a square) with two vertical lines attached to its left and right side.

Brian Havergal 1876–1972. English composer. Largely self-taught, he wrote 32 symphonies in visionary Romantic style, including *Gothic Symphony* 1927 for large choral and orchestral forces.

bridge a support for the strings of an instrument that transmits vibration to the body. In violins, lutes, guitars, and other instruments the bridge is fixed, but in the Indian ◊tambura (long lute) and Japanese ◊koto (zither), bridges are movable to change the tuning.

Bridge Frank 1879–1941. English composer. He was the teacher of Benjamin Britten. His works include the orchestral suite *The Sea* 1912, and *Oration* 1930 for cello and orchestra. After 1920 Bridge's music changed radically, moving from a late Romantic style to one which used elements of ◊atonality, making Bridge one of the first English composers to use it.

Britten (Edward) Benjamin 1913–1976. English composer. Primarily a composer of vocal works, he often wrote for an individual voice; for example, the role in the opera *Peter Grimes* 1945, based on verses by George Crabbe (1752–1834), was created for his life companion Peter ◊Pears. Among his many works are the *Young Person's Guide to the Orchestra* 1946; the chamber opera *The Rape of Lucretia* 1946; *Billy Budd* 1951; *A Midsummer Night's Dream* 1960; and *Death in Venice* 1973.

Born in Lowestoft, Suffolk, he was educated at Gresham's School, Holt, Norfolk. He studied at the Royal College of Music, and was a friend of W H Auden, who frequently collaborated with him. From 1939 to 1942 he worked in the USA, then returned to England and devoted himself to composing at his home in Aldeburgh, Suffolk, where he and Pears established an annual music festival. His oratorio *War Requiem* 1962 was written for the rededication of Coventry Cathedral.

Broadwood make of piano named after John Broadwood (1732–1812), a Scottish-born cabinetmaker who worked in London with the Swiss harpsichordmaker Burkhardt Tschudi (1702–1773), married his daughter, and took over the business when Tschudi retired 1769. The company was one of the first to manufacture a new kind of piano, with a richer tone and different mechanism from the Viennese pianos of the day. It was a forerunner of the modern piano. The present company of John Broadwood & Sons was formed 1951.

Brown Earle 1926– . US composer. He pioneered ◊graph notation and ◊aleatory music during the 1950s, notably in *Available Forms II* 1958 for ensemble and two conductors. He was an associate of John Cage.

Bruch Max 1838–1920. German composer. He wrote three operas, including *Hermione* 1872. Among the most celebrated of his works are the *Kol Nidrei* 1881 for cello and orchestra, violin concertos, and many choral pieces. He became professor of composition at the Berlin Academy 1891. English composer Ralph Vaughan Williams was his pupil for a short period.

Bruckner (Joseph) Anton 1824–1896. Austrian Romantic composer. He was cathedral organist at Linz 1856–68, and from 1868 he was professor at the Vienna Conservatoire. His works include many choral pieces and 11 symphonies, the last unfinished. His compositions were somewhat influenced by Richard Wagner, to whom he dedicated his Third Symphony 1877 (revised 1891).

buffa (Italian 'comic'). See ◊opera buffa.

bugle compact, valveless brass instrument with a shorter tube and less flared bell than the trumpet. Constructed of copper plated with brass, it has long been used as a military instrument for giving a range of signals based on the tones of a ◊harmonic series.

Bull John *c.* 1562–1628. British composer, organist, and virginalist. Most of his output is for keyboard, and includes *God Save the King*. He also wrote sacred vocal music.

bullroarer or *thunder stick* musical instrument of the Australian Aborigines, used for communication and played during religious rites. It consists of a thin piece of wood or stone whirled on a long cord to make a deep whirring noise. It features in a ballet suite *Corroborree* 1946 by Australian composer John Antill (1904–).

It is played in many other parts of the world, including Britain.

Bülow Hans (Guido) Frieherr von 1830–1894. German conductor and pianist. He studied with Wagner and Liszt and in 1857 married Cosima, Liszt's daughter. From 1864 he served Ludwig II of Bavaria, conducting first performances of Wagner's *Tristan und Isolde* 1865 and *Die Meistersinger/The Mastersingers* 1867. His wife left him and married Wagner 1870.

Bush Alan (Dudley) 1900– . English composer. A student of John Ireland, he later adopted a didactic simplicity in his compositions in line with his Marxist beliefs. He has written a large number of works for orchestra, voice, and chamber groups. His operas include *Wat Tyler* 1952 and *Men of Blackmoor* 1956.

Busoni Ferruccio (Dante Benvenuto) 1866–1924. Italian pianist, composer, and music critic. Much of his music was for piano, but he also composed several operas including *Doktor Faust*, completed 1925 by German composer Philipp Jarnach, after Busoni's death. His compositional style ranges from impressionistic to modern. He encouraged the French avant-garde composer Edgard Varèse.

Buxtehude Diderik 1637–1707. Danish composer and organist. In 1668 he was appointed organist at the Marienkirche, Lübeck, Germany. His style attracted and influenced J S Bach and Handel. He is remembered for his organ works and cantatas, written for *Abendmusiken* (evening concerts); he also wrote numerous trio sonatas for two violins, viola da gamba, and harpsichord.

Byrd William 1543–1623. English composer. He was described in his day as 'Father of British music'. His sacred and secular choral music, including over 200 motets, and masses for three, four, and five voices, exemplifies the English polyphonic style.

Probably born in Lincoln, he became organist at the cathedral 1563. He shared with his teacher Thomas Tallis the honorary post of organist in Queen Elizabeth's Chapel Royal, and in 1575 he and Tallis were granted a monopoly in the printing and selling of music.

C

C.A. abbreviation for *col arco* (Italian 'with the bow').

cabaletta a short aria with repeats which the singer could freely embellish as a display of virtuosity. In the 19th century the term came to be used for the final section of an elaborate aria.

caccia (Italian 'hunting') suffix used to describe music or instruments associated with the hunt, for example the oboe da caccia, precursor of the cor anglais, and corno da caccia, or hunting horn.

cadence a chord sequence, of two or more chords linked by a note in common, which defines the completion of a phrase, section, or movement.

A *perfect cadence*, also known as a *full close*, moves from a ♭dominant chord to a ♭tonic one (V–I), a *plagal cadence* also known as a *weak close* is one in which the sub-dominant precedes the tonic (IV–I), and an *imperfect cadence*, also known as a *half close*, ends on the dominant and may be preceded by any chord, though it is often the tonic (I–V). There exist transitional cadences, including the *deceptive cadence* (V–VI and V–IV), resolving on a minor chord, and the *Phrygian cadence* (I–III).

cadenza an exhibition passage, usually unaccompanied, in the style of an improvisation, inserted by the soloist at the climax of a movement especially in a concerto.

The practice of improvising a cadenza largely ceased around 1780, composers thereafter supplying them in written form. Recently, however, the practice of the interpreter composing a cadenza has re-emerged, with Stockhausen writing new cadenzas for Haydn and Mozart and violinist Nigel Kennedy recording Beethoven's 1805 Violin Concerto with a cadenza of his own devising.

Cage John 1912–1992. US composer. His interest in Indian classical music led him to the view that the purpose of music was to change the way people listen. From 1948 he experimented with instruments, graphics, and

methods of random selection in an effort to generate a music of pure inci-
dent. His ideas and collected writings, including *Silence* 1961 and *For the
Birds* 1981, have profoundly influenced late 20th-century aesthetics.

Cage studied briefly with Arnold Schoenberg, also with Henry
Cowell, and joined others in reacting against the European music tradition in favour of a freer idiom open to non-Western attitudes. Working
in films during the 1930s, Cage assembled and toured a percussion
orchestra incorporating ethnic instruments and noisemakers, for which
Double Music 1941 was composed (with Lou Harrison (1917)). He
helped to develop the ◊prepared piano and toured as accompanist with
the dancer Merce Cunningham, a lifelong collaborator. In a later work, *4
Minutes and 33 Seconds* 1952, the pianist sits at the piano reading a
score for that length of time but does not play.

calando (Italian 'lowering') a progressive softening, as in diminuendo,
but sometimes also to an extent a progressive slowing-down, as in ritardando.

Callas Maria. Adopted name of Maria Kalogeropoulos 1923–1977. US
lyric soprano. Born in New York of Greek parents, she had a voice of
fine range and a gift for dramatic expression. She excelled in operas
including Bellini's *Norma* and *La Sonnambula/The Sleepwalker*,
Puccini's *Madame Butterfly* and *Tosca*, and Verdi's *Aïda*.

She debuted in Verona, Italy, 1947 and at New York's Metropolitan
Opera 1956. Although her technique was not considered perfect, she
helped to popularize classical ◊coloratura roles through her expressiveness and charisma.

Campion Thomas 1567–1620. English poet and musician. He was
author of the critical *Art of English Poesie* 1602 and wrote four *Bookes
of Ayres*, for which he composed both words and music. He worked as a
physician and lawyer.

can-can a Parisian dance in fast duple time (2/4), originating in the 19th
century. A famous example is Offenbach's can-can from his operetta
Orphée aux Enfers/Orpheus in the Underworld 1858 (revised 1874).

canon or *round* the strict imitation of two or more voices or instruments, most common in music before 1750. A canon may appear in a
work, which, itself, is not a canon.

Canonic variations may also introduce a difference in starting pitch between the voices, creating ambiguities of tonality. A cryptic form of canon cultivated by composers since 1600 requires the same fragment of music to be performed by different players in different clefs and from different viewpoints, for example Schoenberg's 'Legitimation als Canon/Canonic Licence' from the *Three Satires* 1926, dedicated to George Bernard Shaw (1856–1950).

cantabile (Italian 'singable') a singing and lyrical style (of playing). It implies a full, rich tone and legato touch.

cantata an extended work for voices, from the Italian, meaning 'sung', as opposed to sonata ('sounded') for instruments. A cantata can be sacred or secular, sometimes uses solo voices, and usually has orchestral accompaniment. The first printed collection of sacred cantata texts dates from 1670. In the Baroque period the cantata was one of the most important genres, forming the basis of the Lutheran church service. J S Bach wrote 300 cantatas, both sacred and secular.

canticle in the Roman Catholic or Anglican liturgies, a hymn or song of praise based on scripture and similar to a psalm, but whose text does not originate in the *Book of Psalms*. An example of a canticle is the ◊Magnificat of Anglican evensong.

cantor in Roman Catholic and Jewish music, the soloist responsible for singing solo parts of the chant and also often for leading the congregation; in Protestant churches, the music director.

cantus firmus (Latin 'fixed song') any melody employed in counterpoint as a reference for the invention of an accompanying melody.

canzona (Italian 'ballad') originally a 16th-century vocal form of ◊polyphony, similar to a ◊madrigal, extending, in the 16th and 17th centuries to to instrumental pieces, developing from the vocal form. Notable composers of the instrumental canzona are Frescobaldi, J S Bach, Andrea Gabrieli, and Giovanni Gabrieli. In the 18th and 19th centuries the term broadened to mean a song or instrumental piece of melodic character.

capriccio (Italian 'caprice') an all-purpose name for a lightweight piece, often improvisatory in nature, combining technical virtuosity with entertainment.

Carey Henry 1690–1743. English poet and musician. He is remembered for the song *Sally in Our Alley*; *God Save the King* (both words and music) has also been attributed to him.

carillon a keyboard struck with the side of the hands and connected by wires to bells. The bells are usually hung in a church tower. Carillons are found throughout Europe and the USA; mechanized carillons were the forerunners of musical clocks and boxes.

Carissimi Giacomo 1605–1674. Italian composer. He wrote sacred and secular cantatas and motets. As *maestro di capella* (chapel master) at Sant' Apollinaire, Rome, 1630–74, he pioneered the use of the expressive solo aria as a commentary on the Latin biblical text. He wrote five oratorios, including *Jephtha* 1650.

Carmina Burana medieval Latin verse miscellany compiled from the work of wandering 13th-century scholars and including secular (love songs and drinking songs) as well as religious verse. German composer Carl Orff composed a cantata based on the material 1937.

Carnegie Hall largest concert hall of New York (seating 3,000), opened 1891. It is named after the millionaire philanthropist Andrew Carnegie (1835–1919). It has a distinctive rich ◊acoustic.

carol song that in medieval times was associated with a round dance; today carols are associated with festivals such as Christmas and Easter.

Christmas carols were common as early as the 15th century. The custom of singing carols from house to house, collecting gifts, was called 'wassailing'. Many carols, such as *God Rest You Merry Gentlemen* and *The First Noel*, date from the 16th century or earlier.

Carreras José 1947–   . Spanish operatic tenor. His comprehensive repertoire of roles includes Handel's Samson, and he has made a recording of *West Side Story* 1984 under Leonard Bernstein. His vocal presence, charmingly insinuating rather than forceful, is favoured for Italian and French romantic roles.

In 1987 he became seriously ill with leukaemia, but resumed his career 1988. Together with tenors Placido Domingo and Luciano Pavarotti, he achieved worldwide fame in a recording of operatic hits released to coincide with the World Cup soccer series in Rome 1990.

Carter Elliott (Cook) 1908–   . US composer. After writing first in a
Neo-Classical style, he created intricately structured works using
◊serialism, incorporating 'metrical modulation', an adaptation of standard notation allowing different instruments or groups to remain synchronized while playing at changing speeds. This practice was first
employed in his *String Quartet No 1* 1951, and to dense effect in *Double
Concerto* 1961 for harpsichord and piano. In his eighth decade, his
music has shown a new tautness and vitality, as in *Three Occasions for
Orchestra* 1989.

Caruso Enrico 1873–1921. Italian tenor. His voice had a dark, full-
bodied tone and a remarkable dynamic range. In 1902 he starred, with
Nellie Melba, in Puccini's *La Bohème/The Bohemian*. He was among
the first opera singers to achieve lasting fame through gramophone
recordings.

Casals Pablo 1876–1973. Catalan cellist, composer, and conductor.
He was largely self-taught. As a cellist, he was celebrated for his interpretations of J S Bach's unaccompanied suites. He wrote instrumental
and choral works, including the Christmas oratorio *The Manger*. He was
an outspoken critic of fascism, openly defying Franco, and a tireless cru-
sader for peace.

   Casals' pioneer recordings of Schubert and Beethoven trios 1905,
with violinist Jacques Thibaut (1880–1953) and pianist Alfred Cortot
(1877–1962), launched his international career and established the popularity of the cello as a solo instrument, notably the solo suites of J S
Bach.

castanets Spanish percussion instrument made of two hollowed wooden
shells, held in the palm and drummed
together by the fingers to produce a rhythmic accompaniment to dance.

castanets

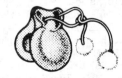

castrato a high male voice of unusual
brilliance and power achieved by castra-
tion before puberty, regarded as the ideal timbre for heroic roles in opera
by composers from Monteverdi to Wagner. Recordings preserve the

voice of Alessandro Moreschi (1858–1922), the last male soprano of the Sistine Chapel.

Women singers superseded the castrato during the 19th century.

Cavalli (Pietro) Francesco 1602–1676. Italian composer and organist. He was the first to make opera a popular entertainment with such works as *Equisto* 1643 and *Xerxes* 1654, later performed in honour of Louis XIV's wedding in Paris. Twenty-seven of his operas survive. He was organist at St Mark's, Venice.

cavatina a short operatic aria, consisting of one section without repetition of text, unlike the aria's usually three-part division; for example *Porgi amor* from Mozart's *Le nozze di Figaro/The Marriage of Figaro* 1786. Also, an instrumental piece of song-like quality, for example a movement of Beethoven's String Quartet No. 13 1826.

cello

Cecilia, St Patron saint of music, celebrated every November 22. She is believed to have been a Christian martyr, killed in about AD 176, but her original connection with music is tenuous. There are many compositions in her honour, for example Purcell's *Ode on St. Cecilia's Day* 1692 and Britten's *Hymn to St. Cecilia* 1942.

celesta keyboard ◊glockenspiel producing high-pitched sounds of glistening purity. It was invented by Auguste Mustel 1886 and first used to effect by Tchaikovsky in the *Nutcracker* ballet 1890.

cello common abbreviation for violoncello, tenor member of the violin family and fourth member of the string quartet. Unlike the violin and viola, the cello is held upright with the ◊tail pin touching the ground. The player sits with the instrument resting between the legs. The cello's solo potential was recognized by J S Bach, and a concerto repertoire extends from Haydn (who also gave the cello a leading role in his string quartets), and Boccherini to Dvořák, Elgar, Britten, Ligeti, and Lukas Foss. The *Bachianas Brasilieras 1* 1945 by Villa-Lobos is scored for eight cellos, and Boulez's *Messagesquisse* 1977 for seven cellos.

cembalo short form of clavicembalo, Italian for harpsichord.

Chabrier (Alexis) Emmanuel 1841–1894. French composer. He wrote *España* 1883, an orchestral rhapsody, and the light opera *Le Roi malgré lui/The Reluctant King* 1887. His colourful orchestration inspired Debussy and Ravel.

chaconne piece of music derived from a Latin American dance form, introduced to Spain in the late 16th century. Constructed over a ◊ground bass in triple time, it is virtually indistinguishable from the ◊passacaglia. Examples include the famous Bach Chaconne (from the Second Violin Partita) and the aria 'Dido's Lament' from Purcell's opera *Dido and Aeneas* 1689, in which the inevitability of the bass line conveys a sense of Dido's inescapable fate.

Chaliapin Fyodor Ivanovich 1873–1938. Russian bass singer, born in Kazan (Tatar Republic). He achieved fame in the West through his charismatic recordings, notably as Boris in Mussorgsky's opera *Boris Godunov*. He specialized in Russian, French, and Italian roles.

chalumeau short thickset double-reed wind instrument, ancestor of the clarinet. It is also the term used to describe the dark lowest register of clarinet tone.

chamber music music originally intended for performance in a small room or chamber, rather than in a church or theatre, and usually written for instrumental combinations, played with one instrument to a part, as in the string quartet.

Chamber music developed as an instrumental alternative to earlier music for voices such as the ◊madrigal, which allowed accompanying instruments little freedom for technical display. At first a purely instrumental style, it developed through Haydn and Beethoven into a private and sometimes experimental medium making unusual demands on players and audiences alike. During the 20th century many composers have favoured the medium, both for economic reasons and exploration of varying ◊timbres. Examples include Stravinsky's *l'Histoire du Soldat/The Soldier's Tale* 1918 and works composed for Peter Maxwell Davies's group *The Fires of London*.

chamber orchestra small orchestra, consisting of about 25 players. This was the standard orchestral size until the 19th century, when expanding wind sections, followed by a compensatory increase in the number of string players, increased the proportions to the size of the modern symphony orchestra. During the 20th century the chamber orchestra has once again become fashionable, partly as a reaction against the Romantic legacy of Wagner (which included the use of large-scale instrumental forces), partly as a result of economic conditions, and partly as a result of the ◊authenticity movement and the interest in ◊early music. Famous chamber orchestras include the Academy of St Martin-in-the-Fields and the Orpheus Chamber Orchestra.

chanson song type common in France and Italy, often based on a folk tune that originated with the ◊troubadours. Guillaume Dufay and Josquin Desprez were chanson composers.

chant Liturgical music, usually sung unaccompanied and in a free rhythm. ◊Ambrosian chant and ◊Gregorian chant are forms of ◊plainsong.

Chapel Royal a group of musicians and clergy serving the English monarch. Dating back at least to 1135, the Chapel Royal fostered many of England's greatest composers, especially prior to the 18th century, when many great musical works were religious in nature. Members of the chapel Royal have included Byrd and Tallis.

Charpentier Gustave 1860–1956. French composer. A pupil of Massenet, he is known chiefly for his opera about Paris working-class life, *Louise* 1900.

Charpentier Marc-Antoine 1645–1704. French composer. He wrote incidental music in Italian style to plays by Molière, including *Le Malade imaginaire/The Hypochondriac* 1673. Later in life, as official composer to the Sainte Chapelle, Paris, he composed sacred music in French style and the opera *Médée* 1693.

Chávez Carlos 1899–1978. Mexican composer and pianist. His music incorporates national and pre-Columbian folk elements, for example *Chapultepec: Republican Overture* 1935. He composed a number of ballets, seven symphonies, and concertos for both violin and piano.

He was founder-director of the Mexico Symphony Orchestra 1928–48.

Cherubini Luigi (Carlo Zanobi Salvadore Maria) 1760–1842. Italian composer. His first opera *Quinto Fabio* 1779 was produced at Alessandria. Following his appointment as court composer to King George III of England 1784–88, he settled in Paris where he produced a number of dramatic works including *Médée* 1797, *Les Deux Journées* 1800, and the ballet *Anacréon* 1803. After 1809 he devoted himself largely to church music.

chest voice the lower register of the human voice, the chest being the source of sound production. In men it contrasts with the high 'falsetto' range, requiring ◊head voice. There has been, in the 19th century and earlier, disagreement concerning the precise use of the term, some claiming that only head (high) and chest voices exist, others claiming that a third, middle register is also available. Today there is less concern about these distinctions.

chitarrone Largest member of the lute family. It incorporates freely vibrating bass strings that are twice the length (sounding an octave lower) of the other strings. It was developed in the 16th century and used by Renaissance and early Baroque ensembles to provide a firm and resonant bass line.

choir body of singers, traditionally of sacred music; also the place in a church or cathedral where the singers are stationed. Choirs may be mixed, comprising men and women, or male, comprising men and boys. A traditional cathedral choir of male voices is required to sing responses (usually ◊plainsong), hymns, and psalms appropriate to the church calendar.

The choir was the principal medium for the development of Renaissance ◊polyphony, with instruments initially reading from vocal parts and only subsequently evolving distinct instrumental styles. During the 19th century choir festivals became a popular feature of musical life, promoting mixed-voice choral singing by amateur groups.

choir organ third manual of an organ, characterized by quiet stops and pipes appropriate for accompanying a church choir. Often the pipes of the choir organ are housed separately from the rest, located behind the organist's back instead of being grouped together with the other pipes, usually in front and above the player.

Chopin Frédéric (François) 1810–1849. Polish composer and pianist. He made his debut as a pianist at the age of eight, although in adulthood he rarely performed in public. His compositions for piano, which were written mostly for piano solo, are characterized by great volatility of mood, lyrical melodies, imaginative harmonies, and rhythmic fluidity. They include waltzes, preludes, polonaises, nocturnes, ballades, mazurkas, and études.

From 1831 he lived in Paris, where he became known in the fashionable salons. In 1836 the composer Liszt introduced him to Madame Dudevant (the author George Sand (1804–1876)), with whom he had a close relationship 1838–46. During this time she nursed him in Majorca for tuberculosis, while he composed intensively and for a time regained his health. But after their break, Chopin's health deteriorated and he died three years later, having written little during this period.

chorale traditional hymn tune of the German Protestant church, usually harmonized in four parts for singing by a congregation.

chord a group of three or more notes sounded together. The chord provides the foundation of harmony.

chorus body of male and female singers of secular music in usually four parts. A stage chorus in opera or musicals provides an accompaniment to principal soloists.

Christoff Boris 1918– . Bulgarian bass singer. He has a voice of soulful, massive tone. His operatic debut 1946 marked him out for darker roles, including Mussorgsky's Boris Godunov, Ivan the Terrible in Rimsky-Korsakov's *The Maid of Pskov*, and the title role in *Mefistofele/Mephistopheles* by the Italian composer Arrigo Boito (1842–1918). His greater range is revealed in recordings of the complete songs of Mussorgsky.

chromaticism the use of pitches and harmonics not included in the diatonic scale (the seven notes of any major or minor key). Although it was practised increasingly in the late 19th century and early 20th century by composers such as Wagner, Skryabin, Ravel, Debussy, and Messiaen in order to increase emotional intensity, its origins lie in the tetrachord (a scale of four notes) of Greek music and ◊musica ficta of the Middle Ages. A famous example from the 18th century is Bach's *Chromatic Fantasia and Fugue c.*1720.

chromatic scale musical scale consisting of 12 consecutive semitones. Works using the ◊twelve-tone system incorporate all the notes of the chromatic scale.

church mode or *authentic mode* one of eight modes or scales developed by the medieval church, centring on the notes D, E, F, or G, and using the notes of the C major scale.

ciaccona Italian spelling of ◊chaconne.

Cimarosa Domenico 1749–1801. Italian composer. Known for his comic operas including *Il Matrimonio segreto/The Secret Marriage* 1792; he also composed orchestral and keyboard music.

cimbalom a Hungarian ◊dulcimer modernized during the 19th century from a gipsy instrument. It consists of a box-shaped resonator over which strings are stretched laterally, the performer playing front to back rather than across. Composers include Stravinsky in *Renard* 1922 and Kodály in the orchestral suite *Háry János* 1927.

cittern

cittern plucked stringed instrument, similar in shape to a lute but with a flat back. It originated about 1500, is easy to play, and was a popular alternative to the lute. Larger forms include the pandora and the orpharion. It was superseded in the 19th century by the guitar.

clarinet any of a family of single-reed woodwind instruments of cylindrical bore. In their concertos for clarinet, Mozart and Weber exploited the instru-

ment's range of tone from the dark low reg- clarinet
ister rising to brilliance, and its capacity for
sustained dynamic control. The ability of
the clarinet both to blend and to contrast
with other instruments make it popular for
chamber music and as a solo instrument. It
is also heard in military and concert bands
and as a jazz instrument.

The clarinet was developed *c.*1700 from
the double-reed chalumeau by German
instrumentmaker J C Denner (1655–1707)
and used in the Baroque orchestra as an
instrument of trumpet-like tone. In the 19th
century Theobald ◊Boehm made the essential modifications in order for the instrument to play in all the keys. A broad range
of clarinets remain in current use, including piccolo E flat and D,
soprano B flat and A (standard orchestral clarinets), alto F (military
band), and B flat bass. The clarinet is capable of ◊glissando, for example
in Gershwin's *Rhapsody in Blue*.

Clarke Jeremiah 1659–1707. English composer. Organist at St Paul's,
he composed 'The Prince of Denmark's March', a harpsichord piece
that was arranged by Henry Wood as a 'Trumpet Voluntary' and
wrongly attributed to Purcell.

Classical term used to refer generally to any 'serious' Western art
music, that is, music whose traditions are traceable from the various
20th-century styles to Romantic, Classical, Baroque, Renaissance, and
medieval music; also used ahistorically and relatively as a comparison
with Romantic to denote a style which emphasizes formal beauty rather
than freedom of personal expression, intellect rather than raw emotion.

Classical the period in music between approximately 1750 and 1820,
in which composers' concerns for form and symmetry were analogous
to those of the ideals of Classical Greek and Roman art and philosophy.
Classical music, as epitomized by the Viennese Classical School of
Haydn, Mozart, and Beethoven, is characterized by the growth of clear

formal and sectional elements, especially ◊sonata form; clear and often symmetrical harmonic and melodic relationships from phrase to phrase and section to section, influenced in part by the study of rhetoric (for example, the use of ◊antecedent/consequent phrases); the development from Baroque ◊polyphony and counterpoint to the melodic homophonic style with distinct and subordinate accompaniments.

clavecin French term for ◊harpsichord.

claves percussion instrument of Latin American origin, consisting of small hardwood batons (7 or 8 inches long), which are struck together.

clavichord small domestic keyboard instrument of variable and delicate tone developed in the 16th century. Notes are sounded by a metal blade striking the string. The sound is clear and precise, and a form of vibrato (◊bebung) is possible by varying finger pressure on the key. It was superseded in the 18th century by the fortepiano.

The first clavichords had few strings, using a keyboard-based array of metal tangents combining the function of plectrum and bridge to define and produce a range of pitches. Later instruments increased the number of strings.

clavier early general term for any ◊keyboard instrument.

Clay Frederic 1838–1889. British composer. Clay wrote popular light operas, and the cantata *Lalla Rookh* 1877, based on a poem by Thomas Moore.

clef a symbol prefixed to a five-line stave indicating the pitch range to which the music applies. Introduced as a visual aid in ◊plainsong notation, *treble clef* is based on G4; *C clefs* (including soprano, alto, and tenor clefs) establish C4 (middle C) as a prime reference pitch, and *bass clef* is based on F3.

The C clefs are now comparatively rare, except for viola and, to a lesser extent, cello, and bassoon; for most other instruments the treble and bass clefs are standard.

Clementi Muzio 1752–1832. Italian pianist and composer. He settled in London 1782 as a teacher and then as proprietor of a successful piano and music business. His sonatas and ◊bel canto approach to keyboard playing were admired by Beethoven. His series of studies, *Gradus ad*

Parnassum 1817, is still in use. He also taught Irish composer and pianist John Field (1782–1837).

click-track in film music, a technique to aid the coordination of music and film action. It was invented by composers Carl Stalling and Scott ◊Bradley. Holes punched in the composer's working print of the sound-track 'click' at a desired tempo measured in frames. A metronome tempo of 144 beats per minute, for example, is equivalent to one hole, or click, every ten frames of film. A composer is then able to construct a musical phrase so that it climaxes at a precise moment in the film action.

cluster the effect of playing simultaneously and without emphasis all the notes within a chosen interval. It was introduced by Henry Cowell in the piano piece *The Banshee* 1925, for which using a ruler on the keys is recommended. Its use in film and radio incidental music symbolizes a hallucinatory or dreaming state, presumably because it resembles an internalized disturbance of normal hearing.

The cluster effect is also heard in *Ecuatorial* 1934 by Varèse, and Ligeti's *Volumina* 1962 for organ, using the player's forearms. Cluster writing for strings features in Penderecki's *Threnody for the Victims of Hiroshima* 1960, and for voices in Ligeti's *Lux Aeterna* 1966.

Coates Eric 1886–1957. English composer. He wrote well-crafted, light music, including the orchestral suites *London* 1933, including the 'Knightsbridge' march; 'By the Sleepy Lagoon' 1939; 'The Dam Busters March' 1942; and the songs 'Bird Songs at Eventide' and 'The Green Hills of Somerset'.

coda (Italian 'tail') a concluding section of a movement added to emphasize the destination key. However, composers such as Beethoven often increased the weight of the coda, introducing new material or developing existing ideas.

col Italian 'with the'; as in col arco, 'with the bow'.

Coleridge-Taylor Samuel 1875–1912. English composer. He wrote the cantata *Hiawatha's Wedding Feast* 1898, a setting in three parts of Longfellow's poem. The son of a West African doctor and an English mother, he was a student and champion of traditional black music.

coloratura rapid vocal ornamentation, consisting of runs and ◊trills (rapid oscillation between adjacent notes). A *coloratura soprano* is a light, high voice suited to such music.

colour one quality or timbre of an instrument or voice. A 'dark' sound denotes a thick, heavy sonority while a 'light' sound describes a thinner, more transparent sonority. Alexander Skryabin invented a keyboard which would project colours on to a screen in order to reflect the mood and character of the music.

combination tone an acoustical phenomenon in which a third faint tone is heard when two notes are sounded loudly together. The frequency of the combination tone is the difference between the numerical frequencies of the two notes (see ◊hertz). For example, given note 1 = 500 Hz, and note 2 = 300 Hz, the combination tone is: 500 Hz – 300 Hz = 200 Hz. Combination tones are often used and manipulated in ◊electronic music.

common time alternative name for 4/4 time. The symbol C that denotes common time is not derived from the first letter of the word, but originates in music of the Middle Ages in which triple time (three beats in a bar) was considered perfect (as it reflected the Holy Trinity) and notated by a circle (the perfect geometric shape), and duple time (two beats in a bar) was considered imperfect and notated by a broken circle.

composition the process of combining sounds creatively to yield a musical work; also, the musical work itself.

compound time a metre in which each beat divides into three units. For example, 6/8 consists of two beats, each of three quavers.

computer-generated music music in which a computer has been used by the composer, generating or synthesizing the properties and timbre of sound; also, music which is generated by a computer's response to a series of commands, which are designed by a composer and fed to the machine on a computer program. A computer is often used in compositions which use elements of chance, as in a ◊stochastic work.

con Italian 'with'; for example *con espressione*, 'with expression'.

concertante the group of instrumental soloists in a ◊concerto grosso, as opposed to the ripieno players (full orchestra); the term is also used more widely to mean 'in the manner of' a concertante, for example a *sinfonia concertante*, a work for solo instruments and orchestra, but resembling a symphony more closely than a concerto.

Concertgebouw (Dutch 'concert building') Amsterdam's principal concert hall, built in 1888. The Concertgebouw Orchestra, conducted by Bernard Haitink, is in residence there.

concertina portable reed organ related to the accordion but smaller in size and hexagonal in shape, with buttons for keys. It was invented in England in the 19th century.

concert master the leader of an orchestra, usually the principal violinist.

concerto composition, usually in three movements, for solo instrument (or instruments) and orchestra. It developed during the 18th century from the concerto grosso form for string orchestra, in which a group of solo instruments (concerto) is contrasted with a full orchestra (ripieno). Bach was one of the first develop the solo concerto in his harpsichord concertos. In the 19th century the solo instrument became increasingly independent from the orchestral texture, often set in heroic opposition to the other instruments.

Recent concertos by György Ligeti (*Double Concerto* 1972 for flute and oboe), Luciano Berio (*Concerto for Two Pianos* 1973), and Elliott Carter (*Violin Concerto* 1990) have developed the concerto relationship along new lines.

concerto grosso A form of concerto most popular in the 17th and 18th centuries, although revived this century by composers such as Schoenberg. The concerto grosso is a composition for a relatively small ensemble featuring a ◊concertante or concertino (solo instrumental group) in opposition to the ripieno musicians (full orchestra).

concert pitch The standard pitch at which the note A (A4) is 440 Hz (hertz, or cycles per second). In practice, there is some variation, some orchestras and musicians preferring 438 Hz. Before 1960 there was no international consensus. Prior to 1700 the pitch standard was local and set by the chapel organ, of which a number of Renaissance and Baroque examples survive with values for A4 between a low extreme of 380 Hz and a high of 610 Hz. In 1862 Herman ◊Helmholtz gave a value for A4 of 431 Hz, an increase on 18th-century concert pitch. The revival of authentic ◊early music practices has led to agreement on standards of 460–465 Hz for High Renaissance music, 415 Hz for Baroque and Classical music, and 430 Hz for Romantic music.

concrete music English translation of ◊musique concrète.

conductor the director of an orchestra who beats time, cues entries, and controls the overall expression and balance of a performance.

Conductors of ballet and opera are normally resident, on a fulltime contract, available for the ongoing preparation of new repertoire. Conductors for symphony orchestras are more often freelance, star performers in their own right, under temporary contract for concert or recording purposes and thus more reliant on the expertise of orchestras.

conga Afro-Cuban barrel drum, long and narrow in shape, played with the fingers and palms; also an Afro-Cuban ballroom dance in duple time (2/4), with a syncopated rhythm.

consequent in musical analysis, the second phrase of a symmetrical two-phrase unit. Following the 'questioning' *antecedent* phrase, the consequent phrase often ends on a more stable harmony. Antecedent/consequent phrases are most typical of Classical-period composition.

conservatory a school or college of music which specializes in preparing students for a career in performance or composition. The term originated in 16th- and 17th-century Italy with orphanages that taught music to a high standard. Famous conservatories include ◊Juilliard in New York, the Conservatoire in Paris, and the ◊Royal College of Music in London.

consonance a combination of two or more tones that is pleasing to the ear. It is the opposite of a ◊dissonance.

consort term for a chamber ensemble of Renaissance or Baroque instruments of uniform sonority, for example recorders or viols. A nonuniform ensemble, comprising instruments of different families, is called a broken consort.

continuo or *thorough bass* (from Italian *basso continuo*) the continuous bass part in concerted works of the 17th and 18th centuries, underlying the musical harmonies that were often indicated by figures (see ◊figured bass).

contra prefix attached to the name of certain instruments, denoting a lower pitch (usually an octave below).

contrabass alternative name for ◊double bass.

contralto a low-register female voice, also called an ◊alto.

contrapuntal of music employing ◊counterpoint, multiple parts of imitative melody.

contrary motion the movement of two voices in opposite directions from each other; the opposite of parallel motion. The strictest form of contrary motion is ◊inversion, in which one voice plays the mirror image of the other. For example, two voices which sing simultaneously: C4-G4-F4 and C4-F3-G3.

Coperario or *Coprario* John. Assumed name of John Cooper *c.*1570–1626. English composer of songs with lute or viol accompaniment. His works include several masques, such as *The Masque of Flowers* 1614, and sets of fantasies for organ and solo viol.

Copland Aaron 1900–1990. US composer. His early works were notoriously dissonant, but he gradually developed a gentler style with a regional flavour drawn from American folk music. Among his works are the ballets *Billy the Kid* 1939, *Rodeo* 1942, and *Appalachian Spring* 1944 (based on a poem by *Hart Crane*), and *Inscape for Orchestra* 1967.

cor anglais

Born in New York, Copland studied in France with Nadia Boulanger, and taught from 1940 at the Berkshire Music Center, now the Tanglewood Music Center, near Lenox, Massachusetts. He took avant-garde European styles and gave them a distinctive American accent. His eight film scores, including *The Heiress* 1949, set new standards for Hollywood.

cor anglais or *English horn* alto oboe in E flat with a distinctive tulip-shaped bell and warm nasal tone, heard to pastoral effect in Rossini's overture to *William Tell* 1829, and portraying a plaintive Sasha the duck in Prokofiev's *Peter and the Wolf* 1936.

corda Italian 'string'; as in *una corda* or ('one string') *u.c.* directing a pianist to depress the ◊soft pedal, which moves the hammers so that they strike only one or two strings per key instead of the usual three. *Tre corde* ('three strings') or *tutte le corde* (all the strings) reverses the marking. (See also ◊due corde.)

Corelli Arcangelo 1653–1713. Italian composer and violinist. He was one of the first virtuoso exponents of the Baroque violin and his music, marked by graceful melody, includes a set of *concerti grossi* and five sets of chamber sonatas.

Born near Milan, he studied in Bologna and in about 1685 settled in Rome, under the patronage of Cardinal Pietro Ottoboni, where he published his first violin sonatas.

cornamuse Renaissance capped double-reed woodwind musical instrument of straight bore and with a clear, reedy tone. In French it can refer to bagpipes, and in Italian to a ◊crumhorn.

cornet three-valved brass band instru- coronet
ment, soprano member in B flat of a
group of valved horns developed in
Austria and Germany about 1820–50 for
military band use. Of partly cylindrical
bore, its compact shape and deep conical
bell allow greater speed and agility of
intonation than the trumpet, at the
expense of less tonal precision and brilliance.

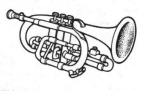

The cornet is typically played with vibrato, and has its own repertoire of virtuoso pieces. The cornet is a featured solo in Stravinsky's ballet *Petrushka* 1911 and *l'Histoire de Soldat/The Soldier's Tale* 1919, though its part is now more usually played by the trumpet.

cornett precursor of the orchestral brass cornet, combining woodwind finger technique with a brass cup mouthpiece. Its highly versatile tone made it a favoured instrument of Renaissance broken consorts (chamber ensembles of mixed instruments) and Baroque orchestras, and although superseded by brass instruments in the 18th century, it remained popular with military and church bands until well into the 19th century. It has also seen a revival this century as a result of the ◊authenticity movement.

Members of the cornett family include the straight soprano *mute cornett*, a curved alto *cornetto*, S-shaped tenor *lysarden*, and double S-shaped *serpent*, and *ophicleide*.

counterpoint (from Latin *punctus contra punctum* 'note against note') the art of simultaneously combining two or more independent lines (vocal or instrumental) with apparent freedom while preserving a harmonious effect. The term is associated most closely with works by composers of the 16th and 17th centuries such as Giovanni Palestrina and J S Bach.

It originated in ◊plainsong, with two independent vocal lines sung simultaneously.

counter-subject a melody which follows the opening subject (principal melody) in a ◊fugue. Typically, when the second voice enters with the subject, the first voice (which previously sang or played the subject) begins the counter-subject as a contrapuntal complement to the subject.

countertenor or *male alto* the highest natural male voice, sung with ◊head voice. It was favoured by the Elizabethans for its heroic brilliance of tone.

It was revived in the UK in the 1940s by singer Alfred Deller.

Couperin François le Grand 1668–1733. French composer. He was the best-known member of a musical family, which included his uncle Louis Couperin (1626–1661), composer for organ and harpsichord. A favoured composer of Louis XIV, François Couperin composed numerous chamber concertos and harpsichord suites, and published a standard keyboard tutor *L'Art de toucher le clavecin/The Art of Playing the Harpsichord* 1716 in which he laid down guidelines for fingering, phrasing, and ornamentation.

courante (French 'running') a dance originating in the 16th century and refined by the 17th century to form one of the standard movements of a Baroque ◊suite. The Italian courante is in quick triple time (3/8 or 3/4), with continuous 'running' figures in the melody. The French courante is a more moderate triple time (3/2) or compound duple time

(6/4), and often exploits the rhythmic disruption of changing from one metre to the other. Bach uses this variety in the courantes of his famous French Suites.

course the rank of strings on a lute, guitar, or mandolin. A course consists of one, two or three strings, tuned to one pitch (sometimes at octaves) and plucked together, as one string. The 12-string guitar is a modern example of a double-course instrument, with each pair tuned to the octave.

While the original purpose of doubling of strings may have been to increase loudness, an additional factor is improved liveliness of tone.

Covent Garden common name of the Royal Opera House in London. The present building was completed 1858 after two previous ones burnt down. The Royal Ballet is also in residence there.

Cowell Henry 1897–1965. US composer and theorist. His pioneering *New Musical Resources* 1930 sought to establish a rationale for modern music. He worked with Percy Grainger 1941 and alongside John Cage. Although remembered as a discoverer of piano effects such as strumming the strings in *Aeolian Harp* 1923 and inventor of the ◊prepared piano, for introducing ◊clusters, and using a ruler on the keys in *The Banshee* 1925, he was also an astute observer and writer on new music developments.

Cowell also wrote chamber and orchestral music and was active as a critic and publisher of 20th-century music.

Cramer John Baptist 1771–1858. German-born English composer, pianist, and teacher. He lived mostly in London and composed in a conservative style for his day, trying to emulate the music of Mozart. He is most famous for his 84 studies for piano 1804 and 1810, which are still used today. As a pianist he was admired for his technical command and ◊legato touch. He was one of a group of composers known as the ◊London Pianoforte School.

crescendo or *cresc.* (Italian 'growing') increase in the loudness of a passage by constant degrees. *Crescendo poco a poco* ('growing little by little') means that the crescendo should progress more gradually. The opposite marking is 'decrescendo' or 'diminuendo'.

Cristofori Bartolommeo di Francesco 1665–1731. Italian harpsichord-maker, inventor of the piano. He constructed 1709 a *gravicembalo col piano e forte* (harpsichord with softness and loudness), consisting of a harpsichord frame with a new ◊action mechanism: hammers hitting the strings instead of plucking them, allowing for the first time a gradation of loud to soft.

Crossley Paul 1944– . British pianist. He was joint artistic director of the London Sinfonietta from 1988. A specialist in the works of such composers as Ravel, Messiaen, and Michael Tippett, he studied with Messiaen and French pianist Yvonne Loriod (1924–).

cross rhythms either the simultaneous presentation of opposing rhythmic patterns within the same metre (for example one part playing two notes per beat while another part plays three notes per beat; '2 against 3'), or the superimposition of at least two different and unrelated metres (for example 3/4 in one part and 4/4 in another).

cross relation alternative name for ◊false relation.

crotchet (US *quarter note*) a note value one quarter the duration of a ◊semibreve. It is written as a filled, black note-head with a stem. It is the basic unit of beat for the most frequently used time signatures (2/4, 3/4, 4/4, etc).

Crumb George Henry 1929– . US composer. His works are reliant on sound imagery, based on unusual and imaginative sonorities such as the ◊musical saw in *Ancient Voices of Children* 1970. He has used electronic and aleatory compositional settings of poems by the Spanish poet Federico García Lorca (1898–1936).

crumhorn

crumhorn ('curved horn') or *krumhorn* any of a Renaissance family of woodwind instruments employing a double-reed enclosed in a 'cap', into which the player blows. It curves upwards, like a hook, and dates from the 15th century. There are soprano, alto, tenor, and bass variants, all of which emit a buzzing tone.

Cui César Antonovich 1835–1918. Russian composer and critic. He is best remembered for his writings in support of the Russian nationalist movement in music. A member of The ◊Five, he composed ten operas (including *Angelo* 1876 and *Le Flibustier/The Buccaneer* 1889) and orchestral and piano pieces of dubious quality, acknowledged so even by members of his own circle.

curtal or *dulcian* Renaissance woodwind instrument, ancestor of the bassoon, employing a double reed enclosed within a 'cap' into which the player blows. It has a mild reedy tone.

Curtis Institute music school in Philadelphia, founded by Mary Bok 1924 in memory of her father Cyrus Curtis. Since 1928 students have not had to pay tuition fees. Directors have included Josef Hofmann and Rudolf Serkin.

Curwen John 1816–1880. English cleric and educator. In about 1840 he established the *tonic sol-fa* system of music notation (a form of ◊solfeggio) in which the notes of the diatonic major scale are named by syllables (doh, ray, me, fah, soh, lah, te) to simplify singing by sight.

Curzon Clifford 1907–1982. English pianist. He made his reputation as a pianist of 18th-century composers, though he also played 19th- and 20th-century works in his early years. He was known as perhaps the greatest Mozartian of his day.

cut time alternative name for ◊alla breve.

cyclic form in musical analysis, a multimovement work in which the same motif, theme, melody or other notable compositional element is used throughout, at times in a different context or manifestation from its original form. Early examples include works by Handel and Vivaldi, but not until the 19th century did this technique reach its fruition, in works including Beethoven's Fifth Symphony 1808, Liszt's Piano Sonata in B minor 1853, and compositions based on the theories of Wagner's ◊leitmotiv and Berlioz's 'idée fixe' (a repeated ◊theme).

cymbal ancient percussion instrument of indefinite pitch, consisting of a shallow circular brass dish suspended at the centre; either used in pairs clashed together or singly, struck with a beater. Smaller finger cymbals or *crotala*, used by Debussy and Stockhausen, are precise in pitch. Turkish or 'buzz' cymbals incorporate loose rivets to extend the sound.

cymbal

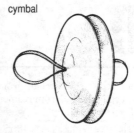

Czerny Carl 1791–1857. Austrian composer and pianist. He wrote an enormous quantity of religious and concert music, but is chiefly remembered for his books of graded studies and technical exercises used in piano teaching, including the *Complete Theoretical and Practical Pianoforte School* 1839 which is still in widespread use. He was taught by Beethoven, and he taught Liszt.

D

da capo or *D.C.* (Italian 'from the top') instructing a player to return to the beginning of the ◊movement. A companion instruction is ◊dal segno ('from the sign').

Dalcroze Emile Jaques 1865–1950. See ◊Jaques-Dalcroze, Emile.

Dallapiccola Luigi 1904–1975. Italian composer. Initially a Neo-Classicist, he adopted a lyrical twelve-tone style after 1945. His works include the operas *Il prigioniero/The Prisoner* 1949 and *Ulisse/Ulysses* 1968, as well as many vocal and instrumental compositions. He opposed the fascist regime in his *Canti di prigionera/Songs of Captivity* 1941.

dal segno or *D.S.* (Italian 'from the sign') instructing a player to return to a point earlier in the music, other than the beginning, indicated in the score by a crossed 'S' sign. A return to the beginning is termed 'da capo' ('from the top') or 'D.C.'.

damper pedal alternative name for the ◊sustaining pedal.

Da Ponte Lorenzo (Conegliano Emmanuele) 1749–1838. Italian librettist. He is renowned for his collaboration with Mozart in *The Marriage of Figaro* 1786, *Don Giovanni* 1787, and *Così fan tutte* 1790. His adaptations of contemporary plays are deepened by a rich life experience and understanding of human nature.

Appointed as a professor in literature at Treviso Seminary 1773, his radical views and immoral behaviour led to his banishment from Venice 1779. Travelling to Vienna, he was appointed as librettist to the New Italian Theatre 1781 on the recommendation of Salieri. After completing successful librettos for Mozart and other composers, he emigrated 1805 to the USA, eventually becoming a teacher of Italian language and literature.

Dart Thurston 1921–1971. English musicologist and harpsichordist. His articles and pioneer reinterpretations of Baroque classics such as

Bach's *Brandenburg Concertos* helped to launch the trend towards ◊authenticity in early music.

David Félicien César 1810–1876. French composer. His symphonic fantasy *The Desert* 1844 was inspired by travels in Palestine. He was one of the first Western composers to introduce oriental scales and melodies into his music.

Davies Henry Walford 1869–1941. English composer and broadcaster. From 1934 he was ◊Master of the King's Musick, and he contributed to the musical education of Britain through regular radio talks.

His compositions include the cantata *Everyman* 1904 and *Solemn Melody* 1908 for organ and strings. He also wrote chamber music and ◊part-songs.

Davies Peter Maxwell 1934– . English composer and conductor. His music combines medieval techniques and ◊serialism with a heightened ◊expressionism, as in his opera *Taverner* 1968. Other works include the opera *The Lighthouse* 1980. He has also composed extensively for his chamber group The Fires Of London. He was appointed conductor of the BBC Scottish Symphony Orchestra 1985.

Davis Colin 1927– . English conductor. He was musical director at Sadler's Wells 1961–65, chief conductor of the BBC Symphony Orchestra 1967–71, musical director of the Royal Opera 1971–86, and chief conductor of the Bavarian Radio Symphony Orchestra from 1986. He is particularly noted for his instinctive and technically fine performances of Berlioz, Mozart, and Michael Tippett.

D.C. abbreviation for ◊da capo (Italian 'from the beginning').

Debussy (Achille-) Claude 1862–1918. French composer. After first admiring Wagner, he broke with German Romanticism and introduced new qualities of ◊impressionism in melody and harmony, often based on the ◊whole-tone scale. His work includes *Prélude à l'après-midi d'un faune/Prelude to the Afternoon of a Faun* 1894, illustrating a poem by Stéphane Mallarmé (1842–1898), and the opera *Pelléas et Mélisande* 1902.

Among his other works are numerous piano pieces, songs, orchestral pieces such as *La Mer* 1905, and the ballet *Jeux* 1913. Debussy also published witty and humorous critical writing about the music of his day, featuring the fictional character Monsieur Croche *antidilettante* (professional debunker), a figure based on Erik Satie.

decibel basic unit for measuring intensity (volume) of sound. It represents approximately the smallest variation of volume that a human ear can perceive.

decrescendo or *decresc.* (Italian 'decreasing') a decrease in the loudness of a passage by constant degrees. *Decrescendo poco a poco* means that the decrescendo should progress more gradually. An alternative marking is 'diminuendo'. The opposite marking is 'crescendo'.

de Falla Manuel 1876–1946. Spanish composer. See ◊Falla, Manuel de.

degree the position of a note in a scale. The first degree of C major is therefore C, the second is D, the third is E, etc. Alternative terms for the seven degrees of a scale are, starting with the first degree: tonic, supertonic, mediant, subdominant, dominant, submediant, and leading note.

Delalande Michel-Richard 1657–1726. French organist and composer. He composed for the court of Louis XIV. His works include grand motets and numerous orchestral suites.

Delibes (Clément Philibert) Léo 1836–1891. French composer. His lightweight, perfectly judged works include the ballets *Coppélia* 1870 and *Sylvia* 1876, and the opera *Lakmé* 1883.

Delius Frederick (Theodore Albert) 1862–1934. English composer. The son of German parents, he wrote haunting, richly harmonious works including the opera *A Village Romeo and Juliet* 1901; the choral pieces *Appalachia* 1903, *Sea Drift* 1904, *A Mass of Life* 1905; orchestral works such as *In a Summer Garden* 1908, *A Song of the High Hills* 1911; chamber music; and songs.

Born in Bradford, he tried orange-growing in Florida, before studying music in Leipzig 1888, where he met Grieg. From 1890 Delius lived mainly in France and in 1903 married the artist Jelka Rosen. Although blind and paralysed for the last ten years of his life, he continued to write music.

Deller Alfred 1912–1979. English countertenor. He was the singer who revived the ◊countertenor voice and repertoire of 16th- to 18th-century music in the UK. He founded the Deller Consort 1948 and made notable recordings of John Dowland, John Blow, and Henry Purcell.

Del Mar Norman (1919–1994). English conductor, composer, and horn player. He founded the Chelsea Symphony Orchestra 1944, and was guest conductor with leading orchestras. He specialized in the late 19th- and 20th-century repertory, and was noted for his clear interpretations of complex scores. He also composed symphonies and a number of works for horn.

demisemiquaver (US *32nd note*) a note value 1/32nd the duration of a ◊semibreve. It is written as a filled, blackened note-head with a stem and three flags (tails).

descant high-pitched line for one or more sopranos, added above the normal soprano line (melody) of a hymn tune; a high-pitched instrument of a family, such as the descant recorder (US soprano recorder); also, an improvised melody sung against a written voice-part (see ◊discant).

Desprez Josquin 1440–1521. Franco-Flemish composer; see ◊Josquin Desprez.

Dessau Paul 1894–1979. German composer. His work includes incidental music to the theatre pieces of Bertolt Brecht (1898–1956); an opera, *Der Verurteilung des Lukullus/The Trial of Lucullus* 1949, also to a libretto by Brecht; and numerous choral works and songs.

development the central section of ◊sonata form, in which thematic material presented in the opening section ('exposition') is reworked in other keys before returning to the tonic in the last section ('recapitulation').

de Vitry Philippe 1291–1361. See ◊Vitry Philippe de.

dhola deep-toned Indian drum, barrel-shaped and played at both ends. It is played with the hands and produces a flexible tone that rises from the bass register to the tenor register.

Diabelli Anton 1781–1858. Austrian publisher and composer. He was the original publisher of Beethoven, Haydn, and Schubert. He is most famous today for appearing in the title of Beethoven's *Diabelli Variations* 1823, which formed part of a contribution by fifty composers, each of whom was asked to compose a piece based on a waltz theme written by Diabelli himself.

diapason the principal stop of an organ, which gives the instrument its characteristic tone quality. Diapasons may be 'open', producing a bright colour, or 'stopped', producing a muffled but sweet tone. The equivalent stop on a German-built instrument is the Prinzipal. In French usage, 'diapason normal' is the equivalent of ◊concert pitch.

diatonic scale a scale of the seven notes of any major or minor key.

didjeridu lip-reed wind instrument made from a hollow eucalyptus branch (1.5 m/4 ft long) and blown to produce rhythmic, booming notes of relatively constant pitch. It was first developed and played by Australian Aborigines.

digital adjective describing a method of sound recording in which audio signals are converted into a series of electronically-represented pulses, determined by the voltage of the sound. This information can be stored for reproduction or manipulation in the case of composition in the electronic medium.

diminished interval a reduction of interval size within a chord. Opposite of ◊augmentation.

diminished seventh an interval consisting of a minor ◊seventh which is contracted (diminished) by one semitone, to create an interval of nine semitones (for example A–G flat); alternatively, a chord consisting of a minor seventh which is contracted (diminished) by one semitone. If every voice of the chord is filled in, there is also a minor third and a diminished fifth, for example A – C – E flat – G flat. This chord, which consists only of a series of minor thirds, is ambiguous harmonically and therefore useful in ◊modulation (moving from one key to another).

diminuendo (Italian 'diminishing') a decrease in the loudness of a passage by constant degrees. *Diminuendo poco a poco* means that the diminuendo should progress more gradually. An alternative marking is 'decrescendo'. The opposite marking is 'crescendo'.

diminution or *divisions* a method of composition and improvising ◊variations by dividing the basic note values of a theme into smaller fractions representing higher tempi in proportion to the original time values, most common before the 18th century.

It can be found in later keyboard variations of Mozart, Beethoven, and Brahms; in the late 20th century Stockhausen has reinvented the concept.

D'Indy Vincent 1851–1931. See ◊Indy, Vincent D'.

dirge (Latin *dirige*, from the office of the dead) song of lamentation for the dead.

discant or *descant* in medieval music, a form of ◊polyphony, originally an improvisation technique in which one voice had the ◊cantus firmus (fixed melody) whilst another or several others extemporized a free accompanying part or parts. It is found in early medieval ◊plainsong, such as ◊organum.

discord a combination of notes jarring to the ear. See ◊dissonance.

dissonance or *discord* a combination of two or more tones displeasing to the ear. It is the opposite of a ◊consonance, and in music before the 20th century was almost invariably resolved.

divertimento a suite of 18th-century music written for light entertainment, usually in four to nine movements, for a small string, wind, or mixed ensemble. Mozart wrote 25, entitling them in addition to 'divertimento', 'serenades' and 'cassations'.

divisi or *div.* (Italian 'divided') in orchestral compositions, associated with passages of double notes, directing players reading one part (for example first violins) to divide into groups and play only one note per instrument, rather than trying to play both notes at once. It appears most often in orchestral string parts.

divisions another name for ◊diminution.

DMus abbreviation for *Doctor of Music*.

dodecaphony music composed according to the ◊twelve-tone system of composition.

Dohnányi Ernst von (Ernö) 1877–1960. Hungarian pianist, conductor, composer, and teacher. His music tends to be less nationalistic than his contemporaries Bartók and Kodály, while still retaining a Hungarian flavour. His compositions include *Variations on a Nursery Song* 1914 and *Second Symphony for Orchestra* 1948.

dolce (Italian 'sweet') sweet, soft expression.

Dolmetsch Arnold 1858–1940. Swiss-born English musician and instrumentmaker. Together with his family, including his son *Carl* (1911–   ), he revived interest in the practical performance of solo and consort music for lute, recorders, and viols, and established the Baroque soprano (descant) recorder as an inexpensive musical instrument for schools. See also ◊authenticity.

dominant the fifth note of the diatonic scale, for example, G in the C major scale.

The chord of the dominant is a triad built upon the dominant note. Music of the 18th century frequently relies on the tension between tonic and dominant keys, extended over the duration of a section or movement, as in ◊sonata form, before the tonic is re-established at the end.

Domingo Placido 1937–   . Spanish lyric tenor. He specializes in Italian and French 19th-century operatic roles to which he brings a finely tuned dramatic temperament. Since his New York debut 1965 he has established a world reputation as a sympathetic leading tenor, and has made many films including the 1988 version of Puccini's *Tosca* set in Rome, and the 1990 Zeffirelli production of Leoncavallo's *I Pagliacci/The Strolling Players*.

He also sang with tenors José Carreras and Luciano Pavarotti in a recording of operatic hits released to coincide with the World Cup soccer series in Rome 1990.

Donizetti Gaetano 1797–1848. Italian composer. He created more than 60 operas, including *Lucrezia Borgia* 1833, *Lucia di Lammermoor* 1835, *La Fille du régiment* 1840, *La Favorite* 1840, and *Don Pasquale* 1843. They show the influence of Rossini and Bellini, and are characterized by a flow of expressive melodies.

Dorati Antál 1906–1988. US conductor, born in Hungary. He toured with ballet companies 1933–45 and went on to conduct orchestras in the USA and Europe in a career spanning more than half a century. Dorati gave many first performances of Bartók's music and recorded all Haydn's symphonies with the Philharmonia Hungarica.

Dorian mode one of the ♭church modes, a scale D – C, centred around and beginning on D, which uses only the notes of the C major scale.

double bass large bowed four-stringed (sometimes five-stringed) musical instrument, the bass of the violin family. It is descended from the *violone*, the double-bass viol. Performers include Domenico Dragonetti, composer of eight concertos, the Russian-born US conductor Serge Koussevitsky (1874– 1951), and the US virtuoso Gary Karr (1941–   ). The double bass features in the well-loved 'Elephants' solo, No 5 of Saint-Saëns' *Carnival of the Animals* 1897.

double bass

double fugue a ♭fugue consisting of two subjects (principal melodies). Of two types, one consists of three sections: a fugue on subject A, a fugue on subject B, and a fugue combining A and B. The other consists of a fugue in which both subjects are introduced at the beginning of the piece and combined throughout.

Dowland John 1563–1626. English composer. He composed lute songs, introducing daring expressive refinements of harmony and ornamentation to English Renaissance style in the service of an elevated aesthetic of melancholy, as in the masterly *Lachrymae* 1605.

downbeat the first or the strong beat of a bar, analogous to the downstroke of a conductor's hand; the opposite of upbeat.

Dragonetti Domenico 1763–1846. Italian-born double bass player and composer. A virtuoso player, he established the instrument's solo credentials in tours of Britain and Europe, performing a repertoire including a transcription for double bass of Beethoven's Cello Sonata in D 1811. His own compositions include eight concertos and numerous string quartets.

drone an accompanying constant tone or harmony to a changing melody. It is a feature of many classical and folk traditions, and is produced by many instruments of folk music, including the Indian vina, bagpipes, and hurdy-gurdy. Drone effects in written music include the organ ◊pedal point and the ◊musette dance form.

Among examples of drone in the concert repertoire are Wagner's overture to *Das Rheingold/The Rhinegold* 1854 and the mystery chord of Schoenberg's third orchestral piece 'Farben/Colours' from the *Five Pieces for Orchestra* 1909.

drum any of a class of percussion instruments including *slit drums* made of wood, *steel drums* fabricated from oil drums, and a majority group of *skin drums* consisting of a shell or vessel of wood, metal, or earthenware across one or both ends of which is stretched a membrane of hide or plastic. Drums are struck with the hands or with a stick or pair of sticks; they are among the oldest instruments known.

Most drums are of indeterminate low or high pitch and function as rhythm instruments. The exceptions are steel drums, orchestral timpani (kettledrums), and Indian tabla, which are tuned to precise pitches. Double-ended African kalungu ('talking drums') can be varied in pitch by the player squeezing on the tension cords. Frame drums including the Irish bodhran and Basque tambour are smaller and lighter in tone and may incorporate jingles or rattles.

Orchestral drums consist of timpani, tambourine, snare, side, and bass drums. Military bands of foot soldiers employ the snare and side drums, and among cavalry regiments a pair of kettledrums mounted on horseback are played on ceremonial occasions.

Recent innovations include the rotary tunable rototoms, electronic drums, and the drum machine, a percussion synthesizer.

D.S. abbreviation for ◊dal segno (Italian 'from the sign').

due corde (Italian 'two strings') directing a pianist to depress the ◊soft pedal halfway (as in Beethoven's Piano Sonata in A flat 1822) so that the hammer hits two of the three strings for each note; or directing a violinist to use two strings, which affects the timbre, even though the passage in question could be played on one string.

duet or *duo* music or ensemble of two voices or instruments. A piano duet is normally two players sharing a single instrument (also called 'piano four-hands'); a piano duo is two players on two pianos.

Dufay Guillaume 1400–1474. Franco-Flemish composer. He wrote secular songs and sacred music, including 84 songs and eight masses. His work marks a transition from the style of the Middle Ages to the expressive melodies and rich harmonies of the Renaissance.

Dukas Paul (Abraham) 1865–1935. French composer and teacher. His scrupulous orchestration and chromatically enriched harmonies were admired by Debussy. His small output includes the opera *Ariane et Barbe-Bleue/Ariane and Bluebeard* 1907, the ballet *La Péri/The Peri* 1912, and the animated orchestral scherzo *L'Apprenti sorcier/The Sorcerer's Apprentice* 1897.

dulcian organ stop of reedy quality, usually of 16-foot pitch (sounding an octave lower than written); also an alternative name for the ¢curtal.

dulcimer a form of zither, consisting of a shallow open trapezoidal soundbox across which strings are stretched laterally; they are horizontally struck by hand-held lightweight hammers or beaters. It produces clearly differentiated pitches of consistent quality and is more agile and wide ranging in pitch than the harp or lyre. In Hungary the dulcimer (a variety known as the cimbalom), is in current use.

Of Middle Eastern origin, the dulcimer spread into Europe about 1100 and was introduced to China and Korea about 1800.

Dunstable John c. 1385–1453. English composer. He wrote most notably masses and motets, and was possibly the first to compose instrumental accompaniments to church music. He is considered one of the founders of Renaissance harmony.

Duparc (Marie Eugène) Henri Fouques 1848–1933. French composer. He studied under César Franck. His songs, though only 15 in number, are memorable for their lyric sensibility.

duple time a metre in which the bar may be divided into two beats, as in 2/4 and 6/8.

Du Pré Jacqueline 1945–1987. English cellist. She was celebrated for her proficient technique and powerful interpretations of the classical cello repertory, particularly of Elgar. She had an international concert career while still in her teens and made many recordings, until stricken with multiple sclerosis. Although confined to a wheelchair for the last 14 years of her life, she continued to work as a teacher and to campaign on behalf of other sufferers of the disease.

dur (German 'hard') German equivalent to 'major' when refering to a key, as in 'C dur' (C major). Opposite of 'moll'.

Dussek Jan Ladislav 1760–1812. Bohemian (Czech) composer and pianist. A virtuoso pianist, his compositions, which include 28 piano sonatas and 15 piano concertos, often display technically challenging passages, by the standard of his day. Composing more fully textured (and often more harmonically adventurous) music than most of his contemporaries, Dussek foreshadowed many of the musical developments of the 19th century. He was one of a group of composers known as the ◊London Pianoforte School.

Dutilleux Henri 1916– . French composer. He wrote instrumental music in elegant Neo-Romantic style. His works include *Métaboles* 1965 for orchestra and *Ainsi la nuit/Thus the Night* 1976 for string quartet.

Dvořák Antonin (Leopold) 1841–1904. Czech composer. International recognition came with two sets of *Slavonic Dances* 1878 and 1886. He was director of the National Conservatory, New York, 1892–95 and works such as his *New World Symphony* 1893 reflect his interest in American folk themes, including black and native American. He wrote nine symphonies; ◊symphonic poems; operas, including *Rusalka* 1900; large-scale choral works; the *Carnival* 1892 and other overtures; violin and cello concertos; chamber music; piano pieces; and songs. His Romantic music reveals the influence especially of Brahms, and also of Czech dance forms.

dynamics terms and notation indicating relative loudness, changes in loudness such as 'crescendo' (growing louder) and 'diminuendo' (getting quieter) or loudness in accentuation such as 'rinforzando'.

Dynamic markings from Monteverdi to J S Bach were primarily objective indicators of tonal change, occasionally spatial and directional in significance. During this period the performer had great freedom to create his or her own dynamics. Dynamic notation emerged slowly during the 18th century as the expressive clavichord and fortepiano appeared, eventually superseding the less responsive harpsichord. After 1950 many composers attempted to bring dynamics under serial control (◊integral serialism), but with only limited success.

E

early music referring to music composed in previous periods. Its meaning has changed over the years: originally it denoted Western music composed from the early Middle Ages to the Renaissance. As the ◊authenticity movement grew during the mid-20th century it came to include music of the Baroque period as well. Today there is no precise limitation regarding the qualification of early music, but it is generally accepted to include music as late as the early 19th century. The journal *Early Music*, established 1973, focuses on ◊performance practice and other musicological issues concerning music prior to the Romantic period.

eighth note US term for ◊*quaver*, a note value one eighth the duration of a ◊semibreve.

Elder Mark 1947– . English conductor. He was music director of the English National Opera (ENO) from 1979 and of the Rochester Philharmonic Orchestra, USA, from 1989.

Elder worked at Glyndebourne from 1970, conducted with the Australian Opera from 1972, and joined the ENO 1974. As principal conductor of the ENO, he specializes in 19th- and 20th-century repertoire.

electronic music term first applied 1954 to edited tape music composed primarily of electronically generated and modified tones, organized in ◊series using objective scales of differentiation to distinguish it from the more intuitive methodology of ◊musique concrète. The term was subsequently extended to include prerecorded vocal and instrumental sounds organized in a similar way, as in Stockhausen's *Gesang der Jünglinge/Song of the Youths* 1955 and Berio's *Differences* 1957 for chamber ensemble and tape. Other pioneers of electronic music are Milton Babbitt and Bruno Maderna.

After 1960, with the arrival of the purpose-built synthesizer developed by *Robert Moog* (1934–), Peter Zinovieff (1934–), and others, interest switched to computer-aided synthesis, culminating in the system installed at ◊IRCAM.

Elgar Edward (William) 1857–1934. English composer. His *Enigma Variations* 1899 brought him fame, and although his celebrated oratorio *The Dream of Gerontius* 1900 (based on the written work by theologian John Henry Newman (1801–1890)) was initially unpopular in Britain, it was well received at Düsseldorf 1902, leading to a surge of interest in his earlier works, including the *Pomp and Circumstance* marches.

Among his later works are oratorios, two symphonies, a violin concerto, chamber music, songs, and the symphonic poem *Falstaff* 1913. His later works, which tend to be more introspective than the earlier ones, culminate in the poignant cello concerto of 1919. After this piece, Elgar published no further music of significance. He concentrated on transcriptions and he made some early gramophone recordings of his own work.

embellishment an alternative name for ◊ornamentation.

embouchure the position of the lips and tension of the facial muscles required to produce a good tone on a brass or woodwind instrument.

encore (French 'again') an unprogrammed extra item, usually short and well known, played at the end of a concert to please an enthusiastic audience.

end pin alternative term for ◊tail pin.

English horn alternative name for ◊cor anglais, musical instrument of the oboe family.

enharmonic describing a note or harmony capable of alternative interpretations, used as a link between passages of normally unrelated key. For example, an enharmonic modulation from C sharp to F major plays on the equivalence, in keyboard terms, of the notes E sharp and F.

ensemble (French 'together') any combination of musicians, a term used especially to refer to chamber music groups in which every performer plays a different part, or in opera to refer to a piece in which several singers perform together.

entr'acte (French 'between acts') orchestral music played between the acts of an opera or play.

episode in a ◊fugue, a passage or section linking appearances of the subject (principal melody), usually non-thematic in nature and often forming sequences in a order to modulate (move from one key to another) before the subject establishes a new key; or in a ◊rondo, one of a variety of sections appearing between and contrasting with the recurring principal theme.

equal temperament a type of ◊temperament (tuning of a scale) in which every semitone within an octave is exactly equal.

espressione Italian 'expression'

espressivo or *espr.* Italian 'expressive'.

étude (French 'study') musical exercise designed to develop technique.

euphonium tenor valved brass band instrument of the bugle type, often mistaken for a tuba, and called a *baryton* in Germany.

eurhythmlcs practice of coordinated bodily movement as an aid to musical development. It was founded about 1900 by the Swiss musician Emil Jaques-Dalcroze, professor of harmony at the Geneva conservatoire. He devised a series of 'gesture' songs, to be sung simultaneously with certain bodily actions.

evensong an evening service of the Anglican church in which most of the liturgy is sung in ◊Anglican chant, it also contains hymns, psalms, and the canticles: ◊Magnificat and ◊Nunc Dimitis.

exposition the first section of a classical sonata, concerto, or symphony first movement, in which the principal themes are clearly outlined. Typically, the themes of the exposition fall into two groups. In the first group, themes appear in the ◊tonic key, while in the second group different themes appear in the ◊dominant.

expression signs or words providing an emotional context for a piece of music. These are indicated by phrasing and dynamic markings, but the most subtle types of expression cannot be represented on the page and must be left to the performer.

expressionism term borrowed from the visual arts to describe music of a deeply subjective nature, in which the composer strives to compose without the mediation of conscious, intellectual control. Applied specifically to pre-serial works of Schoenberg, Webern, and Berg.

F

f abbreviation for ♭forte (loud).

Falla Manuel de (full name Manuel Maria de Falla y Matheu) 1876–1946. Spanish composer. His opera *La vida breve/Brief Life* 1905 (performed 1913) was followed by the ballets *El amor brujo/Love the Magician* 1915 and *El sombrero de tres picos/The Three-Cornered Hat* 1919, and his most ambitious concert work, *Noches en los jardines de España/Nights in the Gardens of Spain* 1916.

Born in Cádiz, he lived in France, where he was influenced by the impressionist composers Debussy and Ravel. In 1939 he moved to Argentina. The folk idiom of southern Spain is an integral part of his compositions. He also wrote songs and pieces for piano and guitar.

false relation or *cross relation* in harmony, the appearance in different voices (independent parts) of two notes which bear the same note-name but not the same pitch, either simultaneously or in close succession; that is, where one is modified by a flat or sharp, and the other is a natural. For example, false relations occur if an E flat in the soprano voice is followed in the next chord by an E natural in the tenor voice. In traditional harmony and counterpoint, false relations are not encouraged because harmonic alterations in one voice, as represented by a modifying sharp or flat, are resolved most smoothly within the same voice.

falsetto a male voice singing in the female (soprano or alto) register, using ♭head voice.

fandango an 18th-century Spanish dance in moderate to fast triple time (3/8 or 3/4), danced by a couple with the accompaniment of a guitar and castanets. Fandangos are found in Mozart's *Marriage of Figaro* 1786, Gluck's *Don Juan* 1761, and Rimsky-Korsakov's *Capriccio espagnol/Spanish Capriccio* 1887.

fanfare a ceremonial short and brilliant tune for trumpets, or a piece for other instruments imitating the effect of trumpets. Written traditionally for valveless (natural) instruments, fanfares typically include notes of the major ◊triad and ◊diatonic scale. An example of a fanfare is the introduction to Act II of Wagner's *Tristan und Isolde* 1865.

fantasia or *fantasy*, *phantasy*, or *fancy* a free-form instrumental composition for keyboard or chamber ensemble, originating in the late Renaissance, and much favoured by English composers Dowland, Gibbons, and Byrd. Intended to sound like an ◊improvisation, some composers such as J S Bach and C P E Bach leave the precise figuration of given harmonic progressions to the performer.

Farnaby Giles 1563–1640. English composer. He wrote madrigals, psalms for the *Whole Booke of Psalms* 1621, edited by Thomas Ravencroft (1582–1633), and music for virginals, over 50 pieces being represented in the 17th-century manuscript collection the ◊*Fitzwilliam Virginal Book*.

Fauré Gabriel (Urbain) 1845–1924. French composer. His music successfully spans the gap between ◊Romanticism and 20th-century harmonic boldness. He is remembered for his songs, chamber music, and a choral *Requiem* 1888. He was a pupil of Saint-Saëns, became professor of composition at the Paris Conservatoire 1896 and its director 1905–20.

Feldman Morton 1926–1988. US composer. An associate of John Cage and Earle Brown in the 1950s, he devised an indeterminate notation based on high, middle, and low instrumental registers and time cells of fixed duration for his *Projection* 1951, a series for various ensembles, later exploiting the freedoms of classical notation in a succession of reflective studies in vertical tone mixtures including *Madame Press Died Last Week at 90* 1970.

feminine adjective describing a cadence or phrase which ends on an unstressed beat of the bar, most typically the second beat.

Ferneyhough Brian 1943– . English composer. His uncompromising, detailed compositions, influenced by Boulez and Stockhausen, include *Carceri d'Invenzione* 1982, a cycle of seven works inspired by the engravings of Piranesi, *Time and Motion Studies* 1977, and string quartets.

Ferrier Kathleen (Mary) 1912–1953. English contralto. She brought warmth and depth of conviction to English oratorio roles during wartime and subsequently to opera and lieder, including Gluck's *Orfeo ed Euridice*, Mahler's *Das Lied von der Erde/The Song of the Earth*, and the role of Lucretia in Benjamin Britten's *The Rape of Lucretia*.

ff abbreviation for fortissimo, very loud.

fiddle generic term for a bowed stringed instrument. It is also applied to specific instruments, usually of foreign origin.

The *American Apache fiddle* has a hollow tubular body, often made of cactus; the *Middle East spike fiddle* rests on the leg and has a dish-shaped soundbox; *African fiddles* take many forms, including the shoe-like *rebab*; *Asian fiddles* include the Japanese *ko-kiu*, the Mongolian *morinchur*, and the Chinese *erh-hu*. *Medieval* and *Renaissance fiddles*, held at the shoulder, are the immediate predecessors of the violin.

Fiedler Arthur 1894–1979. US orchestra conductor. Concerned to promote the appreciation of music among the public, he founded the Boston Pops Orchestra 1930, dedicated to popularizing light classical music through live and televised concert appearances.

Born in Boston and trained at the Academy of Music in Berlin, Fiedler joined the Boston Symphony Orchestra 1916.

Field John 1782–1837. Irish-born composer and pianist. Often regarded as one of a group of composers known as the ◊London Pianoforte School, all of his works include the piano, reaching their peak artistically with his ◊nocturnes, a genre he named and devised. These nocturnes anticipate those by Chopin by twenty years, especially regarding their forward-looking textures and ◊passage work.

As an apprentice to Clementi, he travelled throughout Europe demonstrating instruments for the firm of pianomakers established by his master. He settled in St. Petersburg 1803, where he composed most of his mature music.

fife small transverse flute of similar range to the piccolo, an octave above the standard flute. Swiss in origin, the fife is a popular military band instrument, played with the side drums and associated with historic parades.

fifth an interval of five diatonic notes, consisting of three whole tones and a semitone, for example C – G. A fifth is an example of a 'perfect interval' because it remains the same in both major and minor keys. A fifth may be augmented (by one semitone), for example C – G sharp, or diminished (by one semitone), for example C – G flat.

figured bass in 17th- and 18th-century music, notation for a leading harpsichord or organ part indicating the ♭continuo line in standard notation and the remaining music by numeric chord indications, allowing the player to fill in the appropriate harmonies, usually as accompaniment to other players. The practice declined during the late 18th century, as composers notated more fully the required textures and performers concentrated less on the art of embellishment and improvisation, and more on the acquisition of virtuoso technique. Although the practice never disappeared, it has seen a revival in the ♭authenticity movement of this century.

film score in contemporary usage, music specially written to accompany a film on the soundtrack. In the early days of cinema a ♭symphonic poem was composed as a loosely aligned accompaniment to a major silent film, or background music was improvised or assembled by pit musicians with the aid of a Kinothek theme catalogue. With the arrival of optical sound on film came the fully synchronized Hollywood film score.

Composers for silent films include Saint-Saëns, Arthur Honegger, and Edmund Meisel, whose music for Eisenstein's *Battleship Potemkin* 1925 was banned by the authorities. Composers for sound film include Georges Auric, Aaron Copland, Prokofiev, William Walton, Bernard Herrmann, and Ennio Morricone.

finale a normally fast final movement of a work, or an elaborate conclusion of an opera incorporating a variety of ensembles.

fingerboard upper surface of the neck of a string instrument against which the fingers press to alter the pitch. Violins have smooth fingerboards, allowing the player scope to alter the pitch continuously; other instruments such as the viol, guitar, and lute have frets attached or inlaid to regulate intonation.

fingering notation directing the player to use specific fingers on specific notes. In piano music '1' represents the thumb, '2' the index finger, and so on. In orchestral string music '1' represents the index finger, '2' the middle finger, and so on.

fipple flute an instrument of the flute family that has a plug or 'fipple' in the mouthpiece, directing the flow of air past a rigid and sharp reed-like edge. Instruments include the recorder and various African and Asian pipes.

Fischer-Dieskau Dietrich 1925– . German baritone singer. His intelligently focused and subtly understated interpretations of opera and lieder introduced a new depth and intimacy to a wide-ranging repertoire extending in opera from Gluck to Berg's *Wozzeck*, Henze, and Britten, and from Bach arias to lieder of Schubert, Wolf, and Schoenberg. Since 1973 he has also conducted.

Fitzwilliam Virginal Book manuscript collection of 297 mainly English 17th-century compositions for keyboard instruments copied by Francis Tregian (1574–1619) and acquired by Richard Fitzwilliam (1745–1816) who bequeathed it to Cambridge University. Among composers represented are William Byrd, John Bull, and Giles Farnaby.

Five, The or *The Mighty Five* or *The Mighty Handful* term applied by art critic Vladimir Stasov (1824–1906) to the St Petersburg group of five composers – Balakirev, Borodin, Musorgsky, Rimsky-Korsakov, and Cui – whose establishment of a distinctively Russian nationalist idiom (built on Russian folk elements) he promoted.

flageolet whistle flute popular in France and England as a town band instrument during the 17th–19th centuries.

flamenco music and dance of the Andalusian gypsies of S Spain, evolved from Andalusian and Arabic folk music. The *cante* (song) is sometimes performed as a solo but more often accompanied by guitar music and passionate improvised dance. Hand clapping, finger clicking (castanets are a more recent addition), and enthusiastic shouts are all features. Male flamenco dancers excel in powerful, rhythmic footwork while the female dancers place emphasis on the graceful and erotic movements of their hands and bodies.

flat a note or a key that is played a semitone lower in pitch than the written value, indicated by a flat sign or key signature. It is cancelled by a ♮natural sign. It can also refer to inaccurate intonation by a player.

flue pipes the majority of pipes in an organ, which generate sound by directing air over a narrow rigid edge (as when a person blows across the top of a bottle). The other pipes are known as reeds. See ▷organ.

flugelhorn alto valved brass band instrument of the bugle type. In B flat, it has a similar range to the cornet but is of mellower tone. In the classical repertory it is found in Vaughan Williams's Ninth Symphony 1957 and Stravinsky's cantata *Threni* 1958.

flute or *transverse flute* side-blown soprano woodwind instrument of considerable antiquity. The player blows across an end hole, the air current being split by the opposite edge which causes vibrations within the tube. The fingers are placed over holes in the tube to create different notes.

flute

The flute has a extensive concert repertoire, including familiar pieces by J S Bach, Mozart, and the pastoral refrain of Debussy's *Prélude à l'après-midi d'un faun/Prelude to the Afternoon of a Faun* 1894. Vivaldi wrote a number of concertos for piccolo, and Bruno Maderna has composed for alto and bass flutes.

Flutes first existed in Asia about 900 BC. European flutes can be traced back to about 1100, and include the military fife, subsequently developed by the Hotteterre family of instrumentmakers into the single-key Baroque flute. Today's orchestral chromatic flutes with extensive keywork derive from further modifications in the 19th century by Theobald Boehm. They include the soprano flute, the higher piccolo, the alto, and the bass flute, a rarity in the orchestra but much in vogue during the avant-garde 1950s.

folk music body of traditional music, originally transmitted orally. Many folk songs originated as a rhythmic accompaniment to manual work or to mark a specific ritual. Folk song is usually melodic, not harmonic, and the modes used are distinctive of the country of origin.

A burgeoning interest in ballad poetry in the later 18th century led to the discovery of a rich body of folk song in Europe. The multi-ethnic background of the USA has conserved a wealth of material derived from European, African, and Latin American sources. Throughout the 18th and 19th centuries many composers have been aware of national folk-styles and dances, but the systematic notation of folk melodies began only at the turn of the 20th century by ethnomusicologists such as Bartók.

form the large-scale structure and overall design of a composition, providing a coherent framework for the effective presentation of musical ideas. Short pieces do not require complicated forms because the thematic material is usually sufficiently coherent in itself. The simplest forms are *binary form*, which consists of two sections often separated by a double bar (marking-off a section), and simple *ternary* form, which consists of one section followed by a contrasting section, followed by the return of the first section. Most larger-scale forms are expansions and developments of these two basic types, carefully using a balance of thematic development and transformation, repetition, variation, and contrast. Examples include *sonata form* and *rondo form*. During the 19th century, when Romantic composers such as Wagner fought against standard Classical forms, the alternative structure of a literary text or idea often came to replace the traditional, more technical, compositional forms.

forte or *f* (Italian 'strong') loud.

fortepiano a piano of the 18th and early 19th century, invented 1709 by Italian maker Bartolomeo Cristofori, having small leather-bound hammers and harpsichord strings. Over the following 150 years the instrument evolved until it began to resemble the piano of today. However, the fortepiano has seen a revival this century as a result of the ♭authenticity movement. Specialist performers include Malcolm Bilson and Melvyn Tan.

forte piano or *fp* (Italian 'loud, soft') of dynamics, loud then immediately soft.

fortissimo or *ff* (Italian 'very strong') very loud.

Foss Lukas 1922– . US composer and conductor. His stylistically varied works, including the cantata *The Prairie* 1942 and *Time Cycle*

1960 for soprano and orchestra, express an ironic view of tradition.

Born in Germany, he studied in Europe before settling in the USA 1937. A student of Hindemith, he composed vocal music in Neo-Classical style; in the mid-1950s he began increasingly to employ improvisation. Foss has also written chamber and orchestral music in which the players reproduce tape-recorded effects.

fourth an interval of four diatonic notes consisting of two whole tones and a semitones, for example C – F. A fourth is an example of a perfect interval because it remains the same in both major and minor keys. A fourth may be augmented (increased by a semitone), for example C – F sharp.

fp abbreviation for *forte piano*, loud then immediately soft.

Franck César Auguste 1822–1890. Belgian composer and organist. His music, mainly religious and Romantic in style, includes the Symphony in D minor 1868, *Symphonic Variations* 1885 for piano and orchestra, the Violin Sonata in A 1886, the oratorio *Les Béatitudes/The Beatitudes* 1879, and many organ pieces. His organ style left its mark on following generations of French organists and composers, up to Messiaen

Frankel Benjamin 1906–1973. English composer and teacher. His output includes chamber music and numerous film scores, notably *The Man in the White Suit* 1951 and *A Kid for Two Farthings* 1955.

Frankl Peter (1935–   ). Hungarian-born British pianist. Both a solo and chamber-music pianist, Frankl's wide repertory ranges from Mozart to Bartók. He is noted for both his technique and sensitivity of expression.

free-reed instrument wind instrument such as the mouth organ, accordion, or harmonium, employing tuned metal tongues, vibrating at a predetermined frequency, as valves controlling the escape of air under pressure. Free reeds do not overblow (produce higher harmonics), but the mouth organ can be made to 'bend' the pitch by varying the air pressure.

French horn

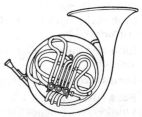

French horn musical brass instrument, a descendant of the natural hunting horn, valved and curved into a circular loop, with a funnel-shaped mouthpiece and wide ♭bell.

Until the early 19th century, the horn lacked valves and could deviate from the ♭harmonic series only by 'hand stopping', the placement of the arm over the bell. Although the horn was capable of playing chromatically with the addition of valves, it lost some purity of tone.

Frescobaldi Girolamo 1583–1643. Italian composer and keyboard player. His fame rests on numerous keyboard toccatas, fugues, ricercares, and capriccios in which he advanced keyboard technique and exploited ingenious and daring modulations of key. He was organist at St Peter's, Rome 1608–28.

fret inlaid ridge of ivory or metal, or a circlet of nylon, on the fingerboard of a plucked or bowed string instrument, against which a string is pressed to change its pitch.

fugue (Latin 'flight') a contrapuntal form with one subject (principal melody) or more, and a number of parts, which enter in succession in direct imitation of each other or transposed to a higher or lower key, and may be combined in augmented form (using longer time values). It represents the highest form of contrapuntal ingenuity in works such as J S Bach's *Das musikalische Opfer/The Musical Offering* 1747, on a theme of Frederick II of Prussia, and *Die Kunst der Fuge/The Art of the Fugue* 1751, and Beethoven's *Grosse Fuge/Great Fugue* for string quartet 1826.

full close alternative name for a perfect ♭cadence, in which the ♭dominant chord resolves to the ♭tonic.

full organ directing an organist to couple the manuals (keyboards) together and use all the louder stops.

full score a complete transcript of a composition showing all parts individually, as opposed to a *short score* or *piano score* which are condensed into fewer lines of music.

fundamental in musical ♭acoustics, the lowest harmonic of a musical tone, corresponding to the audible pitch.

Furtwängler (Gustav Heinrich Ernst Martin) Wilhelm 1886–1954. German conductor. Leader of the Berlin Philharmonic Orchestra

1924–54, his interpretations of Wagner, Bruckner, and Beethoven were valued expressions of national grandeur, and preserved on record. He also gave first performances of Bartók, Schoenberg's *Variations for Orchestra* 1928, and Hindemith's opera *Mathis der Maler/Mathis the Painter* 1934, a work implicitly critical of the Nazi regime. He was a master of moulding phrases through subtle fluctuations of tempo.

He ascended rapidly from theatre to opera orchestras in Mannheim 1915–20 and Vienna 1919–24, then to major appointments in Leipzig and Vienna.

Fux Johann Joseph 1660–1741. Austrian composer and theorist. His rules of ♭counterpoint, compiled in his *Gradus ad Parnassum*, are still used as a teaching formula by many music schools. He wrote a considerable quantity of sacred music, including 50 masses and ten oratorios.

G

Gabrieli Giovanni *c.* 1555–1612. Italian composer. He succeeded his uncle *Andrea Gabrieli* (*c.*1533–1585) as organist of St Mark's basilica, Venice. He developed the use of antiphony (music using widely spaced choirs and groups of instruments), making particular use of St Mark's architecture. His sacred and secular works include numerous madrigals, motets, the antiphonal *Sacrae Symphoniae* 1597 (sacred canzonas and sonatas for brass, choirs, strings, and organ).

galliard a lively dance originating in Italy before the 16th century. It consists of compound duple time (6/8) with bars of simple triple time (3/4) intermingled to upset the pulse. The galliard is often coupled to a ◊pavane, of contrasting common time (4/4).

Galway James 1939– . Irish flautist. Born in Belfast, he played with the London Symphony Orchestra 1966, Royal Philharmonic Orchestra 1967–69, and was principal flautist with the Berlin Philharmonic Orchestra 1969–75 before taking up a solo career.

gamba, da (Italian 'on the leg') suffix used to distinguish a viol, played resting on the leg, from a member of the violin family, played under the chin, or 'on the arm' (da braccio).

gamelan Indonesian orchestra employing tuned gongs, xylophones, metallophones (with bars of metal), cymbals, drums, flutes, and fiddles, the music of which has inspired such Western composers as Debussy, Colin McPhee, John Cage, Benjamin Britten, and Philip Glass.

The music is improvised and based on interlocking tonal and rhythmic patterns. Javanese gamelan music uses a seven-tone *pelog* scale, Balinese preferring a five-tone *slendro* scale. The scales of gongs vary in precise pitch, but incorporate matched pairs that deviate slightly in pitch.

gamut in medieval musical theory, the lowest note (G2); also a generic term for scale, or for the entire spectrum of pitches, from the lowest to the highest.

Gardiner John Eliot (1943–). English conductor. He first made his mark establishing the Monteverdi Choir 1966, which he continues to conduct. He is an authority on 17th- and 18th-century music, and an exponent of the ◊authenticity movement. He has also recorded modern music.

Gardner John 1917– . English composer. Professor at the Royal Academy of Music from 1956, he has produced a symphony 1951; the opera *The Moon and Sixpence* 1957, based on a Somerset Maugham novel; and other works, including film music.

gavotte a French dance of the 17th century in moderate common time (4/4). It begins with an ◊upbeat of two crotchets, and the phrases usually begin and end in the middle of each bar. It became popular at the court of Louis XIV (Lully composing several), later becoming an optional movement of the Baroque ◊suite. The gavotte has been revived by some 20th-century composers, including Prokofiev and Schoenberg, who uses one in his *Suite* 1934.

Geminiani Francesco 1687–1762. Italian violinist and composer. His treatise *The Art of Playing the Violin* 1740 was the first violin tutor ever published. His music was influenced by Corelli and is typically brilliant in fast movements and expressive in slow movements. He lived in London, Paris, and Dublin.

gemshorn an obsolete type of recorder made from an animal's horn (especially a cow- or goat-horn), which disappeared from use during the 16th century; also, an organ stop of light, sweet tone, with conical pipes and usually 4-foot pitch (one octave above that written).

general pause or *G.P.* in orchestral works, a rest of at least one full bar for the entire orchestra, often appearing suddenly after a climax. It originated in 18th-century Germany.

Gerhard Roberto 1896–1970. Spanish-born British composer. He studied with Enrique Granados and Arnold Schoenberg and settled in England 1939, where he composed twelve-tone works in Spanish style. He composed the *Symphony No 1* 1955, followed by three more symphonies and chamber music incorporating advanced techniques.

German Edward 1862–1936. English composer. He is remembered for his operettas *Merrie England* 1902 and *Tom Jones* 1907, and he wrote many other instrumental, orchestral, and vocal works.

Gershwin George 1898–1937. US composer. He wrote concert works such as the ◊symphonic poems *Rhapsody in Blue* 1924 and *An American in Paris* 1928, and popular musicals and songs, many with lyrics by his brother Ira Gershwin (1896–1983), including 'I Got Rhythm', ''S Wonderful', and 'Embraceable You'. His opera *Porgy and Bess* 1935 incorporated jazz rhythms and popular song styles in an operatic format.

Gesualdo Carlo 1560–1613. Italian composer and lutenist. His compositions, which comprise sacred and secular vocal music, and some instrumental pieces, are noted for their complex (modern-sounding) harmonic structure, most unlike the work of his contemporaries. His books of madrigals were highly regarded by Stravinsky.

Gibbons Orlando 1583–1625. English composer. One of the greatest early English composers of sacred anthems, instrumental fantasias, and madrigals, including *The Silver Swan* for five voices 1612. From a family of musicians, he became organist at Westminster Abbey, London, 1623.

gigue a dance form, which developed in two directions, one French, one Italian (*giga*), probably from the 16th-century English jig. The French variety is in a moderate or fast tempo (6/4 or 6/8) and the writing is characterized by wide leaps and dotted rhythms. It is more contrapuntal than most other dance forms of the period, similar in style to a ◊fugue with an inverted subject (principal melody) for the second theme. The Italian variety is quicker (12/8) with 'running' figures and few leaps. It is non-fugal with a more obvious harmonic framework. The gigue came to be used, more often than not, as the last movement of a Baroque ◊suite. Composers of the more common French form include Bach, Handel, and Froberger.

Ginastera Alberto 1916–1983. Argentinian composer. His early works, including his *Pampeana No. 3* 1954, are mostly in a nationalistic style, but after 1958 he turned to modern techniques of ◊serialism, aleatory rhythms (see ◊aleatory music), and the use of microtones. He is most famous for his operas *Don Rodrigo* 1964, *Bomarzo* 1967, and *Beatrix Cenci* 1971.

giocoso (Italian 'jocose') merry, humorous.

Giulini Carlo Maria 1914– . Italian conductor. He was joint musical director of the Los Angeles Philharmonic Orchestra 1978–84. As principal conductor at La Scala, Milan, 1953–55 he worked with soprano Maria Callas, as well as film directors Franco Zeffirelli (1923–), and Luchino Visconti (1906–1976). He is noted for interpretations of Verdi, Bach, Mozart, and Beethoven, blending romantic lyricism with a musical integrity not unlike Toscanini. At Milan Radio 1946–51 he revived rare operas by Scarlatti, Malapiero, and Bartók; his 1951 radio production of Haydn's opera *Il mondo della luna/The World on the Moon* 1777 attracted Toscanini who recommended his appointment at La Scala. Since 1967 he has concentrated on the concert repertory.

giusto Italian 'just', 'strictly'; as in tempo giusto ('in strict time').

Glass Philip 1937– . US composer. Educated first in the conservatory tradition, he was then strongly influenced by Indian music after studying with Ravi Shankar; his work is characterized by repeated rhythmic figures that are continually expanded and modified. His compositions include the operas *Einstein on the Beach* 1975, *Akhnaten* 1984, *The Making of the Representative for Planet 8* 1988, and the *'Low' Symphony* 1992 on themes from *Low*, a record album by pop singer/songwriter David Bowie (1947–).

glass harmonica or *armonica* musical instrument based on the principle of playing a wine glass with a wet finger. It consists of a graded series of glass bowls nested on a spindle and resting in a trough part-filled with water. Rotated by a foot-pedal, it emits pure tones of unchanging intensity when touched. It was devised by Benjamin Franklin; Mozart, Beethoven, and Schubert all wrote pieces for it.

Glazunov Alexander Konstantinovich 1865–1936. Russian composer. He achieved fame with his first symphony, which was written when he was only 17. He absorbed a range of influences, from his teacher Rimsky-Korsakov's orchestrational skill to Tchaikovsky's lyricism. His own style fits between that of the Russian national school of The ◊Five and that of the Western European 'cosmopolitan' composers. He made a significant impact as a teacher on the following generation of composers, including Prokofiev and Shostakovich.

Glinka Mikhail Ivanovich 1804–1857. Russian composer. One of the first Russian composers to be recognized outside his country, he broke away from the prevailing Italian influence and turned to Russian folk music, as in his opera *A Life for the Tsar* (originally *Ivan Susanin*) 1836. He is regarded as the founder of a Russian national style of music. His later works include the opera *Ruslan and Lyudmila* 1842 and the instrumental fantasia *Kamarinskaya* 1848.

glissando a rapid uninterrupted scale produced by sliding the finger across a keyboard or harp strings, or along the fingerboard of a violin or guitar. In wind instruments, a famous example is the clarinet glissando at the start of Gershwin's *Rhapsody in Blue* 1924.

glockenspiel percussion instrument of light metal bars mounted on a carrying frame for use in military bands or on a standing frame for use in an orchestra. The bars are arranged in the manner of a keyboard, and when struck with small handheld hammers, produce a high-pitched, bell-like tone.

glockenspiel

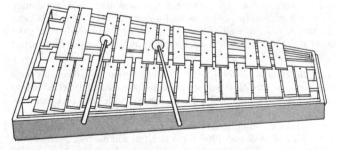

Gluck Christoph Willibald von 1714–1787. German composer who settled in Vienna as ◊kapellmeister (chapel master) to Maria Theresa 1754. His *Orfeo ed Euridice/Orpheus and Eurydice* 1762 revolutionized the 18th-century conception of opera by seeking a 'beautiful simplicity' of melody, and striving to unite the music with the dramatic and poetic content of the libretto. His 100 operas influenced future composers, including Mozart and Beethoven. *Orfeo* was followed by *Alceste/Alcestis* 1767 and *Paride ed Elena/Paris and Helen* 1770.

Glyndebourne site of an opera house near Lewes, East Sussex, England, established 1934 by John Christie (1882–1962). Operas are staged at an annual summer festival and a touring company is also based there. Extensive rebuilding work took place 1992–94 .

Goehr (Peter) Alexander 1932– . British composer, born in Berlin, professor of music at Cambridge from 1976. A lyrical but often hard-edged serialist (see ◊serialism), he nevertheless usually remained within the forms of the symphony and traditional chamber works, and more recently turned to tonal and even Neo-Baroque models. Works include the opera *Arden muss sterben/Arden Must Die* 1966, the music theatre piece *Naboth's Vineyard* 1968, and *Metamorphosis/Dance* 1974.

gong percussion instrument originating in ancient China, consisting of a round sheet of metal with a turned-up rim. It is hit with a felt-covered hammer. A large gong is also called a ◊tam-tam.

Goodman Benny 1909–1986. US clarinettist and jazz musician. Known primarily as a jazz clarinettist, he was also a highly-regarded classical musician. He commissioned concertos from Copland 1947 and Hindemith 1947, as well as Bartók's *Contrasts* 1938 in which he gave the first performance, with the composer as pianist and with violinist Joseph Szigeti (1892–1973).

Górecki Henryk Mikolaj 1933– . Polish composer. His study with Messiaen and exposure to avant-garde influences after 1956 led him to abandon a more conformist Neo-Classical style and seek out new sonorities. He later adopted a slow-moving tonal idiom appealing to revived religious tradition, often on tragic themes from Polish history, as in *Old Polish Music* 1969 for orchestra, and his Symphony No. 3 1976, which propelled him to fame in the West 1992, even appearing in the popular music charts.

Gottschalk Louis Moreau 1829–1869. US pianist and composer.

Gottschalk toured extensively as a composer and his playing was praised by Chopin. His often sentimental compositions include *Souvenir d'Andalousie/Souvenir of Andalusia* 1851 for piano and orchestra and numerous piano pieces, which include *The Dying Poet* 1864.

Gould Glenn 1932–1982. Canadian pianist. He was launched to fame with his first recording of Bach's *Goldberg Variations*, and built his reputation as one of the greatest interpreters of that composer. His eccentricities, especially his unusual choice of tempo, ultimately led to his giving up live performance in favour of making recordings.

Gounod Charles François 1818–1893. French composer and organist. His operas, notably *Faust* 1859 and *Roméo et Juliette* 1867, and church music, including *Messe solennelle/Solemn Mass* 1849, combine graceful melody and elegant harmonization. His *Méditation sur le prélude de Bach/Meditation on Bach's 'Prelude'* 1889 for soprano and instruments, based on Prelude No. 1 of Bach's *Well-Tempered Clavier*, achieved popularity as 'Gounod's *Ave Maria*'.

G.P. abbreviation for ⃟general pause, a short period where all players are silent.

grace alternative name for embellishment or ⃟ornamentation.

grace note an ornamental note written in small type to show that its duration is not counted as a part of the metre of the bar, but must be subtracted from either the following or the preceding full note. When appearing singly, written as a quaver or sometimes a crotchet, it can indicate an *appoggiatura* ('leaning' note), requiring up to half the value of the next note. If it appears as a semiquaver or as a quaver with a stroke through the stem, it generally appears just on or before the beat, as in the manner of an *acciaccatura* ('crushed' note). When appearing in a large group of grace notes, as in a cadenza by Beethoven or a melody by Chopin, the grace notes usually fill in the duration of a single note in the melody, and may (if time permits) be played with greater rhythmic flexibility than if notated in standard notation.

Grainger Percy Aldridge 1882–1961. Australian-born composer and pianist. He is remembered for piano transcriptions, songs, and short instrumental pieces drawing on folk idioms, including *Country Gardens*

1925, and for his collections and settings of folk songs, such as *Molly on the Shore* 1921.

He studied in Frankfurt, moved to London, then settled in the USA 1914. Grainger shared his friend Ferruccio Busoni's vision of a free music, devising a synthesizer and composing machine far ahead of its time.

Granados Enrique 1867–1916. Spanish composer and pianist. His piano-work *Goyescas* 1911, inspired by the art of the artist Goya, was converted to an opera 1916. He also wrote seven operas and two ◊symphonic poems.

grand opera type of ◊opera seria without any spoken dialogue (unlike the ◊opéra-comique), as performed at the Paris Opéra in the 1820s to 1880s. Grand operas were extremely long (five acts), and included incidental music and a ballet.

Composers of grand opera include D F E Auber, Giacomo Meyerbeer, and Ludovic Halévy; examples include Verdi's *Don Carlos* 1867 and Meyerbeer's *Les Huguenots* 1836.

graph notation The notational representation of music by visual analogy. It is commonly used in the scores of electronic works, for which classical notation is not suitable. In 1940 Villa-Lobos composed *New York Skyline* based on the outline of a photograph projected onto graph paper and thence to music manuscript. Development of the sound spectrograph 1944 by engineers at Bell Telephone Laboratories introduced a much improved visual projection of audio events in pitch and time, providing a model for Stockhausen's iconic score *Elektronische Studie II/Electronic Study II* 1954. John Cage's graphic scores of the 1950s revive memories of film experiments in the 1930s, as may be said of many European composers of graph scores from the period 1959–70. A form of graph notation for speech patterns used in phonetics was adopted by Stockhausen in *Carré/Squared* 1960.

grazioso Italian 'graceful'.

great organ principal manual of an organ, characterized by the most powerful pipes and stops of the instrument. It often has the greatest number of stops, ranging from a wide variety of ◊flue pipes to a selection of reeds.

Gregorian chant any of a body of ◊plainsong choral chants associated with Pope Gregory the Great (540–604), which became standard in the Roman Catholic Church. Most of the repertory derives from manuscripts of the 9th and 10th centuries.

Grieg Edvard Hagerup 1843–1907. Norwegian nationalist composer. Much of his music is small scale, particularly his songs, dances, sonatas, and piano works, strongly identifying with Norwegian folk music. Among his orchestral works, which are characterized by lyrical qualities, are the Piano Concerto in A Minor 1869 and the incidental music for Ibsen's *Peer Gynt* 1876, commissioned by playwright Henrik Ibsen (1828–1906) and the Norwegian government.

Grieg studied at the Leipzig Conservatoire and in Copenhagen. He was a director of the Christiania (Oslo) Philharmonic Society 1866 and was involved in the formation of the Norwegian Academy of Music.

ground bass a bass line that repeats cyclically, over which an evolving harmonic and melodic structure is laid. Examples are the ◊chaconne and ◊passacaglia.

Grove Charles 1915– . English conductor. Known both as a choral and symphonic conductor, he is an outstanding interpreter of British music, especially the works of Delius.

Grove George 1820–1900. English scholar. He edited the original *Dictionary of Music and Musicians* 1889, which in its expanded and revised form is still one of the standard music reference sources. He was, in addition, the first director of the ◊Royal College of Music.

Grumiaux Arthur 1921–1986. Belgian violinist. He was admired for his purity of tone and controlled intensity. He excelled in the 18th-century repertory, and is famous for his recordings of the unaccompanied Bach violin sonatas, and the Mozart and Beethoven violin/piano sonatas with Romanian pianist Clara Haskil (1895–1960). In addition he played the 20th-century concertos of Bartók, Berg, and Stravinsky.

gruppetto (also *gruppo*, *groppo*) one of several similar Italian terms used in the 16th century for ◊trills (rapid oscillation between adjacent notes), and later for the turn (a form of melodic pirouette around a note). As a turn, the *gruppetto* designates a four-note figure consisting of the note above the principal note, the note itself, the note below, and the note itself. It was often used as an extemporized embellishment, especially by singers.

Guarneri family of stringed-instrument makers of Cremona, Italy. *Giuseppe 'del Gesù' Guarneri* (1698–1744) produced the finest models.

guitar six-stringed, or twelve-stringed, flat-bodied musical instrument, plucked or strummed with the fingers. The *Hawaiian guitar*, laid across the lap, uses a metal bar to produce a distinctive gliding tone; the solid-bodied *electric guitar*, developed in the 1950s by Les Paul and Leo Fender, mixes and amplifies vibrations from electromagnetic pickups at different points to produce a range of tone qualities.

Derived from a Moorish original, the guitar spread throughout Europe in medieval times, becoming firmly established in Italy, Spain, and the Spanish American colonies. Its 20th-century revival owes much to Andrés Segovia, Julian Bream, and John Williams. The guitar's prominence in popular music can be traced from the traditions of the US mid-West; it played a supporting harmony role in jazz and dance bands during the 1920s and adapted quickly to electric amplification. Classical composers for electric guitar include Frank Martin, Pierre Boulez, and Luciano Berio.

H

H German equivalent of B natural.

habanera a Cuban dance named after the city of Havana. The most popular dance in Latin America during the 19th century, it was the ancestor of other dance forms, including the Argentinian tango. The habañera is always in moderate common time (4/4) and uses a variety of standard rhythms. A famous example is that from Bizet's *Carmen* 1875.

Haitink Bernard 1929– . Dutch conductor. Associated with the ◊Concertgebouw Orchestra, Amsterdam 1958–88, and the London Philharmonic Orchestra 1967–79; musical director at Glyndebourne 1977–87 and at the Royal Opera House, Covent Garden, London, from 1987. A noted interpreter of Mahler and Shostakovitch, he also conducted Mozart's music for the film *Amadeus*, after the play by Peter Schaffer (1926–).

half note US term for ◊minim, a note value half the duration of a ◊semibreve.

half tone or *half step* alternative terms for ◊semitone.

Hallé Charles 1819–1895. German conductor and pianist. Settling in England 1848, he established and led Manchester's Hallé orchestra 1858, until his death. As a pianist, he was the first to play all 32 Beethoven piano sonatas in London (also in Manchester and Paris).

Hamilton Iain Ellis 1922– . Scottish composer. His intensely emotional and harmonically rich works include striking viola and cello sonatas; the ballet *Clerk Saunders* 1951; the operas *Pharsalia* 1968 and *The Royal Hunt of the Sun* 1969, which renounced melody for inventive chordal formations; and symphonies.

Hammond organ electric organ invented in the USA by Laurens Hammond 1934 and widely used in gospel music. It incorporates a distinctive tremulant using rotating speakers. The Hammond organ was a precursor of the synthesizer.

hand bells small hand-held bells of various pitches that are rung by a group of performers. In addition to providing a form of practice for 'change ringing' (a team method of ringing full-size church bells using hand-ropes), many pieces of music are easily transcribed for hand bells, including Christmas carols.

Handel Georg Friedrich 1685–1759. German composer who became a British subject 1726. His first opera, *Almira*, was performed in Hamburg 1705. In 1710 he was appointed ♭kapellmeister (chapel master) to the elector of Hanover (the future George I of England). In 1712 he settled in England, where he established his popularity with such works as the *Water Music* 1717 (written for George I). His great choral works include the *Messiah* 1742 and the later oratorios *Samson* 1743, *Belshazzar* 1745, *Judas Maccabaeus* 1747, and *Jephtha* 1752.

Born in Halle, he abandoned the study of law 1703 to become a violinist at Keiser's Opera House in Hamburg. Visits to Italy (1706–10) inspired a number of operas and oratorios, and in 1711 his opera *Rinaldo* was performed in London. *Saul* and *Israel in Egypt* (both 1739) were unsuccessful, but his masterpiece the *Messiah* was acclaimed on its first performance in Dublin 1742. Other works include the pastoral *Acis and Galatea* 1718 and a set of variations for harpsichord that were later nicknamed 'The Harmonious Blacksmith'. In 1751 he became totally blind.

Harewood George Henry Hubert Lascelles, 7th Earl of Harewood 1923– . Administrator, critic, and writer. Artistic director of the Edinburgh Festival 1961–65, he was also director of the English National Opera 1972–85, and a governor of the BBC 1985–87.

harmonica pocket-sized free-reed wind instrument blown directly from the mouth, invented by Charles Wheatstone 1829. See ♭mouth organ.

The ♭glass harmonica (or armonica) is based on an entirely different principle.

harmonic minor scale a kind of minor scale in which the seventh degree is raised by a semitone from its original 'natural' position.

harmonic series or *overtone series* a series of partial vibrations that combine to form a musical tone. The number and relative prominence of harmonics produced determines an instrument's tone colour (timbre). An oboe is rich in harmonics, the flute has few. Harmonics exist because a string or air column vibrates as a whole (the ◊fundamental) and also simultaneously in halves (second harmonics), thirds (third harmonics), quarters etc.

harmonium keyboard reed organ of the 19th century, powered by foot-operated bellows and incorporating lever-action knee swells to influence dynamics. It was invented by Alexandre Debain (1809–1877) in Paris *c.*1842.

Widely adopted in the USA as a home and church instrument, in France and Germany the harmonium flourished as a concert solo and orchestral instrument, being written for by Karg-Elert, Schoenberg (*Herzgewächse/Heart's Bloom* 1907), and Stockhausen (*Der Jahreslauf/The Course of the Years* 1977).

harmony any simultaneous combination of sounds, as opposed to melody, which is a succession of sounds. Although the term suggests a pleasant or agreeable sound, it is applied to any combination of notes, whether consonant or dissonant. The theory of harmony deals with the formation of chords and their interrelation and logical progression.

Influential treatises on harmony have been written by Rameau, Schoenberg, Hindemith, and Heinrich Schenker (1868–1935).

Harnoncourt Nikolaus 1929–   . German conductor, cellist, and musicologist. A leading figure in the ◊authenticity movement, he established the Vienna Consensus Musicus 1953, an ensemble playing early music on period instruments. He has conducted notable recordings of Montiverdi's operas and Bach's choral and orchestral music. Since 1969 his wife, violinist Alice Harnoncourt (1930–   ), has led Consensus Musicus.

harp plucked musical string instrument, with the strings stretched vertically within a wood and brass soundbox of triangular shape. The orchestral harp is the largest instrument of its type. It has up to 47 diatonically tuned strings, in the range B0–C7 (seven octaves), and seven double-action pedals to alter pitch. Composers for the harp include Mozart, Ravel, Carlos Salzedo, and Heinz Holliger.

Recorded from biblical times, the harp existed in the West as early as the 9th century, and it was common among medieval minstrels. At that time it was quite small, and was normally placed on the knees. It evolved in size because of a need for increased volume following its introduction into the orchestra in the 19th century. The harp has also been used in folk music, as both a solo and accompanying instrument, and is associated with Wales and Ireland.

harpsichord keyboard instrument developed in the 15th century, used in ensembles and as a solo instrument. The strings are plucked by 'jacks' made of leather or quill, and multiple keyboards offering variation in tone are common. It remained popular until the late 18th century, when the piano superseded it. The revival of the harpsichord repertoire in the 20th century owes much to Wanda Landowska and Ralph Kirkpatrick (1911–1984).

A modern repertoire has developed for the concert harpsichord, with concertos by Elliott Carter 1961, Frank Martin 1952, and *Continuum* 1968 for solo harpsichord by György Ligeti.

Harris Roy 1898–1979. US composer. Born in Oklahoma, he combined American folk tunes with modern compositional techniques. Among his works are the 10th Symphony 1965 (known as 'Abraham Lincoln') and the orchestral *When Johnny Comes Marching Home* 1935.

Harvey Jonathan Dean 1939– . English composer. His use of avant-garde and computer synthesis techniques is amalgamated with a tradition of visionary Romanticism in works such as *Inner Light II* 1977 for voices, instruments, and ◊tape music and *Mortuos plango, vivos voco/I Mourn the Dead, I Call the Living* 1980 for computer-manipulated concrete sounds, realized at ◊IRCAM.

Hauptwerk German equivalent of the ◊great organ, the manual of the most powerful pipes and stops.

hautbois (French 'high-wood' or 'loud-wood') term for smaller members of the ◊shawm family, used in England and France after 1500; 'Hautboy' was the English term for oboe (the shawm's descendant) in the 17th and 18th centuries.

Haydn Franz Joseph 1732–1809. Austrian composer. He was a major exponent of the classical ◊sonata form in his numerous chamber, solo keyboard, and orchestral works (he wrote more than 100 symphonies). He also composed choral music, including the oratorios *The Creation*

1798 and *The Seasons* 1801. He was the first great master of the string quartet, and for working extensively with symphony, developing it formally and expressively, he is known popularly today as the 'father' of the genre (although he did not actually invent it). His music is marked by elegance, wit, and a sense of drama. His technique of motivic development was continued further by his pupil Beethoven.

Born in Lower Austria, he was ◊kapellmeister (chapel master) 1761–90 to Prince Esterházy. His work also includes operas, church music, and songs, and the Emperor's Hymn, adopted as the Austrian, and later the German, national anthem.

head voice the upper register of the human voice, refering to the head as the area of sound production. The head voice of a male singer is called ◊falsetto. However, there has been disagreement (in the 19th century and earlier) concerning the precise use of the term, some claiming that only head voice and ◊chest voice (the lower register) exist, others claiming that a third middle register is also important. Today, there is less concern about these distinctions.

heckelphone wide-bore baritone oboe in B flat, introduced by the German maker Wilhelm Heckel (1856–1909) and adopted by Richard Strauss in the opera *Salome* 1905.

heel the part of the bow (at one of its ends) held by a player.

Heifetz Jascha 1901–1987. Russian-born US violinist. One of the great virtuosos of the 20th century. He first performed at the age of five, and before he was 17 had played in most European capitals, and in the USA, where he settled 1917. His technical finesse and characteristic vibrato was well suited to the Romantic repertory.

Helmholtz Hermann (Ludwig Ferdinand), von 1821–1894. German scientist. His work on ◊acoustics, entitled *On the Sensations of Tone* 1875 formed the basis of later research. He discovered the relationship between harmonics and timbre, explained systems of ◊temperament, and founded the physiology of hearing.

hemidemisemiquaver (or US *64th note*) a note value 1/64th the duration of a ◊semibreve. It is written by a filled, blackened note-head with a stem and four flags (tails).

hemiola a rhythmic device based on the ratio 3:2, in which two bars of triple time are articulated in the manner of three bars in duple time. It was much favoured by Brahms, and also by Baroque composers for use in passages approaching a ◊cadence.

Henze Hans Werner 1926–   . German composer. His immense and stylistically restless output is marked by a keen literary sensibility and seductive use of orchestral coloration, as in the opera *Elegy for Young Lovers* 1961 and the cantata *Being Beauteous* 1963. Among recent works are the opera *Das Verratene Meer/The Sea Betrayed* 1992.

  Following the student unrest of 1968 he suddenly renounced the wealthy musical establishment in favour of a militantly socialist stance in works such as the abrasive *El Cimarrón* 1970 and *Voices* 1973, austere settings of 22 revolutionary texts in often magical sonorities. In 1953 he moved to Italy where his music became more expansive, as in the opera *The Bassarids* 1966.

Herbert Victor 1859–1924. Irish-born US conductor and composer. He is known for his operettas including *Babes in Toyland* 1903 and *Naughty Marietta* 1910. He was conductor of the Pittsburgh Philharmonic 1898–1904, and helped to found the American Society of Composers, Authors, and Publishers (ASCAP) 1914.

Herrmann Bernard 1911–1975. US film composer. His long career began with *Citizen Kane* 1940 and included collaborations with Alfred Hitchcock (1899–1980) (*North by Northwest* 1959 and *Psycho* 1960) and François Truffaut (1932–1984) (*Fahrenheit 451* 1966). He wrote his best scores for thriller and mystery movies, and was a major influence in the establishment of a distinctively American musical imagery.

hertz or *Hz* measurement of musical pitch, corresponding to cycles per second, and named after the German physicist Heinrich Hertz (1857–1894). For example, the term 'A 440Hz' (as in ◊concert pitch) means the note A (A4) has a frequency of 440 cycles per second.

Heseltine Philip (Arnold) 1894–1930. Real name of the English composer Peter ◊Warlock.

Hess Myra 1890–1965. British pianist. She is remembered for her morale-boosting National Gallery concerts in World War II, her transcription of the Bach chorale *Jesu, Joy of Man's Desiring*, and her interpretations of Beethoven.

heterophony form of improvisation found in folk music worldwide, in which the same melody line is presented by different players simultaneously in plain and individually embellished forms.

hexachord not a chord in the true sense, but a group of six individual notes. Introduced in the 11th century as a method of sight-singing, a series of overlapping scalar hexachords embraced the entire compass of notes. In the 20th century the term has been redefined by composers using the ◊twelve-tone system, particularly Schoenberg and Webern, as being half of a twelve-tone (twelve-note) row, allowing further compositional manipulation.

Hildegard of Bingen 1098–1179 German abbess, writer, and composer. A lyric poet, Hildegard collected her work in the 1150s into one volume, providing each individual text with music. The poetry is vivid, reflecting the visions she experienced throughout her life. Her melodic structure is based on a small number of patterns (similar to ◊motifs) which are repeated in different modes.

Hindemith Paul 1895–1963. German composer, teacher, and violist. His operas *Cardillac* 1926 (revised 1952), and *Mathis der Maler/Mathis the Painter* 1935, are theatrically astute and politically aware; as a teacher in Berlin 1933 he encouraged the development of a functional modern repertoire ('*Gebrauchsmusik*'/'utility music') for home and school.

Following Nazi persecution, he emigrated to the USA 1940, where he was influential in promoting a measured tonal idiom of self-evident contrapuntal mastery but matter-of-fact tone, exemplified in *Ludus Tonalis* for piano 1942 and the *Symphonic Metamorphoses on Themes of Carl Maria von Weber* 1944. In later life he revised many of his earlier compositions to conform with his own theory of harmony.

Hoffmann E(rnst) T(heodor) A(madeus) 1776–1822. German writer and composer. He composed the opera *Undine* 1816, but is chiefly remembered both as an essayist and librettist of fairy stories, including *Nussknacker/Nutcracker* 1816. His stories inspired Offenbach's *Les Contes d'Hoffmann/Tales of Hoffmann* 1881.

Hofmann Josef 1876–1957. Polish-born US pianist and composer. One of the great pianists of the Romantic repertory, his interpretation of Chopin and Liszt was considered to be his strongpoint. He influenced many young pianists as director of the ◊Curtis Institute 1925–1938.

Holborne Anthony 1584–1602. English composer. He was in the service of Queen Elizabeth I. His collection *The Cittharn Schoole* 1597 contains pieces for viol consort, lute, bandora, and cittern. A further collection, *Pavans, Galliards, Almains and Other Short Aeirs*, was published 1599.

Holliger Heinz 1939–   . Swiss oboist and composer. His avant-garde works, in lyric expressionist style, include *Siebengesang/Sevensong* 1967 for amplified oboe, voices, and orchestra. He has given first performances of Luciano Berio, Ernst Krenek, Hans Werner Henze, and Stockhausen.

Holst Gustav(us Theodore von) 1874–1934. English composer. He wrote operas, including *Sávîtri* 1908 and *At the Boar's Head* 1924; ballets; choral works, including *Hymns from the Rig Veda* 1912 and *The Hymn of Jesus* 1917; orchestral suites, including *The Planets* 1916; and songs. He was a lifelong friend of Ralph Vaughan Williams, with whom he shared an enthusiasm for English folk music. His musical style, although tonal and at times drawing on folk song, tends to be more severe than Vaughan Williams'.

He was the father of Imogen Holst (1907–   ), musicologist and the writer of his biography.

homophony music comprising a melody and an accompanying harmony, in contrast to ◊heterophony and ◊polyphony in which different melody lines of equal importance are combined. There is no rhythmic independence between the parts or voices in homophony.

Honegger Arthur 1892–1955. Swiss composer. He was one of the group of composers known as Les ◊Six. His work was varied in form, for example, the opera *Antigone* 1927, the ballet *Skating Rink* 1922, the oratorio *Le Roi David/King David* 1921, programme music *Pacific 231* 1923 (which depicts a locomotive), and the *Symphonie liturgique/ Liturgical Symphony* 1946. His style varied from mechanical to Neo-Romantic, but remained tonal throughout.

horn member of a family of brass instruments originally used for signalling and ritual, consisting of a coiled conical tube ending in a bell (a flared opening). The lips vibrate in the mouthpiece to sound the instrument. The modern valve horn is a 19th-century hybrid B flat/F instrument; the name *French horn* strictly applies to the earlier *cor à pistons* which uses lever-action rotary valves and produces a lighter tone. The *Wagner tuba* is a horn variant in tenor and bass versions devised by Wagner to provide a fuller horn tone in the lower range. Composers for horn include Mozart, Haydn, Richard Strauss (*Till Eulenspiegel* 1895), Ravel, and Benjamin Britten (*Serenade for Tenor, Horn, and Strings* 1943).

Many horns are based on animal horns, for example the shofar of Hebrew ritual and the medieval oliphant and gemshorn, or shells, for example the conch shell of Pacific island peoples. Horns in metal originated in South America and also Central Asia (Tibet, India, Nepal), and reached Europe along with the technology of metalwork in the Bronze Age. The familiar hunting horn, unchanged for many centuries, was adapted and enlarged in the 18th century to become an orchestral instrument, its limited range of natural harmonics extended by a combination of lip technique and hand stopping within the bell and the use of extension crooks for changes of key. The basset horn and English horn (cor anglais) are in fact not brass but woodwind instruments.

hornpipe an English dance popular between the 16th and 19th centuries, associated especially with sailors. During the 18th century it changed from triple time (3/4) to common time (4/4). Examples include those by Purcell and Handel.

Horowitz Vladimir 1904–1989. Russian-born US pianist. He made his US debut 1928 with the New York Philharmonic Orchestra. A leading interpreter of Liszt, Schumann, and Rachmaninov, he toured worldwide until the early 1950s, when he retired to devote more time to recording. His rare concert appearances 1965–86 displayed undiminished brilliance.

Hotteterre Jacques-Martin 1674–1763. French flautist, bassoonist, and instrumentmaker. He came from a family of woodwind instrumentmakers and composers responsible for developing the orchestral Baroque flute and bassoon from folk antecedents. A respected performer and teacher, he wrote a tutor for the transverse flute and composed trio sonatas and suites for flute and bassoon.

Howells Herbert 1892–1983. English composer, organist, and teacher. His works are filled with an 'English' quality, as with those of Elgar and Vaughan Williams. Often elegiac in expression, as in some of the *Six Pieces for Organ* 1940, much of his music after the mid-1930s reflects his mourning over the death of his son. He wrote choral and chamber music, as well as solo works, both sacred and secular.

Hummel Johann Nepomuk 1778–1837. Austrian composer and pianist. Following in the steps of Mozart (his teacher), his melodies are graceful if somewhat overly symmetrical and 'square'. He was known as a conservative in his lifetime, clinging to a decaying tradition in the face of growing Romanticism. In addition to his keyboard works, which include seven concertos, he wrote choral and chamber works, and operas.

humoresque a 19th-century French and English title (German *Humoreske*) for a short instrumental piece characterized by a lively and capricious nature. Famous examples include humoresques for piano by Schumann 1839 and Dvořák 1894.

Humperdinck Engelbert 1854–1921. German composer. He studied in Cologne and Munich and assisted Wagner in the preparation of *Parsifal* 1879 at Bayreuth. He wrote the musical fairy operas *Hänsel und Gretel* 1893 and *Königskinder/King's Children* 1910.

hurdy gurdy

hurdy-gurdy musical stringed instrument dating from the 12th century, resembling a violin in tone but using a form of keyboard to play a melody and ◊drone strings to provide a continuous harmony. An inbuilt wheel, turned by a handle, acts as a bow.

hymn a song of praise to a god. Usually associated with chorale-style settings of texts used by the Christian church, the first hymns were in fact written in honour of the god Apollo in 150 BC. The earliest sources of modern hymn melodies can be traced to the 11th and 12th centuries, and the earliest polyphonic settings date from the late 14th century. Modern composers have written hymns: Vaughan Williams edited the *English Hymnal* 1906, writing new hymns as well as giving new arrangements to many existing ones. Less conventional is Britten's Hymn to St Cecilia 1942.

Ibert Jacques François Antoine 1890–1962. French composer. Although writing in a variety of genres and styles, his music is generally considered light, due in large part to his seven often witty operas. However, his music reflects its subject matter: in his ◊symphonic poem *La Ballade de la geôle de Reading* he captures the horror of Oscar Wilde's poem; while in his Flute Concerto 1934, he involves the full technical range of the solo instrument.

imitation a ◊contrapuntal device in which a theme or motive is repeated in different vocal or instrumental parts. The strictest form of imitation is the ◊canon, in which every voice has, in turn, exactly the same notes and rhythms as the one before it. In a ◊fugue the subject (principal melody) is treated imitatively, before a greater degree of contrapuntal freedom occurs in a non-thematic episode (a passage linking appearances of the subject). The use of imitation in composition can be traced back to early forms of ◊polyphony from about AD 1200.

impressionism a term borrowed from 19th-century painting, used to describe a French style of musical composition at the turn of the 20th century, which emphasizes instrumental colour and texture. It was first applied to the music of Debussy, who broke free from the German Romantic tradition, as influenced by Wagner.

impromptu a 19th-century character piece in the style of an improvisation. Composers of piano impromptus include Schubert and Chopin.

improvisation or *extemporization* a principal means of artistic expression among oral cultures, including popular music and jazz in the West. It is based on standard models, including modes and ◊raga (Indian scales), and on standard rhythms, or familiar melodies combining modal and rhythmic components.

A composer/performer creates a fresh and personal interpretation of a model at each performance. Successful improvisation relies on the

awareness of an audience, knowing the prototype, and freely responding
to refinements of artistic variation. In the current Western tradition,
organists are taught improvisation as a technique (in the playing of
◊voluntaries), and in the days of silent films, improvisation was a principal technique of accompaniment. In the 18th century and earlier, improvisation was used in playing ◊cadenzas and in embellishing existing
melodies.

incidental music accompanying music to stage or film drama that, in
addition to setting a mood (see ◊background music), can also be part of
the action, as in Thomas Arne's music (including songs) for the stage,
music for ◊masques, and so on.

indeterminacy the absence of specific instruction concerning a significant element of a composition. A piece of ◊aleatory music is unspecific
in terms of the order of sections; a ◊graph score is indeterminate in notation or timing. All music is indeterminate to some degree, since no two
live performances can be totally alike.

Indeterminacy as an aesthetic goal of the avant-garde *c.*1950–70
aims, by stripping away the means of achieving an exact performance,
to re-establish extemporization as an element of virtuosity, and to provoke new discoveries. Composers of indeterminate music include
Luciano Berio, Stockhausen, and the Polish composer Roman
Haubenstock-Ramati (1919–   ). After 1970 indeterminacy became a
music education cause, aimed at releasing repressed creativity.

Indian music classical musical culture represented in North India,
Pakistan, Nepal, and Bangladesh by the Hindustani tradition, and in
South India and Sri Lanka by the Karnatic tradition. An oral culture of
great antiquity, allied to Muslim traditions of the Middle East and
Central Asia, it resembles the medieval European troubadour tradition
of composer-performer, being an art of skilful extemporization in a
given mood (rasa), selecting from a range of melody prototypes (ragas)
and rhythmic formulae (talas), understood in the same way as in the
West certain popular genres, such as 'blues', define a mood, a scale, and
a form, and 'boogie-woogie' an associated rhythm.

Indian music is geared to the time of day, and a composition/perfor-
mance is not fixed in duration. An ensemble consists of a melody section,

featuring voice, ◊sitar, ◊sarod, surbahar, violins, shrill reed woodwinds, or harmonium, solo or in combination; a drone section featuring the ◊vina or ◊tambura, providing a resonant harmonic ground; and a rhythm section of high and low tuned hand drums. The music has a natural buoyancy, the melody effortlessly rising, in contrast to the tonal gravitational pull exerted in European tonal music. The sounds of Indian music are rich in high frequencies, giving an impression of luminous radiance. Popular awareness of Indian music in the West increased after world tours since the 1950s by virtuosos Ravi Shankar, a sitar player, and Ali Akhbar Khan (1922–   ), a sarod player. In Britain, a tradition of popular music thrives among expatriate communities and in schools.

Indy (Paul Marie Théodore) Vincent d' 1851–1931. French composer and biographer. He studied under César Franck and was one of the founders of the *Schola Cantorum*. His works include operas (*Fervaal* 1897), symphonies, ◊symphonic poems (*Istar* 1896), and chamber music. He wrote biographies of Beethoven and Franck.

inner part in polyphonic music (see ◊polyphony), the voices (independent parts) whose registers (instrumental or vocal ranges) are neither the highest nor lowest. In a four-voice choir, for example, the alto and tenor sing inner parts, their registers falling between the soprano and bass. In a string quartet usually the second violin and viola are inner parts between the first violin and cello.

instrumentation the art of composing for particular instruments in a manner appropriate to their range and sound. ◊Orchestration is similar in meaning, usually refering specifically to instruments in an orchestral setting.

integral serialism a type of ◊serialism pioneered by Boulez and Stockhausen in the early 1950s that brings as many musical elements as possible under serial control. This technique applies not only to pitch, but also to dynamics, duration, and timbre.

interlude a piece or passage of music played between two other works or sections. This may occur between scenes of an opera, for example, as in Britten's 'Sea Interludes' from *Peter Grimes* 1945. In the 18th century, interludes were played between the verses of a hymn or psalm. In the latter case, the organist often improvised passages and so there are few remaining printed examples. Exceptions include certain organ chorales, such as Bach's *In dulci jubilo*.

intermezzo a one-act comic opera, often placed between the acts of a serious opera, such as Pergolesi's *La Serva Padrona/The Maid as Mistress* 1732; also a short orchestral interlude played between the acts of an opera to denote the passage of time. By extension, an intermezzo can also be a short movement to be played between others.

interpretation the manner in which a performer plays a work of music. Except in the case of pre-recorded electronic music, which excludes the performer altogether, the limitations of notation mean that a composer cannot indicate the most subtle levels of dynamics, expression, articulation, and other details of ◊performance practice. Inevitably the performer is responsible for these, although during some periods it was the convention for the musician to take greater liberties than during others. For instance, the 18th-century performer had much greater freedom than has the 20th-century performer, not only to alter a composer's dynamics and articulation without criticism, but also, to a degree, to change the notes themselves.

interval the pitch difference between two notes, expressed in terms of the diatonic scale, for example a fifth (C–G, D–A etc), or as a harmonic ratio, 3:2. A *perfect interval* remains the same in both major and minor keys (the fourth, fifth, and octave). An *imperfect interval* varies.

intonation the extent to which a performer is in tune or not, that is whether their notes are accurate or not. For string instruments, pitch is adjustable by finger positioning. Woodwind instruments are of relatively fixed pitch, but a note may 'bend' using a combination of finger and breath technique. Trumpets are equipped with a tuning slide, controlled by the little finger; horns can be modified in pitch by inserting the left hand into the bell. See also ◊beat frequency.

introduction a section preceding the main body of a musical work. Many symphonies of the 18th century featured a slow introduction (including works by Haydn, Mozart, and Beethoven), and this practice was sometimes transferred to quartets and keyboard works, as in

Beethoven's, *Sonata Pathétique* 1799. The introduction may be related motivically or thematically to the rest of the work, as in *Pathétique*, or it may be more independent, as in Elgar's *Introduction and Allegro* 1905 for strings.

invention a term not commonly used by composers, but made famous by Bach in his *15 Inventions* for keyboard 1720. In two parts, each composition is contrapuntal and highly imitative, based upon a short melodic motif or phrase. Bach's so-called 'three-part inventions' were not named as such by the composer, but rather the term 'sinfonia' was used instead (*15 Sinfonias* 1723).

inversion the mirror-image of a melody used in both traditional counterpoint and the ◊twelve-tone system, in which up becomes down and vice versa; also describes a chord in which the original order of notes is rearranged, or alternatively one not in root position.

ionian mode equivalent to the major scale. On a piano, the scale from C – B using only the white notes.

IRCAM acronym for *Institut de Recherche et de Coordination Acoustique-Musique* (Institute for Musico-Acoustic Research and Coordination), organization founded 1977 in Paris for research into electronic music, using computers, synthesizers, and so on. Its director is Pierre Boulez. There is a remarkable live recording studio with programmable acoustic and movable floor and ceiling panels. IRCAM is housed beneath the Pompidou Arts Centre.

The principal computing facility is the 4X series synthesizer developed by Pepino di Giugno.

Ireland John (Nicholson) 1879–1962. English composer. His works, influenced more by French music than English, include the mystic orchestral prelude *The Forgotten Rite* 1917 and the piano solo *Sarnia* 1941. Benjamin Britten was his pupil.

isorhythm a form in which a given rhythm cyclically repeats, although the corresponding melody notes may change. It was used in European medieval music, and is still practised in classical Indian music. The composers Alban Berg, John Cage, and Olivier Messiaen used isorhythmic procedures.

Ives Charles (Edward) 1874–1954. US composer. He experimented with ♭atonality, quarter tones, clashing time signatures, and quotations from popular music of the time. He wrote five symphonies, including *Holidays Symphony* 1913; chamber music, including the *Concord Sonata*; and two orchestral works including *Three Places in New England* 1914. His pioneering work into modern techniques at times pre-dates their 'discovery' by European composers.

J

Janáček Leoš 1854–1928. Czech composer. He became director of the Conservatoire at Brno 1919 and professor at the Prague Conservatoire 1920. His music, highly original and influenced by Moravian folk music, includes arrangements of folk songs, operas (*Jenůfa* 1904, *The Cunning Little Vixen* 1924), and the choral *Glagolitic Mass* 1926.

Janequin Clément *c.*1472–*c.*1560. French composer. He wrote chansons and psalms. His songs of the 1520s–30s are witty and richly textured in imitative effects, for example *Le Chant des oiseaux/Birdsong, La Chasse/The Hunt,* and *Les Cris de Paris/Street Cries of Paris.*

Jaques-Dalcroze Emile 1865–1950. Swiss composer and teacher. He is remembered for his system of physical training by rhythmical movement to music (◊eurhythmics), and founded the Institut Jaques-Dalcroze in Geneva 1915.

Jarnach Philipp 1892–1982. German composer. After studies in Paris he met Ferruccio Busoni in Zurich 1915 and remained to complete the latter's opera *Doktor Faust* 1925 after Busoni's death. His own works, in Italianate Neo-Classic style, include orchestral and chamber music.

Järnefelt (Edvard) Armas 1869–1958. Finnish-born Swedish composer. He is chiefly known for his *Praeludium* 1907 and the lyrical *Berceuse* 1909 for small orchestra, from music for the drama *The Promised Land.*

jazz a style of music originating in America during the 19th century. Developing from ◊blues and spirituals (religious folk-songs) sung by American slaves in the southern states, it first came to prominence in the early 20th century in New Orleans, St Louis, and Chicago, with a distinctive flavour in each city. Traits common to all types of jazz are the modified rhythms of West Africa; the emphasis on improvisation; Western European harmony emphasizing the dominant seventh and the clash of major and minor thirds; characteristic textures and ◊timbres, first exemplified by a singer and rhythm section (consisting of a piano, bass, drums, and guitar or a combination of these instruments), and later by the addition of other instruments such as the saxophone and various brass instruments, and later still by the adoption of electrically amplified instruments.

Different styles of jazz include *ragtime*, popularized at the turn of the 20th century by Scott Joplin (1868–1917) and others; *dixieland* or 'trad' (traditional) jazz of the New Orleans style; *swing*, which consists of a lilting dotted triplet rhythm; *big band* jazz which reached its peak in the 1940s under musicians such as Glenn Miller (1904–1944); *be-bop* which is characterized by its fast tempos, popularized by Charlie 'The Bird' Parker (1920–1955); and *fusion*, which blends elements of jazz and rock, pioneered by musicians including Miles Davis (1926–1991). Today, no single style is paramount, as jazz has reached a ◊post-modernist stage of development, in which music of every style is considered valid.

Jew's harp musical instrument found throughout Europe and Asia. It consists of a metal frame inserted between the teeth, and a springlike tongue plucked with the finger. The resulting drone excites resonances in the mouth, which, acting as a sound box, can provide a melody.

jig a dance popular in the British Isles during the 16th century, which is thought to have developed into the ◊gigue, later commonly used as the last movement of a Baroque ◊suite.

Joachim Joseph 1831–1907. Austro-Hungarian violinist and composer. He studied under Mendelssohn and founded the Joachim Quartet (1869–1907). Joachim was noted for his performances of the music of his friend Brahms. His own compositions include pieces for violin and orchestra, chamber, and orchestral works.

Josephs Wilfred 1927–   . British composer. As well as film and television music, he has written nine symphonies, concertos, and chamber music. His works include the *Jewish Requiem* 1969 and the opera *Rebecca* 1983.

Josquin Desprez or *des Près* 1440–1521. Franco-Flemish composer. His synthesis of Flemish structural counterpoint and Italian harmonic expression, acquired in the service of the Rome papal chapel

1484–1503, marks a peak in Renaissance vocal music. His work became known throughout western Europe and served as a model for composers and theorists. In addition to masses on secular as well as sacred themes, including the *Missa 'L'Homme armé'/Mass on 'The Armed Man'* 1504, he wrote secular and sacred motets, and chansons such as 'El Grillo/The Cricket', employing imitative vocal effects.

Joyce Eileen 1912–1991. Australian concert pianist. Her playing combined subtlety with temperamental fire. Her immense repertoire included over 70 works for piano and orchestra. She made her UK debut 1930 and retired in the early 1960s.

Juilliard music school and college founded in New York 1924, financed by the will of Augustus D. Juilliard, a cotton merchant. One of the world's leading conservatories, it moved 1969 to its current location, the newly-built Lincoln Center. The Juilliard Quartet was founded 1946 by the school's president William Schumann (1910–   ), and became famous initially for its interpretation of Bartók's works.

K

Kabelevsky Dmitri Borisovich 1904–1987. Russian composer and pianist. Famous in the West for his keyboard and instrumental works, his reputation in the USSR was based upon vocal works, including the opera *The Taras Family* 1947. Kabelevsky's work mirrored the Soviet authorities' policy of 'Socialist Realism' in his transparent Neo-Classical style. As a result, it is more immediately accessible than the music of his contemporaries Prokofiev and Shostakovich, who were frequently criticized by the government. He helped guide the official course of music in the USSR after World War II.

kapellmeister (German 'chapel master') chief conductor and chorus master, in some cases also resident composer for a private chapel, responsible for musical administration.

Karajan Herbert von 1908–1989. Austrian conductor. He dominated European classical music performance after 1947. He was principal conductor of the Berlin Philharmonic Orchestra 1955–89, artistic director of the Vienna State Opera 1957–64, and of the ◊Salzburg Festival 1956–60. A perfectionist, he cultivated an orchestral sound of notable smoothness and transparency; he also staged operas and directed his own video recordings. He recorded the complete Beethoven symphonies three times, and had a special affinity with Mozart and Bruckner, although his repertoire extended from Bach to Schoenberg.

Karg-Elert Sigfrid 1877–1933. German composer. After studying at Leipzig he devoted himself to the European harmonium. His numerous concert pieces and graded studies, including *66 Choral Improvisations* 1910, exploit a range of impressionistic effects.

kazoo simple wind instrument adding a buzzing quality to the singing voice on the principle of 'comb and paper' music.

Kempe Rudolf 1910–1976. German conductor. Renowned for the clarity and fidelity of his interpretations of the works of Richard Strauss and

Wagner's *Ring* cycle, he conducted Britain's Royal Philharmonic Orchestra 1961–75 and was musical director of the Munich Philharmonic from 1967.

Kempff Wilhelm (Walter Friedrich) 1895–1991. German pianist and composer. He concentrated on the 19th-century classical repertory of Beethoven, Brahms, Chopin, and Liszt. He resigned as director of the Stuttgart Conservatory when only 35 to concentrate on performing; he later played with Pablo Casals, Yehudi Menuhin, and Pierre Fournier.

Kennedy Nigel 1956– . British violinist. He is credited with expanding the audience for classical music. His 1986 recording of Vivaldi's *Four Seasons* sold more than 1 million copies.

By cultivating a media image that challenges conventional standards of dress and decorum, he has succeeded in attracting young audiences to carefully understated performances of Bach, Max Bruch, and Alban Berg. His repertoire of recordings also includes jazz.

kettledrum alternative name for ◊timpani.

key in tonal music, the ◊diatonic scale around which a piece of music is written; for example, a work in the key of C major gravitates around and resolves upon the notes of the C major scale.

key the lever activated by a keyboard player, such as a piano key, or the finger control on a woodwind instrument.

Key Francis Scott 1779–1843. US lawyer and poet. He wrote the song 'The Star-Spangled Banner' while Fort McHenry, Baltimore, was besieged by British troops 1814; since 1931 it has been the national anthem of the USA.

keyboard set of keys (levers worked by the fingers or feet) arranged in order, forming part of various instruments and enabling the performer to play a much larger number of strings or reeds than could otherwise be controlled. The keyboard is a major innovation of Western music, introduced to medieval instruments of the organ type, including the portative organ (small enough to carry) and the reed organ (a ◊free-reed instrument), and subsequently transferred to Renaissance stringed instruments such as the ◊clavichord and ◊hurdy-gurdy. Keyboard instruments were designed to enable precise and objective reproduction of musical intervals, without the intervention of ♭portamento. Other examples of keyboard instruments include the harpsichord, piano, and a variety of electric keyboards.

key signature sharps or flats indicating a prevailing key; the symbols for these are inserted on the score at the beginning of a musical stave, after the ♭clef. A key signature without sharps or flats signifies C major or A minor, or that the music is ♭atonal.

A change of key signature during a piece is indicated by a double bar at which any cancellation of elements of the previous key signature is shown by natural signs prior to or incorporated in the new key signature.

Khachaturian Aram Il'yich 1903–1978. Armenian composer. Much of his music reflects colourful folk themes, as in the ballets *Gayaneh* 1942, which includes the 'Sabre Dance', and *Spartacus* 1956. Its accessability rendered most of his works acceptable to the Soviet authorities, although his Second Symphony 1943 and Violin Concerto 1945 were condemned.

Kirckman Jacob 1710–1792. German-born organist and composer. He settled in London about 1730 and founded a family firm of harpsichord-makers which dominated the British market during the late 18th century.

kithara ancient Greek instrument resembling a lyre but with a flat back. It was strung with wire and plucked with a ♭plectrum or (after the 16th century) with the fingers. The *bandurria* and *laud*, still popular in Spain, are instruments of the same type.

Klemperer Otto 1885–1973. German conductor. He was celebrated for his interpretation of contemporary and Classical music (especially Beethoven and Brahms). He conducted the Los Angeles Orchestra 1933–39 and the Philharmonia Orchestra, London, from 1959. Although partially paralysed 1939 he continued conducting. He has also composed a mass and two symphonies.

Knipper Lev Konstantinovich 1898–1974. Soviet composer. His early works were modernist, but following Party policy after 1932 he wrote in a more popular idiom, as in the symphony *Poem of Komsomol Fighters* 1934 with its mass battle songs. He is known in the West for his song Cavalry of the Steppes.

Kodály Zoltán 1882–1967. Hungarian composer and educator. With Béla Bartók, he recorded and transcribed Magyar folk music, the scales and rhythm of which he incorporated in a deliberately nationalist style. His works include the cantata *Psalmus Hungaricus* 1923, a comic opera *Háry János* 1927, and orchestral dances and variations. His Kodály Method of school music education is widely practised.

Korngold Erich Wolfgang 1897–1957. Austrian-born US composer. He achieved early recognition when his opera *Die tote Stadt/Dead City* was premiered simultaneously in Hamburg and Cologne 1920. In 1934 he moved to Hollywood to become a composer for Warner Brothers. His film scores, in richly orchestrated and romantic style, include *The Adventures of Robin Hood* 1938 and *Of Human Bondage* 1945.

koto Japanese musical instrument; a long zither of ancient Chinese origin, having 13 silk strings supported by movable bridges. It rests on the floor and the strings are plucked with ivory finger plectra, producing a brittle sound.

koto

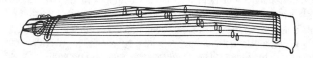

Koussevitsky Serge 1874–1951. Russian musician and conductor. He established his own orchestra in Moscow 1909, introducing works of Prokofiev, Rachmaninov, and Stravinsky. After the Revolution 1917 Koussevitsky left the USSR for the USA, becoming director of the Boston Symphony Orchestra 1924.

Koussevitsky was trained at a conservatory in Moscow, becoming a recognized virtuoso on the double bass. He first appeared as a conductor in Berlin 1908. In 1934 he founded the annual Tanglewood summer music festival in W Massachusetts.

Kreisler Fritz 1875–1962. Austrian-born US violinist and composer. His prolific output of recordings in the early 20th century introduced a wider public to classical music from old masters such as J S Bach and François Couperin to moderns such as Manuel de Falla and Rachmaninov. He also composed and recorded romantic pieces in the style of the classics, often under a pseudonym.

He gave the first performance of Elgar's *Violin Concerto* 1910, dedicated to him by the composer.

Krenek Ernst 1900– . Austrian-born US composer and theorist. Following early popular success with jazz-influenced operas *Jonny spielt auf/Johnny Strikes Up* 1926 and *Leben des Orest/Life of Orestes* 1930, he supported himself as a critic while working on the ambitious twelve-tone opera *Karl V/Charles V* 1938. He remained in contact with postwar developments in ◊integral serialism and ◊aleatory music with *Quaestio Temporis/In Search of Time* 1957, and with electronic music in *Spiritus intelligentiae sanctus* 1956.

His writings include the study *Johannes Ockeghem* 1953 and *Horizon Circled* 1974.

Kreutzer Rodolphe 1766–1831. French violinist and composer. Beethoven dedicated his Violin Sonata 1803, known as the *Kreutzer Sonata*, to him.

krumhorn German spelling of ◊crumhorn, a Renaissance double-reed woodwind instrument.

Kubelik Jan 1880–1940. Czech violinist and composer. He performed in Prague at the age of eight, and became one of the world's greatest virtuosos; he also wrote six violin concertos.

Kubelik Rafael 1914– . Czech conductor and composer, son of violinist Jan Kubelik. His works include symphonies and operas, such as *Veronika* 1947. He was musical director of the Royal Opera House, Covent Garden, London, 1955–58.

Kyrie Eleison (Latin 'Lord have mercy') part of the Roman Catholic Ordinary Mass, following the Introit. It has three parts of text: Kyrie Eleison, Christe Eleison, Kyrie Eleison, each of which is repeated three times, reflecting the Holy Trinity.

L

Labèque Katia (1950–) and Marielle (1952–). French pianist duo. They are sisters, whose career began 1961. Their repertoire has encompassed works by classical composers (Bach, Mozart, Brahms) as well as modern pieces (Stravinsky, Messiaen, Boulez). They also play ragtime, a form of ◊jazz.

lacrimoso Italian 'tearful'.

Lalo (Victor Antoine) Edouard 1823–1892. French composer. His Spanish ancestry and violin training are evident in the *Symphonie Espagnole* 1873 for violin and orchestra, and *Concerto for Cello and Orchestra* 1877. He also wrote operas, including *Le Roi d'Ys/The King of Ys* 1887, a ballet, and chamber music.

Landowska Wanda 1877–1959. Polish harpsichordist and scholar. Although not a perfomer associated with the ◊authenticity movement, she almost single-handedly renewed public interest in the harpsichord as a cogent instrument. She inspired concertos by Manuel de Falla and Poulenc.

langsam German 'slow'; *langsamer* 'slower'.

Lanier Sidney 1842–1881. US flautist and poet. His *Poems* 1877 contain interesting metrical experiments, in accordance with the theories expounded in his *Science of English Verse* 1880, on the relation of verse to music.

Larsson Lars-Erik 1908–1986. Swedish composer, conductor, and critic. His works vary between traditional and more modern styles. For instance, the ten *Two-Part Piano Pieces* 1932 introduced the ◊twelve-tone system to Swedish music, while his *Sinfonietta*, composed in the same year, is contrapuntal and Neo-Baroque in style. However, despite the dichotomy, one trend threading Larsson's music together is his gift of lyricism.

Lassus Roland de. Also known as *Orlando di Lasso* c.1532–1594. Franco-Flemish composer. One of the great masters of 16th-century ♭polyphony. His works include sacred music, songs, and madrigals, including settings of poems by his friend Pierre de Ronsard (1524–1585) such as 'Bonjour mon coeur/Good day my heart' 1564.

Lawes Henry 1596–1662. British composer. His works include music for Milton's masque *Comus* 1634. He also composed songs and madrigals. His brother William Lawes (1602–1645) was also a composer, notably for ♭viol consort.

leading note the seventh note of an ascending ♭diatonic scale, so-called because it 'leads' inevitably to the upper tonic or key note, a semitone above.

The leading note is very dissonant in relation to the tonic, but consonant in relation to the chord of the fifth, or dominant. Typically the transition from leading note to tonic is expressed in the 'perfect' ♭cadence.

Leclair Jean-Marie 1697–1764. French violinist and composer. Originally a dancer and ballet-master, he composed ballet music, an opera, *Scilla et Glaucus* 1746, and violin concertos. He was known as 'the elder', as his younger brother bore the same name and profession.

ledger line or *leger line* notation used to indicate exceptionally high or low notes, consisting of short lines added above or below the ♭stave. In music prior to the Classical period it was common to change clefs in order to avoid using ledger lines. For example, if a part reading bass clef became too high, the composer would notate tenor clef. This practice is continued for cello and bassoon writing but not for other instruments such as the keyboard. The first known example of a ledger line occurs in an organ book of 1523.

legato (Italian 'tied') indicating smooth and continuous phrasing.

leggiero Italian 'light'; *leggieramente* ('lightly'), often implies a detached articulation.

legno (Italian 'wood') from the term *col legno* ('with the wood'), instructing a string player to tap the string with the wooden part of the bow rather than to draw the bow across the string in the usual manner.

Lehár Franz 1870–1948. Hungarian composer. He wrote many operettas, among them *The Merry Widow* 1905, *The Count of Luxembourg* 1909, *Gypsy Love* 1910, and *The Land of Smiles* 1929. He also composed songs, marches, and a violin concerto.

leitmotiv (German 'leading motive') a recurring theme or motive used in opera to illustrate a character or idea. Many composers have used leitmotivs in their works, but none to the extent of Wagner in his *Der Ring des Nibelungen* 1876. It was later adopted in music for film.

lento (Italian 'slow') slightly slower than, or approximately the same tempo as ◊adagio, depending on the historical period in which the music was written.

Lenya Lotte. Adopted name of Karoline Blamauer 1905–1981. Austrian actress and singer. Married to Kurt Weill, she appeared in several of the Brecht-Weill operas, notably *Die Dreigroschenoper/The Threepenny Opera* 1928.

Her plain looks and untrained singing voice brought added realism to her stage roles.

Leoncavallo Ruggiero 1857–1919. Italian operatic composer. He played the piano in restaurants, composing in his spare time, until the success of *I Pagliacci/The Strolling Players* 1892. His other operas include *La Bohème/Bohemian Life* 1897 (contemporary with Puccini's version) and *Zaza* 1900.

Leppard Raymond 1927– . English conductor and musicologist. His imaginative reconstructions of Monteverdi and Cavalli operas did much to generate popular interest in early opera and to stimulate academic investigation of the performance implications of ◊early music manuscript scores.

Les Six (French 'the six') a group of French 20th-century composers; see ◊Six, Les.

L.H. abbreviation for 'left hand', directing a pianist to use the left hand, usually in order to facilitate a technically difficult passage, dividing the notes between both hands rather than playing the passage solely with the right hand. It can also be notated in French as M.G. (*main gauche*) or in Italian as M.S. (*mano sinistra*). The opposite of R.H. ('right hand').

libretto (Italian 'little book') the text of an opera or other dramatic vocal work, or the scenario of a ballet.

licenza (Italian 'licence', 'freedom') from the term *con licenza* ('with freedom'), directing the performer to take liberties with the tempo, using ◊rubato and other forms of expression.

lieder (German 'songs'; singular *lied*) musical dramatization of poems, usually for solo voice and piano, composers of which include Schubert, Schumann, Brahms, and Hugo Wolf.

ligature notation of the 13th to 16th centuries in which two or more notes are combined to form a single symbol. Depending on the shape of the ligature, the same group of notes could indicate different rhythms. In addition to its rhythmic implications, a ligature indicates that only one syllable is to be sung for the duration of its notes, similar in function to a modern slur marking in vocal works (also known as a ligature, or ◊tie).

ligature the adjustable metal brace used to attach the reed to the mouthpiece of an instrument of the clarinet family.

Ligeti György (Sándor) 1923– . Hungarian-born Austrian composer. He developed a dense, highly chromatic style known as micropolyphony, in which individual strands of melody and rhythm are sometimes lost in shifting block-textures of sound. He achieved international prominence with *Atmosphères* 1961 and *Requiem* 1965, which achieved widespread fame as background music for Stanley Kubrick's film epic *2001: A Space Odyssey* 1968. Other works include an opera *Le Grand Macabre* 1978, and *Poème symphonique* 1962, for 100 metronomes.

Lind Jenny 1820–1887. Swedish soprano of remarkable range, nicknamed the 'Swedish nightingale'. She toured the USA 1850–52 under the management of circus promoter P T Barnum.

Lipatti Dinu 1917–1950. Romanian pianist. He perfected a small repertoire, notably of the works of Mozart, Schumann, and Chopin.

l'istesso tempo (Italian 'the same tempo') direction given when a change is indicated in the time signature, the composer intending the music remain at the same pace despite the new rhythm.

Liszt Franz 1811–1886. Hungarian composer and pianist. An outstanding virtuoso of the piano, possibly the greatest of all time, he was an established concert artist by the age of 12, impressing Beethoven and Czerny. His expressive, romantic, and frequently chromatic works include piano music (*Transcendental Studies* 1851), masses and oratorios, songs, organ music, and a symphony. Much of his music is programmatic; he also originated the ♭symphonic poem. His works were progressive for the period, and as musical director and conductor at Weimar 1848–59 he championed the music of Berlioz and Wagner, causing a rift with more conservative composers, such as Brahms.

Retiring to Rome, he turned again to his early love of religion, and in 1865 became a secular priest (adopting the title Abbé), while continuing to teach and give concert tours for which he also made virtuoso piano arrangements of orchestral works by Beethoven, Schubert, and Wagner. He died at Bayreuth in Germany.

liturgy a written, authorized version of a Christian service, especially of the Roman Catholic ♭Mass. Its development over the centuries has had a direct impact on music and composition, because until the Renaissance the Church had a near monopoly on skilled musicians and composers, whose work therefore catered to the service.

Lloyd Webber Andrew 1948– . English composer. A writer of hugely successful musicals, of which the early hits (with lyrics by Tim Rice) include *Joseph and the Amazing Technicolor Dreamcoat* 1968 and *Jesus Christ Superstar* 1970. He also wrote *Cats* 1981, based on T S Eliot's *Old Possum's Book of Practical Cats*, and *The Phantom of the Opera* 1986.

Other works include *Variations for Cello* 1978, written for his brother Julian Lloyd Webber (1951–), a solo cellist, and a *Requiem Mass* 1985.

loco (Italian 'place') a term used to counteract previous notation '8ve' calling for the performance of music at an octave higher or lower than normal; it indicates that the music is to return to its normal 'place' on the stave.

London Pianoforte School term applied to a group of composer-pianists working in London at the turn of the 19th century who pioneered the Romantic style of keyboard playing, based on a ♭legato touch, and who began to develop a more complex harmonic language that ultimately replaced the Classical style. Composers of the London Pianoforte School include Muzio Clementi, Jan Dussek, John Field, and John Cramer.

Los Angeles Victoria de 1923– . Spanish soprano. She is renowned for her elegantly refined interpretations of Spanish songs and for the roles of Manon and Madame Butterfly in Puccini's operas.

Luening Otto 1900– . US composer. He was appointed to Columbia University 1949, and in 1951 began a series of pioneering compositions for instruments and tape, some in partnership with US composer *Vladimir Ussachevsky* (1911–1990) (*Incantation* 1952, *A Poem in Cycles and Bells* 1954). In 1959 he became codirector, with Milton Babbitt and Ussachevsky, of the Columbia-Princeton Electronic Music Center.

Lully Jean-Baptiste. Adopted name of Giovanni Battista Lulli 1632–1687. French composer of Italian origin. He was court composer to Louis XIV, composing music for the ballet and for the plays of *Molière* (1622–1673). He established French opera with such works as *Alceste* 1674 and *Armide et Rénaud* 1686. He was also a ballet dancer. As a conductor he revolutionized bowing technique, but he died from blood poisoning after hitting his foot with a staff he used for beating time on the floor.

lunga pausa ('Italian long pause') a long ♭rest.

Lupu Radu 1945– . Romanian pianist. He favours the standard 19th-century repertory, from Schubert to Brahms, and plays with a lyrical and expressive tone.

lute member of a family of stringed musical instruments, including the mandore, theorbo, and chitarrone. The lute has a pear-shaped body with up to seven courses of strings (single or double), plucked with the fingers, and music for

lute

the instrument is written in special notation called ◊tablature. Dating back over 3,000 years, the lute's popularity peaked in the 16th and 17th centuries. Modern lutenists include Julian Bream and Anthony Rooley (1944–   ).

Members of the lute family were used both as solo instruments and for vocal accompaniment, and were often played in addition to, or instead of, keyboard instruments in larger ensembles and in opera.

Lutosławski Witold 1913–   . Polish composer and conductor, born in Warsaw. His fastidious output includes three symphonies, *Paroles tissées/Teased Words* 1965 for tenor and chamber orchestra, dedicated to Peter Pears, and *Chain I* 1981 for orchestra.

His early major compositions, such as *Variations on a Theme of Paganini* 1941 for two pianos and *First Symphony* 1947, drew some criticism from the communist government. After 1956, under a more liberal regime, he adopted avant-garde techniques, including improvisation and the use of aleatory textures (where instrumental lines are not exactly synchronized), in *Venetian Games* 1961.

Lutyens (Agnes) Elisabeth 1906–1983. English composer. Her works, using the ◊twelve-tone system, are expressive and tightly organized, and include chamber music, stage, and orchestral works. Her choral and vocal works include a motet setting of the *Tractatus* by Austrian philosopher *Ludwig Wittgenstein* (1889–1951) and a cantata *The Tears of Night*. She also composed much film and incidental music.

Lydian mode one of the church modes, a scale F – E, centred around and beginning on F, which uses only notes of the C major scale. Also a scale of ancient Greece, the equivalent of the modern major scale.

lyre stringed instrument of great antiquity. It consists of a soundbox with two curved arms extended upwards to a crosspiece to which four to ten strings are attached. It is played with a plectrum or the fingers. It originated in Asia, and was widespread in ancient Greece and Egypt. Unlike the harp, the lyre's strings are of the same length and therefore must be tuned at different tensions.

lyrical of melodic, songful quality.

Maazel Lorin (Varencove) 1930– . US conductor and violinist. He was musical director of the Pittsburgh Symphony Orchestra from 1986. A wide-ranging repertoire includes opera, from posts held at Berlin, Vienna, Bayreuth, and Milan, in addition to the symphonic repertoire, in particular Sibelius and Tchaikovsky. His orchestral preparation is noted for its inner precision and dynamic range.

McCabe John 1939– . English pianist and composer. He specializes in Haydn and the English 20th-century repertory. His works include three symphonies, two violin concertos, an opera *The Play of Mother Courage* 1974, and orchestral works including *The Chagall Windows* 1974 and *Concerto for Orchestra* 1982. He was director of the London College of Music 1983–90.

MacDowell Edward Alexander 1860–1908. US Romantic composer. His works include the *Indian Suite* 1896 and piano concertos and sonatas. Influenced by Liszt, he was at his best with short, lyrical piano pieces, such as 'To a Wild Rose' from *Woodland Sketches* 1896.

McPhee Colin 1900–1964. Canadian-born US composer. His studies of Balinese music 1934–36 produced two works, *Tabuh-tabuhan* 1936 for two pianos and orchestra and *Balinese Ceremonial Music* 1940 for two pianos, which influenced Benjamin Britten, also John Cage and later generations of US composers.

Machaut Guillame de 1300–1377. French composer and poet. Born in Champagne, he was in the service of John of Bohemia for 30 years and, later, of King John the Good of France. He gave the forms of the ballade (vocal piece based on a story) and ◊rondo (where verses alternate with a refrain) a new individuality and ensured their lasting popularity. His *Messe de Nostre Dame c.*1360, written for Reims Cathedral, is an early masterpiece of the ◊*ars nova* style, exploiting unusual rhythmic complexities.

Mackerras Charles 1925– . Australian conductor. He has helped to make the music of the Czech composer Janáček better known. He was conductor of the English National Opera 1970–78.

Maderna Bruno 1920–1973. Italian composer and conductor. He collaborated with Luciano Berio in setting up an electronic studio in Milan. His compositions combine techniques of ♭aleatory music and graphic techniques (see ♭graph notation) with an elegance of sound. They include a pioneering work for live and prerecorded flute, *Musica su due dimensioni* 1952, numerous concertos, and *Hyperion* 1964, a 'mobile opera', consisting of a number of composed scenes that may be combined in several ways.

madrigal form of secular song, most often in four or five parts, richly polyphonic, and usually sung without instrumental accompaniment. It originated in 14th-century Italy and developed into the early cantata of the 17th century. Madrigal composers include Andrea Gabrieli, Monteverdi, Thomas Morley, and Orlando Gibbons.

Maelzel Johann Nepomuk 1772–1838. German inventor. His name is invariably linked to the ♭metronome. He did not invent the machine, but appropriated the idea, developing it in 1814.

maestoso Italian 'majestic', 'dignified'. When used as part of a tempo marking, for example *allegro maestoso*, it modifies it, directing the performer to maintain a dignified character.

maestro di capella (Italian 'chapel master') Italian equivalent of ♭kapellmeister.

maggiore Italian 'major key'.

Magnificat a ♭canticle of the Virgin Mary based on text from Luke 1:46–55 (My soul doth magnify the Lord...). It is sung at Roman Catholic vespers and Anglican evensong, either in ♭plainsong or to a composer's setting, as in works by Monteverdi, Bach, Palestrina, and Vaughan Williams.

Mahler Alma (born Schindler) 1879–1964. Austrian pianist and composer. She wrote lieder. She abandoned composing when she married the composer Gustav Mahler 1902. After Mahler's death she lived with the architect Walter Gropius (1883–1969); their daughter Manon's death inspired Alban Berg's *Violin Concerto* 1935.

Mahler Gustav 1860–1911. Austrian composer and conductor. He composed epic symphonies expressing a world-weary Romanticism in visionary tableaux incorporating folk music and pastoral imagery. He wrote 10 symphonies, many with voices, including *Symphony No 2 'Resurrection'* 1886 (revised 1896), also orchestral lieder including *Das Lied von der Erde/The Song of the Earth* 1909 and *Kindertoten-lieder/Dead Children's Songs* 1904.

For many years Mahler composed intensively only during the summer months, as the rest of the year he was too busy conducting. Many of his works were not well received during his lifetime, but subsequently have been recognized as works of genius.

main droite or *M.D.* French 'right hand' (see ◊R.H.).

main gauche or *M.G.* French 'left hand' (see ◊L.H.).

malagueña a Spanish dance, named after the town of Malaga, in moderate to fast ◊triple time (3/8 or 3/4). It can refer to several varieties: an 18th-century dance related to the ◊fandango; an older kind of dance based on a ◊chaconne, with a repeating accompaniment of four harmonies and an improvised melody; or a kind of freely formed emotional song. An example of a stylized malagueña can be found in Albéniz's *Iberia* 1909.

Malipiero Gian Francesco 1882–1973. Italian composer and editor of Monteverdi and Vivaldi. His own works show the influence of early Italian masters, Debussy, and Janáček, and include operas based on Shakespeare's *Julius Caesar* 1935 and *Antony and Cleopatra* 1937.

Manchester School a group of composers who attended the Royal Manchester College during the late 1950s, namely Peter Maxwell Davies, Harrison Birtwistle, Alexander Goehr, and John Ogdon. They later formed the British avant-garde, working with the latest serial techniques and sometimes employing electronic procedures.

mandolin plucked string instrument smaller than the lute, its name deriving from its almond-shaped body (Italian *mandorla* 'almond'), with four to six pairs of strings (courses). It flourished between the 17th and 19th centuries. Vivaldi composed two concertos for the mandolin *c.*1736.

The ***Neapolitan mandolin***, a different instrument which appeared about 1750, is played with a plectrum usually in a ◊tremolo style and has metal strings. Composers include Beethoven, Hummel, Schoenberg, and Stravinsky in *Agon* 1957.

mano destra or **M.S.** Italian 'right hand' (see ◊R.H.).

mano sinistar or **M.D.** Italian 'left hand' (see ◊L.H.).

manual any of the keyboards of a multi-keyboard instrument played by the hands. A harpsichord often has two manuals, an organ has up to four (◊great organ, ◊swell organ, ◊choir organ, ◊solo organ). The pedal keyboard (pedalboard) of the organ is not a manual.

maraca one of usually a pair of Latin American percussion instruments, consisting of a gourd partly filled with dry seeds or beans (although there are modern-material versions). Maracas are shaken to produce noise and traditionally form part of the rhythm section of Latin American bands. Classical composers who have written for maracas include Prokofiev in *Romeo and Juliet* 1935.

mandolin

maracas

march or (Italian) *marcia* a piece originally intended to accompany marching soldiers or other people in procession, facilitating a regular and repeated drum rhythm. One of the earliest known forms of music, they are usually in duple time (2/4) or common time (4/4), with a strongly marked beat and regular phrasing. There are various types, distinguished by tempo: the funeral march, slow march, quick march, and, occasionally, double-quick march. The earliest examples of the march in art music are found in the work of Lully and Couperin in the 17th century. The march has been used ever since, from Mozart operas as in *Die Zauberflöte/The Magic Flute* 1791, to Beethoven's *Eroica* symphony 1804, to Elgar's *Pomp and Circumstance Marches* 1901.

marimba bass xylophone of Latin American and African origin with wooden rather than metal tubular resonators.

Markevich Igor 1912–1983. Russian-born conductor and composer. His austere ballet *L'Envol d'Icare/The Flight of Icarus* 1932 influenced Bartók. After World War II he concentrated on conducting, specializing in Russian and French composers 1880–1950.

Marriner Neville 1924– . English conductor and violinist. He founded the Academy of St Martin- in-the-Fields 1956. He is an authority on 17th- and 18th-century music, forming the Jacobean Ensemble with Thurston Dart to perform ◊early music.

martellato (Italian 'hammered') percussive, with sharp attacks and detached articulation. The term usually appears in compositions for strings or for piano.

Martin Frank 1890–1974. Swiss composer, pianist, and harpsichordist. His works are characterized by delicate colouring in instrumentation and an expressive quality combined in later works with a loosely interpreted ◊twelve-tone system. Composing for both large- and small-scale forces, from orchestra to chamber music, his best known works are the operas *The Tempest* 1956 and *Monsieur Pourceaugnac* 1962.

Martinů Bohuslav (Jan) 1890–1959. Czech composer. His music is rhythmically vital, richly expressive, and though at times it exhibits a wide range of dissonance, it is basically diatonic. His works include the operas *Julietta* 1937 and *The Greek Passion* 1959, symphonies, and chamber music. He settled temporarily in New York after the Nazi occupation of Czechoslovakia 1939.

Mascagni Pietro 1863–1945. Italian composer and conductor. The success of his first opera, the one-act *Cavalleria rusticana/Rustic Chivalry* 1890 which was composed in the new ◊verismo or realistic style, overshadowed his later operas, including *L'Amico Fritz* 1891 and *Nerone* 1935.

masque a lavish stage production of the 16th and 17th centuries that combined poetry, music (vocal and instrumental), dancing, and acting, for the entertainment of the aristocracy. Originating in Italy, where members of the court actively participated in the performances, the masque was introduced to England in the 16th century, where it flourished during the 17th century. It developed in part from the influence of medieval mystery plays and from the talent of great writers such as Ben Jonson (1572–1637). Composers of masques include John Coperario and Thomas Campion.

Mass the musical setting of the invariable parts of the Roman Catholic Ordinary Mass, that is the Kyrie, Gloria, Credo, Sanctus with Benedictus, and Agnus Dei. A notable example is Bach's *Mass in B Minor* 1733. The Mass Proper, which varies by day and by season, is usually chanted ◊plainsong if not spoken. Another type of mass is the ◊requiem or Mass for the Dead.

Massenet Jules Emile Frédéric 1842–1912. French composer. He wrote operas, notably *Manon* 1884, *Le Cid* 1885, and *Thaïs* 1894; among other works is the orchestral suite *Scènes pittoresques* 1874. Massenet incorporated Wagnerian ◊leitmotivs into his works, but his style is sweeter than Wagner's.

Master of the King's Musick or *Master of the Queen's Musick* honorary appointment to the British royal household, the holder composing appropriate music for state occasions. The first was Nicholas Lanier (1588–1666), appointed by Charles I 1626; later appointments have included Elgar and Arthur Bliss. The present holder, Malcolm Williamson, was appointed 1975.

mastersinger English for ◊Meistersinger.

Masur Kurt 1928– . German conductor. Music director of the New York Philharmonic from 1990, his speciality is late Romantic and early 20th-century repertoire, in particular Mendelssohn, Liszt, Bruch, and Prokofiev.

He was prominent in the political campaigning that took place prior to German unification.

matins the first Roman Catholic office (or non-Eucharistic service) of the day. It is also used by the Anglican church to refer to Morning Prayer.

Mayer Robert 1879–1985. German-born British philanthropist. He founded the Robert Mayer Concerts for Children and the Transatlantic Foundation Anglo-American Scholarships.

mazurka a family of traditional Polish dances. In triple time (3/4), it is characterized by dotted rhythms and the accentuation of weak beats, on which phrases also begin and end. It is found at a variety of speeds, but is usually not as fast as the waltz, which is also formally a more rigid dance than the mazurka. During the 18th and 19th centuries, it spread throughout Europe and in art music was made famous by Chopin's approximately 60 works in the genre. Other composers of the mazurka include Karol Szymanowski, Glinka, and Mussorgsky.

measure US for ◊bar.

mediant third note or degree of the ◊diatonic scale, for example E in the C major scale. A chord of the mediant is a ◊triad (chord of three notes) built upon the mediant note.

Mehta Zubin 1936–   . Indian-born US conductor. He has been music director of the New York Philharmonic from 1978. He specializes in robust, polished interpretations of 19th- and 20th-century repertoire, including contemporary US compositions.

Meistersinger (German 'master singer') one of a group of German lyric poets, singers, and musicians of the 14th–16th centuries, who formed guilds for the revival of minstrelsy. Hans ◊Sachs was a Meistersinger, and Wagner's opera *Die Meistersinger von Nürnberg/The Mastersingers of Nuremberg* 1868 depicts the tradition.

melodic minor scale a kind of minor scale in which the sixth and seventh degrees are raised by a semitone when ascending and returned to their original 'natural' positions when descending.

melodrama a stage presentation which consists of spoken words with an accompaniment of music contributing to the dramatic effect. It became popular in the late 18th century, due to works like *Pygmalion* 1770 by philosopher and composer Jean-Jacques Rousseau 1712–1778. In melodramas of this period there was no direct correlation between the free rhythm of the actor's voice and the music which was played in strict ◊metre. In addition to self-contained melodramas, some operas of the period included scenes of this style, as in the gravedigging scene in Beethoven's *Fidelio* 1805. Schoenberg developed the genre in his *Pierrot Lunaire* 1912, by the inclusion of semi-musical speech called ◊*Sprechgesang* (German 'speech-song').

melody (Greek *melos* 'song') a distinctive sequence of notes traditionally sounded consecutively within an orderly pitch structure such as a scale or a mode. A melody may be a tune in its own right, or it may form a theme running through a longer piece of music.

Melody, harmony, rhythm, and texture are the basic components of Western music.

Mendelssohn (-Bartholdy) (Jakob Ludwig) Felix 1809–1847. German composer, pianist, and conductor. His music has the textural lightness and charm of classical music, applied to romantic harmonies and descriptive subjects. He was a child prodigy, writing *A Midsummer Night's Dream* 1827 when he was only 17. Other famous works include: the *Fingal's Cave* overture 1832; and five symphonies, which include the *Reformation* 1830, the *Italian* 1833, and the *Scottish* 1842. He was instrumental in promoting the revival of interest in J S Bach's music.

meno Italian 'less'; as in *meno mosso* '(less moved'), meaning slower.

Menotti Gian Carlo 1911– . Italian-born US composer. He is a writer of small-scale realist operas in a melodic tonal idiom, including *The Medium* 1946, *The Telephone* 1947, *The Consul* 1950, *Amahl and the Night Visitors* 1951 (the first opera to be written for television), and *The Saint of Bleecker Street* 1954. He has also written orchestral and chamber music.

He was co-librettist with Samuel Barber for the latter's *Vanessa* 1958 and *A Hand of Bridge* 1959 .

Menuhin Yehudi 1916– . US-born violinist and conductor. His solo repertoire extends from Vivaldi to George Enescu (1881–1955). A child prodigy, he recorded the Elgar Violin Concerto 1932 with the composer conducting, and commissioned the *Sonata* 1944 for violin solo from an ailing Bartók. He has appeared in concert with sitar virtuoso Ravi Shankar, and with jazz violinist Stephane Grappelli (1908–).

In 1959 he moved to London, becoming a British subject 1985. He founded the Yehudi Menuhin School of Music, Stoke d'Abernon, Surrey, 1963.

Messager André Charles Prosper 1853–1929. French composer and conductor. He studied under Saint-Saëns. Messager composed light operas, such as *La Béarnaise* 1885 and *Véronique* 1898.

Messiaen Olivier 1908–1992. French composer, organist, and teacher. His music is mystical in character, vividly coloured through the use of modes, orchestral timbre, and occasionally the ◊ondes Martenot (an electronic musical instrument), and incorporates transcriptions of birdsong. Among his works are the *Quartet for the End of Time* 1941, the large-scale *Turangalîla Symphony* 1949, and solo organ and piano pieces. As a teacher at the Paris Conservatoire from 1942, he influenced three generations of composers.

His theories, often drawing on medieval and oriental music, have inspired contemporary composers such as Boulez and Stockhausen, especially regarding the serial organization of dynamics and rhythm (see ◊integral serialism).

mesto Italian 'mournful', 'sad'.

metre or *time* the timescale represented by a regular beat. Metre can be *simple* as in 2/4, 3/4, 2/2 and so on, where each beat divides into two subbeats; *compound metre* as in 6/8, 9/8, 12/16, and so on, consists of subbeats of 'compounded' or aggregated units of three. The numerical sign for metre is a *time signature*, of which the upper number represents the number of beats in the bar, the lower number the type of beat, expressed as a fraction of a unit (semibreve). Hence 3/4 is three crotchet beats to the bar and 6/8 is two beats each of three quavers. (See also ◊duple time and ◊triple time.)

metronome clockwork device, patented by Johann Maelzel 1815, using a sliding weight to regulate the speed of a pendulum to assist in setting tempo. Today electronic metronomes are also used.

Metropolitan Opera Company foremost opera company in the USA, founded 1883 in New York City. The Metropolitan Opera House (opened 1883) was demolished 1966, and the company moved to the new Metropolitan Opera House at the Lincoln Center.

Meyerbeer Giacomo. Adopted name of Jakob Liebmann Beer 1791–1864. German composer. He is known for his operas, written in the style of Rossini, which include *Robert le Diable* 1831 and *Les Huguenots* 1836. From 1826 he lived mainly in Paris, returning to Berlin after 1842 as musical director of the Royal Opera.

mezzo- or *mezza-* (Italian 'half') prefix indicating a reduction, as in mezzoforte (mf), meaning less loud, and mezzopiano (mp), meaning less soft. 'Mezzo' stands for ◊mezzo-soprano.

mezzo-soprano female singing voice (approximate range C4–F5), between soprano and contralto. Janet Baker is a well-known mezzo-soprano.

mf abbreviation of mezzo forte (Italian 'half loud') medium loud.

microtone any precisely determined division of the octave smaller than a semitone.

Examples of quarter-tone divisions are heard in the violin solo parts of Bartók's Violin Concerto No 2 1938, Berg's *Chamber Concerto* 1925, and Boulez's cantata *Le Visage nuptial/The Bridal Countenance* 1946 (revised 1951). Since 1984 Stockhausen has developed notations of up to 1/16th of a tone for basset horn and flute, for example in *Xi* 1986 for basset horn. Microtones are also found in non-Western music, such as that of India.

middle C white note (C4) at the centre of the piano keyboard, indicating the division between left- and right-hand regions and between the treble and bass staves of printed music. Middle C is also the pitch indicated by a C clef, for example, for viola.

MIDI acronym for *musical instrument digital interface*, a manufacturer's standard allowing different pieces of digital music equipment used in composing and recording to be freely connected.

The information-sending device (any electronic instrument) is called a controller, and the reading device (such as a computer) the sequencer. Pitch, dynamics, decay rate, and stereo position can all be transmitted via the interface. A computer with a MIDI interface can input and store the sounds produced by the connected instruments, and can then manipulate these sounds in many different ways. For example, a single keystroke may change the key of an entire composition. Even a full written score for the composition may be automatically produced.

Mighty Five, The or *The Mighty Handful* alternative names for The ◊Five.

Milhaud Darius 1892–1974. French composer and pianist. A member of Les ◊Six, he was extremely prolific in a variety of styles and genres, ranging from works influenced by jazz, the rhythms of Latin America, and electronic composition. He is noted for his use of ◊polytonality (the simultaneous existence of two or more keys), as in the *Saudades do Brasil* 1921 for orchestra and *L'homme et son désir* 1918. A pastoral element also runs through many of his works, as in his six chamber symphonies 1917–22 or first string quartet 1912. His Jewish ancestry is evident in his cantata *Ani maamiu* written for the Festival of Israel 1973.

minim or US ***half note*** a note value, half the duration of a ◊semibreve. It is written as an empty white note-head with a stem. It is the basic unit of beat for the following metres: 2/2, 4/2, cut time ◊alla breve.

minimalism a musical style which developed in the third quarter of the 20th century. It is usually tonal or even diatonic, and highly repetitive, based on a few 'minimal' musical ideas. The composers Philip Glass and Steve Reich are exponents of this style.

minnesinger (German 'love-singer') one of a group of 12th- to 14th-century German lyric poets and musicians. They represent a continuation of the French ◊troubadour tradition, but their musical and literary styles diverged. Many were of noble birth, unlike the later ◊Meistersingers (German 'mastersingers') who were from the middle classes.

minstrel a professional entertainer of any kind, but particularly a musician, existing in the 12th to 17th centuries. Most common in the Middle Ages, minstrels were usually in the service of a court or of a member of the aristocracy.

minstrel one of a group of white entertainers popular in the USA during the 19th century who painted their faces black and impersonated the music and humour of slaves from the Southern plantations.

minuet French country dance in three time adapted as a European courtly dance of the 17th and 18th centuries. The music was also used as the third movement of a classical four-movement symphony or sonata where its gentle rhythm provided a foil to the slow second movement and fast final movement. Beethoven began the trend of replacing the minuet with a scherzo (a lively piece, usually in rapid triple (3/4) time).

Miserere title of a work using the text of *Psalm 51*, *'Miserere mei, Deus ...'* (Latin 'have mercy upon me, O God ...'). It is sung (often in ◊plainsong) during the Roman Catholic office (or non-Eucharistic service) of Lauds, at sunrise, during the week preceding Easter Sunday. Simple polyphonic settings of the text have been made by early composers such as Josquin Desprez and Gregorio Allegri (the latter work famous for its embellishments and popular with modern audiences). Later composers have set Misereres, including Verdi in the opera *Il Trovatore* 1853.

mixolydian mode one of the ◊church modes, the mode or scale from G – F centred around and beginning on G, that uses only notes of the C major scale. Originally a scale of ancient Greece equivalent to the white notes of a piano from B–A.

mixture an organ stop, controlling at least two rows of very high-pitched pipes. It is not used alone, but in conjunction with lower-pitched pipes in order to enrich the tone quality of a pre-existing combination of stops.

mobile form an alternative term for ◊*aleatory music*, named after the mobile sculpture created by Alexander Calder (1898–1976).

mode a form of scale, with five or more pitches to the octave, originating with the ancient Greeks and later adapted by medieval composers, for ecclesiastical music in particular (called *church modes*). They are often identified with a particular emotion, ritual function, time, or season, to which music is composed or improvised.

moderato Italian 'moderate'; between ◊andante (walking pace) and ◊allegro (lively).

modulation movement from one key to another through harmonic progressions. In classical dance music, modulation is a guide to phrasing rhythm to the step pattern.

Electronic modulation of live or prerecorded instrumental sound is also used to create unusual timbres, as in Stockhausen's *Mixtur* 1967 for instrumental groups and ring modulation.

moll (German 'soft') German equivalent to 'minor' when referring to ◊key, as in B moll (B minor). Opposite of dur ('hard', 'major').

molto Italian 'much', 'very'; as in *allegro molto* 'very quickly'.

monochord (Greek 'one string') ancient scientific instrument consisting of a single string stretched over a soundbox, with a movable bridge. The monochord may be used to demonstrate the existence of harmonics, and the proportional relations of intervals.

monody Italian song for an accompanied solo voice, used at the turn of the 16th and 17th centuries. A reaction against ◊polyphony, the style was also adopted for instruments in trio sonatas by Salamone Rossi (?1570–c.1630) and Biagio Marini (c.1587–1663).

monothematic in musical analysis, of a composition based on a single theme. In the 18th century Haydn experimented with the technique: several finales of his symphonies are composed monothematically. Composers of the 19th-century were also interested in the idea, sometimes involving it as a means of creating coherent ◊cyclic form. Schubert's *Fantasia* ('Wanderer') 1822 may be argued to approach monothematicism, as may Liszt's Sonata in B minor for piano 1854, which presents themes derived from possibly a single ◊motif. Some compositions using the ◊twelve-tone system have another type of monothematic construction, in which only one twelve-note row is manipulated in the work.

Monteux Pierre 1875–1964. French conductor. Ravel's *Daphnis and Chloe* 1912 and Stravinsky's *The Rite of Spring* 1913 were first performed under his direction. He conducted Diaghilev's Ballets Russes 1911–14 and 1917, and the San Francisco Symphony Orchestra 1935–52.

Monteverdi Claudio (Giovanni Antonio) 1567–1643. Italian composer. His place in the development of Renaissance music cannot be overstated. He transformed virtually every genre with which he worked. He contributed to the development of the dramatic opera with *La favola d'Orfeo/The Legend of Orpheus* 1607 and *L'incoronazione di Poppea/ The Coronation of Poppea* 1642. His harmonic language and use of instruments as an orchestral force were advanced for his period. He also wrote madrigals, motets, and sacred music, notably the *Vespers* 1610.

Born in Cremona, he was in the service of the Duke of Mantua about 1591–1612, and was director of music at St Mark's, Venice, from 1613.

Moog syntheziser any of a family of inexpensive analogue ◊synthesizers produced since 1965 by Robert Moog (1934–), incorporating transistorized electronics and voltage control, which brought electronic music synthesis within the reach of composers, performers, and academic institutions.

Moore Gerald 1899–1987. British pianist. He was renowned as an accompanist of Elizabeth Schwarzkopf, Kathleen Ferrier, Heddle Nash (1896–1961), and other singers, a role he raised to equal partnership.

mordent a specific type of ◊ornamentation which consists of the rapid alternation (usually only once) of the written note with the note a semitone or whole-tone below it. It begins on the beat rather than before it.

morendo (Italian 'dying') becoming softer.

Morley Thomas 1557–1602. English composer. He wrote consort music, madrigals, and airs including the lute song *It was a lover and his lass* for Shakespeare's play *As You Like It* 1599. He edited a collection of Italian madrigals *The Triumphs of Oriana* 1601, and published an influential keyboard tutor *A Plaine and Easie Introduction to Practicall Musicke* 1597. He was also organist at St Paul's Cathedral, London.

mosso Italian 'moved'; as in *più mosso* ('more moved') meaning faster.

motet an elaborate, usually polyphonic, composition in Latin, which originated in the 13th century. It is sung at some point during the course of the Roman Catholic Mass, but does not form part of the liturgy. The Anglican ◊anthem was derived from it.

motif or *motive* a group of at least two notes forming an intelligible characteristic figure, which through repetition and development forms a foundation for larger figures and themes; one of the most basic units of composition. Often, a single motif will serve as the building block for a variety of themes and accompaniment figures.

Beethoven was one of the greatest masters of motivic composition. The first movement of his Fifth Symphony 1808 us a famous example of the constant recurrence of the four-note motif which forms the first four notes of the piece. Throughout the 19th century, composers relied on motifs to provide compositional coherence in an era in which traditional large-scale structures such as sonata form were beginning to lose their relevance. Motifs continued to be an essential compositional tool to early 20th-century artists, including Schoenberg and Stravinsky. Since the evolution of chance procedures and other avant-garde techniques introduced in the 1950s, many composers have abandoned the motif, but it still remains a vital instrument.

moto Italian 'motion'; as in *andante con moto* ('andante with motion'), meaning faster than the usual ◊andante tempo.

motoric rhythm 20th-century term for rhythm based on one specific note value (quavers, for example) usually in order to sustain or generate energy. ◊Ostinatos (repeating melodic or rhythmic figures) often form motoric rhythms, as in Stravinsky's *The Rite of Spring* 1913.

mouth organ any of a family of small portable free-reed wind instruments originating in Eastern and South Asia. The compact *harmonica*, or European mouth organ, developed 1829 by Charles Wheatstone, has tuned metal free reeds of variable length contained in a narrow rectangular box and is played by blowing and sucking air while moving the instrument from side to side through the lips.

movement usually a self-contained composition of specific character, a constituent piece of a suite, symphony, sonata, or similar work, with its own tempo, distinct from that of the other movements. Occasionally, two movements are connected, without the players pausing.

Moyse Marcel 1889–1984. French flautist. Trained at the Paris Conservatoire, he made many recordings and was an eminent teacher.

Mozart Wolfgang Amadeus 1756–1791. Austrian composer and pianist. He showed astonishing precocity as a child and was an adult virtuoso. He was trained by his father, Leopold Mozart (1719–1787). From an early age he composed prolifically, his works including 27 piano concertos, 23 string quartets, 35 violin sonatas, and more than 50 symphonies including the E flat K543, G minor K550, and C major K551 ('Jupiter') symphonies, all composed 1788. His operas include *Idomeneo* 1780, *Entführung aus dem Serail/The Abduction from the Seraglio* 1782, *Le Nozze di Figaro/The Marriage of Figaro* 1786, *Don Giovanni* 1787, *Così fan tutte/Thus Do All Women* 1790, and *Die Zauberflöte/The Magic Flute* 1791. Together with Haydn, Mozart's music marks the height of the Viennese Classical style in its purity of melody and form. His impact on later composers, especially regarding opera, the concerto, the quartet, and the symphony, is immense.

Mozart's career began when he was taken on a number of tours 1762–79, visiting Vienna, the Rhineland, Holland, Paris, London, and Italy. In 1772 he was appointed master of the archbishop of Salzburg's court band but he found the post uncongenial and in 1781 was suddenly dismissed. He married Constanze Weber 1782, settled in Vienna, and embarked on a punishing freelance career as concert pianist, composer, and teacher that brought lasting fame but only intermittent financial security. His *Requiem*, unfinished at his death, was completed by a pupil.

mp abbreviation of *mezzo piano* (Italian 'half soft'), less soft.

multiphonics a technique of ◊overblowing a woodwind instrument combined with unorthodox fingering to produce a complex dissonance. Composers of multiphonics include Luciano Berio and Heinz Holliger, and the technique is also used by jazz saxophonists.

musette small French bagpipes popular in the 17th and 18th centuries; also a dance movement or character piece which incorporates a ◊drone accompaniment, imitative of bagpipes, as in Vaughan Williams's oboe concerto 1944.

Musgrave Thea 1928– . Scottish composer. Her works, ranging in style from diatonicism to ◊serialism, include concertos for horn, clarinet, and viola; string quartets; and operas, including *Mary, Queen of Scots* 1977.

music art of combining sounds into a coherent perceptual experience, typically in accordance with conventional patterns and for an aesthetic purpose. Music is generally categorized as classical, jazz, pop music, country and western, and so on.

The Greek word *mousike* covered all the arts presided over by the Muses. The various civilizations of the ancient and modern world developed their own musical systems. Eastern music recognizes subtler distinctions of pitch than does Western music but lacks complex varieties of harmony and ◊polyphony, and also differs from Western music in that the absence, until recently, of written notation ruled out the composition of major developed works; it fostered melodic and rhythmic patterns, freely interpreted (as in the Indian raga) by virtuosos.

Western classical music
Middle Ages The documented history of Western music since Classical times begins with the liturgical music of the medieval Catholic church, derived from Greek and Hebrew antecedents. The four scales, or modes, to which the words of the liturgy were chanted were traditionally first set in order by St Ambrose AD 384. St Gregory the Great added four more to the original Ambrosian modes, and this system forms the basis of Gregorian ◊plainsong, still used in the Roman Catholic Church. The organ was introduced in the 8th century, and in the 9th century harmonized music began to be used in churches, with notation developing

towards its present form. In the 11th century ◊counterpoint was introduced, notably at the monastery of St Martial, Limoges, France, and in the late 12th century at Notre Dame in Paris (by Léonin and Pérotin). In the late Middle Ages the Provençal and French ◊troubadours and court composers, such as Guillaume Machaut, developed a secular music, derived from church and folk music.

15th and 16th centuries Growth of contrapuntal or polyphonic music in Europe. One of the earliest composers was the English musician John Dunstable, whose works inspired the French composer Guillaume Dufay, founder of the Flemish school; its members included Dufay's pupil Joannes Ockeghem and the Renaissance composer Josquin Desprez. Other composers of this era were Palestrina from Italy, Roland de Lassus from Flanders, Victoria from Spain, and Thomas Tallis and William Byrd from England. ◊Madrigals were written during the Elizabethan age in England by such composers as Thomas Morley and Orlando Gibbons.

17th-century The Florentine Academy, a group of artists and writers, aimed to revive the principles of Greek tragedy. This led to the invention of dramatic ◊recitative and the beginning of opera. Monteverdi was an early operatic composer; by the end of the century the form had evolved further in the hands of Alessandro Scarlatti in Italy and Jean-Baptiste Lully in France. In England the outstanding composer of the period was Purcell.

18th century The early part of the century was dominated by J S Bach and Handel. Bach was a master of harmony and counterpoint. Handel is renowned for his dramatic oratorios. Bach's sons C P E Bach and J C Bach reacted against contrapuntal forms and began to develop ◊sonata form from existing Baroque ◊binary forms, the basis of the classical sonata, quartet, and symphony. In these types of composition, the Viennese composers Haydn and Mozart achieved unsurpassed formal beauty and simplicity. With Beethoven, music assumed an increased range of dynamic and expressive functions, influencing all composers of the 19th century.

19th century Romantic music, represented in its early stages by Weber, Schubert, Schumann, Mendelssohn, and Chopin, tended to be subjectively emotional. Orchestral colour was increasingly exploited – most notably by Berlioz – and harmony became more chromatic. Nationalism became prominent at this time, as evidenced by the intense Polish nationalism of Chopin; the exploitation of Hungarian music by Liszt; the

Russians Rimsky-Korsakov, Borodin, Mussorgsky, and, less typically, Tchaikovsky; the works of the Czechs Dvořák and Smetana; and the Norwegian Grieg. Revolutionary changes rooted in the music of Liszt and Berlioz were brought about by Wagner in the field of opera, although traditional Italian lyricism continued in the work of Rossini, Verdi, and Puccini. Wagner's contemporary Brahms championed the Classical discipline of form combined with Romantic feeling. The Belgian César Franck, with a newly chromatic idiom, also renewed the tradition of polyphonic writing.

20th century Around 1900 a reaction against Romanticism became apparent in the ◊impressionism of Debussy and Ravel, and the exotic ◊chromaticism of Stravinsky and Scriabin. In Austria and Germany, the tradition of Bruckner, Mahler, and Richard Strauss faced a disturbing new world of atonal ◊expressionism in Schoenberg, Berg, and Webern. After World War I Neo-Classicism, represented by Stravinsky, Prokofiev, and Hindemith, attempted to restore 18th-century principles of objectivity and order while maintaining a distinctively 20th-century tone. In Paris 'Les Six' adopted a more relaxed style, while composers further from the cosmopolitan centres of Europe, such as Elgar, Delius, and Sibelius, continued loyal to the Romantic symphonic tradition. The rise of radio and recorded media created a new mass market for classical and Romantic music, but one initially resistant to music by contemporary composers. Organizations such as the International Society for Contemporary Music became increasingly responsible for ensuring that new music continued to be publicly performed.

The second half of the 20th century has seen dramatic changes in the nature of composition and in the instruments used to create sounds. Following the 1950s vogue of total ◊integral serialism (that is, serialization of pitch, dynamics, duration, and timbre) composers searched for new modes of expression. Some, such as Ligeti, explored new textural possibilities. Many others, such as Peter Maxwell Davies, began on occasion to return to tonally-based harmonic systems, especially during and after the 1970s. Still others experimented with the medium of electronic music. The recording studio has facilitated the development of ◊*musique concrète* (concrete music), based on recorded natural sounds, and electronic music, in which sounds are generated electrically, thereby allowing the creation of music as a finished object without the need for interpretation by live performers. Chance music, promoted by John Cage, introduced the notion of a music designed to provoke unforeseen results and thereby make new connections; ◊aleatory music, developed by Pierre Boulez, introduced performers to freedom of choice from a range of options. Since the 1960s the computer has become a focus of attention for developments in the synthesis of musical tones, and also in the automation of compositional techniques, most notably at Stanford University and MIT in the USA, and at ◊IRCAM in Paris.

musica ficta (Latin 'feigned music') in music of the Middle Ages, the theory of non-diatonic notes (those notes not normally present in a simple C major scale). B flat was the first non-diatonic note allowed, in order to avoid the ◊tritone B – F. Other notes later became sharpened or flattened for similar reasons. Musica ficta also introduced non-diatonic notes in order to create a semitone between the ◊leading note (seventh note of a scale) and ◊tonic (first note of a scale). For example, when the tonic is G the leading note F must become F sharp in order to have the desired semitone. Musica ficta was not always written using ◊accidentals (sharp, flat, or natural signs), rather it required precise knowledge by the performer of correct theory and practice.

musical 20th-century form of dramatic musical performance, combining elements of song, dance, and the spoken word, often characterized by lavish staging and large casts. It developed from the operettas and musical comedies of the 19th century. Modern examples include Bernstein's *West Side Story* and Lloyd Webber's *Phantom of the Opera*.

The ◊operetta is a light-hearted entertainment with extensive musical content: Jaques Offenbach, Johann Strauss, Franz Lehár, and Gilbert and Sullivan all composed operettas. The *musical comedy* is an anglicization of the French *opéra bouffe*, of which the first was *A Gaiety Girl* 1893, mounted by George Edwardes (1852–1915) at the Gaiety Theatre, London.

musical saw instrument made from a hand saw. The handle is clasped between the knees with the top of the blade held in one hand so that it forms an S-curve. A cello bow is played with the other hand across the back edge of the blade to produce an eerie wailing sound. The pitch is altered by varying the curvature of the blade. Composers include George Crumb.

musical science In general, musical science is the rationalization of ◊pitch, first into ◊modes, then into scales and ◊temperament, and to quantify ◊timbre, to account for differences between sounds of the same pitch, and to analyse the structure of sound itself.

music hall British light theatrical entertainment, in which singers, dancers, comedians, and acrobats perform in 'turns'. The music hall's heyday was at the beginning of the 20th century, with such artistes as Marie Lloyd (1870–1922), Harry Lauder (1870–1950), and George Formby (1904–1961). The US equivalent is ◊vaudeville.

musicology the academic study of music, including music history, music analysis, music aesthetics, and ◊performance practice. All areas of music fall under the category of musicology except composition, performance studies, and practical music teaching (pedagogy).

music theatre staged performance of vocal music that deliberately sets out to get away from the grandiose style and scale of traditional opera.

Its origins can be traced to the 1920s and 1930s, to plays with music like Kurt Weill's *Mahagonny-Songspiel*, but it came into its own as a movement in the 1960s. It includes not just contemporary opera (such as Alexander Goehr's *Naboth's Vineyard* 1968) but also works like Peter Maxwell Davies' *Eight Songs for a Mad King* 1969.

musique concrète (French 'concrete music') music created by electronically reworking natural sounds recorded on disc or tape, developed 1948 by Pierre Schaeffer and Pierre Henry in the drama studios of Paris Radio. *Concrete sound* is pre-recorded natural sound used in electronic music, as distinct from purely synthesized tones or noises.

Mussorgsky Modest Petrovich 1839–1881. Russian composer. A nationalist, he was a member of the group of five composers 'The ◊Five'. His opera masterpiece *Boris Godunov* 1869 touched a political nerve and employed realistic transcriptions of speech patterns. Many of his works, including *Pictures at an Exhibition* 1874 for piano, were 'revised' and orchestrated by others, including Rimsky-Korsakov, Ravel, and Shostakovich, and some have only recently been restored to their original harsh beauty.

He was influenced by both folk music and literature. Among his other works are the incomplete operas *Khovanshchina* and *Sorochintsy Fair*, the orchestral *Night on the Bare Mountain* 1867, and many songs. Mussorgsky died in poverty, from alcoholism.

mutation an organ ◊stop which produces a ◊pitch other than the normal wavelength pitch (8 ft) or one related by octave (16 ft, 4 ft, 2 ft, or 1 ft). For example, a Quint stop (2 $^2/_3$ ft) produces a pitch an octave and a fifth higher than the depressed key (for example the C4 key sounds at G5).

mute any device used to dampen the vibration of an instrument and so affect the tone. Orchestral strings apply a form of clamp to the bridge – the change is used to dramatic effect by Bartók in the opening bars of *Music for Strings, Percussion, and Celesta* 1936. Brass instruments use the hand or a plug of metal or cardboard inserted in the bell.

Although the word implies a reduction of volume, a variety of mutes used in big band jazz are used principally to vary the quality of tone, as in Stravinsky's *Ebony Concerto* 1945.

Muti Riccardo 1941–   . Italian conductor. Artistic director of La Scala, Milan, from 1986. He is equally at home with opera or symphonic repertoire, performed with bravura, energy, and scrupulous detail, and is known as a purist.

Nancarrow Conlon 1912– . US composer. He experimented with mathematically derived combinations of rhythm and tempo in *37 Studies for Piano-Player* 1968, works of a hypnotic persistence that aroused the admiration of a younger generation of minimalist composers. He settled in Mexico 1940.

nationalism the adoption by composers, most prominently during the 19th and early 20th centuries, of folk idioms with which an audience untrained in the classics could identify. Nationalism was encouraged by governments in the 20th century for propaganda purposes in times of war and political tension. Composers of nationalist music include Smetana, Sibelius, Grieg, Dvořák, Nielsen, Kodály, Copland, Elgar, Shostakovich, and Stephen Foster.

natural a sign cancelling a sharp or flat. A *natural trumpet* or *horn* is an instrument without valves, thus restricted to playing natural harmonics.

neck on a string instrument, the narrow piece of wood which projects from the ◊soundbox, supporting the ◊fingerboard. At its end is the peg box, which secures the strings.

Neo-Classical in 20th-century music, a term denoting a trend against music of either the late 19th century or of atonality, describing a deliberate combination of Baroque or Classical forms such as sonata form, fugue, and so on, and modern harmony, for example Prokofiev's 'Classical' Symphony No 1 1917, Stravinsky's ballet *Apollo* 1928, and Busoni's opera *Doktor Faust* 1924.

Nielsen Carl (August) 1865–1931. Danish composer. His works, which were not immediately recognized outside Denmark, reveal inventiveness, as in his First Symphony 1892 which begins and ends in different keys, and his Fifth Symphony 1922 which employs an early example of aleatory technique in the percussion. He also wrote four other symphonies, two operas, concertos, chamber and piano music, numerous songs, and incidental music on Danish texts.

Nilsson Birgit 1918– . Swedish soprano. One of the greatest singers of Wagner, she is best remembered for her roles in his operas: Brünhilde in *Der Ring des Nibelungen/The Nibelung's Ring* 1854 and Isolde in *Tristan und Isolde*. Her voice was pure and perfect in intonation, with a phenomenal range which was consistently smooth.

nocturne literally a 'night piece', a reflective character piece, often for piano, introduced by Irish composer and pianist John Field and adopted and developed by Chopin. Debussy wrote three orchestral nocturnes 1900.

Nono Luigi 1924–1990. Italian composer. He wrote works such as *Il Canto Sospeso/Suspended Song* 1956 for soloists, chorus, and orchestra, in which influences of Webern and Gabrieli are applied to issues of social conscience. After the opera *Intolleranza 1960/Intolerance 1960* his style became more richly expressionist, and his causes more overtly polemical.

Norman Jessye 1945– . US soprano. She is acclaimed for her majestically haunting interpretations of German opera and lieder (songs), notably Wagner, Mahler, and Richard Strauss, but she is equally at home with the songs of Ravel and Ernest Chausson (1855–1899), and gospel music.

Born in Augusta, Georgia, she made her operatic debut at the Deutsche Oper, Berlin, 1969.

Norrington Roger 1934– . English conductor. An ◊early music enthusiast, he has promoted the use of period instruments in his many recordings. He is noted for his interpretations of the Mozart and Beethoven symphonies, which he often takes at unusually fast tempos, drawing criticism from some that the expressive intensity in the music is thereby lost.

notation a system representing music graphically as successive values in pitch and time. By 1700 modern notation had displaced ◊plainsong and ◊tablature notations, making possible the coordination under one system of orchestras of increasing size, and also making possible the composition of large-scale musical forms.

note the written symbol indicating pitch and duration, the sound of which is a tone.

note row alternative term for ◊series.

Novello Vincent 1781–1861. English publisher and organist of Italian origin. He established the firm Novello and Co. 1811, originally to publish sacred music in order to facilitate his duties as a choirmaster. He later published the music of Purcell, Mozart, Haydn, and Beethoven and handed the firm to his eldest son Alfred (1810–1896).

Nunc Dimitis music set to St Luke's *Song of Simeon* ('Lord, now lettest thou thy servant depart in peace'). It is sung at Roman Catholic compline and Anglican evensong, either in ◊plainsong or to a composer's polyphonic setting. It is often linked compositionally with the Anglican ◊Magnificat.

nut on a string instrument, the ridge at one end of the ◊fingerboard, next to the peg box, which raises the strings from the surface of the fingerboard. On some instruments, such as the ◊ukelele, there is a movable nut, which raises the pitch of the entire instrument.

nut the name given to the part of a bow which secures the horsehair and, by incorporating a screw mechanism, allows the tension of the hairs to be adjusted.

Nyman Michael 1944– . British composer. His highly stylized music is characterized by processes of gradual modification by repetition of complex musical formulas. His compositions include scores for the British filmmaker Peter Greenaway (1942–); a chamber opera, *The Man Who Mistook His Wife for a Hat* 1989; and three string quartets.

O

o abbreviation of ◊open string, marked over a note in music for a string player; or an indication that a harmonic is to be played (see ◊harmonic series).

obbligato (Italian 'obligatory') indicating that an instrument or voice is essential and not to be omitted. However, some composers have used this term with the opposite meaning in mind: that an instrument or voice may be omitted if so desired. Generally the older the notation, the more likely it is that obbligato retains its original meaning of an 'obliged', essential part.

Oberwerk German for ◊swell organ, the second manual (keyboard) of an organ.

oboe instrument of the woodwind family, a refined treble ◊shawm of narrow tapering bore and exposed double reed. The oboe was developed by the ◊Hotteterre family of makers about 1700 and was incorporated in the court ensemble of Louis XIV. The modern oboe was refined during the next 150 years. Oboe concertos have been composed by Vivaldi, Albinoni, Richard Strauss, and others. Heinz Holliger is a modern virtuoso oboist.

◊Alto variants oboe d'amore and oboe da ◊caccia feature in the work of J S Bach and other 18th-century composers, superseded by the 19th-century cor anglais in the modern orchestra. The rarely heard heckelphone is a baritone deviation.

Obrecht Jacob c. 1450–1505. Flemish

oboe

composer. One of the outstanding composers of his day, his mostly poly-phonic sacred music (which in style predates that of Josquin Desprez) centred on the Mass, of which he wrote 24. He was innovative, developing borrowed material, and using a secular fixed ◊*cantus firmus* (Latin 'fixed song') in his *Missa super Maria zart*. He also wrote motets and secular works. He worked as a ◊kapellmeister (chapel master) in Utrecht, Antwerp, and Bruges. He died of the plague.

Ockeghem Johannes (Jean d') *c.*1421–1497. Flemish composer. He wrote church music, including the antiphon *Alma Redemptoris Mater* and the richly contrapuntal *Missa Prolationum/Prolation Mass* employing complex canonic imitation in multiple parts at different levels. He was court composer to Charles VII, Louis XI, and Charles VIII of France.

octatonic scale a scale of eight notes, consisting of a series of intervals: tone, semitone, tone, semitone, etc (for example: C – D – E flat – F – G flat – A flat – A – B). There are only three octatonic scales: the ones beginning on C, C sharp, and D. Octatonic scales beginning on other notes are simply transformations of one of these basic types.

octave a span of eight notes as measured on the white notes of a piano keyboard. It corresponds to the consonance of first and second harmonics.

octet an ensemble of any eight instruments, or the music written for such a group. The most common combination of instruments is the string octet for four violins, two violas, and two cellos, as in Mendelssohn's String Octet in E flat 1830. Stravinsky wrote an Octet 1923 for a wind ensemble. A mixture of strings and winds is also possible, as in Schubert's Octet in F 1824, scored for two violins, viola, cello, double bass, clarinet, bassoon, and horn.

oeuvre (French 'work') alternative term for ◊opus.

Offenbach Jacques 1819–1880. French composer. He wrote light opera, initially for presentation at the *Bouffes parisiens*. Among his works are *Orphée aux enfers/Orpheus in the Underworld* 1858, *La Belle Hélène* 1864, and *Les Contes d'Hoffmann/The Tales of Hoffmann* 1881.

Offertory the fourth part of the Roman Catholic Mass Proper, in which the bread and wine are placed on the altar, preceding the Credo and Communion. In musical terms a psalm in the form of a ◊chant was originally sung, but composers including Palestrina and Lassus have written polyphonic works for the Offertory. The term is also used in other denominations of the Christian Church.

Ogdon John 1937–1989. English pianist and composer. He won early recognition at the Moscow Tchaikovsky Piano Competition 1962 and went on to become an ebullient champion of neglected virtuoso repertoires by Alkan, Bartók, Busoni, and Sorabji.

For a number of years unable to perform as a result of depression, he recovered to make a successful return to the concert hall shortly before his death.

Oistrakh David Fyodorovich 1908–1974. Soviet violinist. He was celebrated for performances of both standard and contemporary Russian repertoire. Shostakovich wrote both his violin concertos for him. His son Igor (1931–) is renowned as a violinist and conductor.

ondes Martenot (French 'Martenot waves') electronic musical instrument invented by Maurice Martenot (1898–1980), a French musician, teacher, and writer who first patented his invention 1922. A series of notes of considerable range and voicelike timbre are produced by sliding a contact along a conductive ribbon, the left hand controlling the tone colour.

In addition to inspiring works from Messiaen, Edgard Varèse, André Jolivet (1905–1974), and others, the instrument has been in regular demand among composers of film and radio incidental music.

open string the string of an instrument which is played without the finger touching it, allowing it to vibrate along its entire length. It is notated by an 'o' above the note. Open strings of the violin are: G3-D4-A4-E5, of the viola: C3-G3-D4-A4, of the cello: C2-G2-D3-A3, of the double bass: E1-A1-D2-G2.

opera dramatic musical work in which singing takes the place of speech. In opera the music accompanying the action has paramount importance, although dancing and spectacular staging may also be invlolved. Opera originated in late 16th-century Florence when the musical declamation, lyrical monologues, and choruses of Classical Greek drama were reproduced in current forms.

One of the earliest opera composers was Jacopo Peri (1561–1633), whose *Euridice* influenced Monteverdi. At first solely a court entertainment, opera soon became popular, and in 1637 the first public opera house was opened in Venice.

In the later 17th century the elaborately conventional aria of ◊seria opera (Italian 'serious opera'), designed to display the virtuosity of the singer, became predominant, overshadowing the dramatic element. Composers of this type of opera included Cavalli, Cesti, and Alessandro Scarlatti. In France opera was developed by Lully and Rameau, and in England by Purcell, but the Italian style retained its ascendancy, as exemplified by Handel.

◊*Opera buffa* (or *comic opera*) was developed in Italy by such composers as Pergolesi, while in England *The Beggar's Opera* 1728 by John Gay started the vogue of the *ballad opera*, using popular tunes and spoken dialogue. ◊*Singspiel* was the German equivalent (although its music was newly composed). A lessening of artificiality began with Gluck, who insisted on the pre-eminence of the dramatic over the purely vocal element. Mozart learned much from Gluck in writing his serious operas, but also excelled in Italian opera buffa. In works such as *The Magic Flute* 1791, he laid the foundations of a purely German-language opera, using the *Singspiel* as a basis. This line was continued by Beethoven in *Fidelio* and by the work of Weber, who introduced the Romantic style for the first time in opera.

The Italian tradition, which placed the main stress on vocal display and melodic suavity (◊bel canto), continued unbroken into the 19th century in the operas of Rossini, Donizetti, and Bellini. It is in the Romantic operas of Weber and Meyerbeer that the work of Wagner has its roots. Dominating the operatic scene of his time, Wagner attempted to create, in his 'music-dramas', a new art form, and completely transformed the 19th-century conception of opera. In Italy, Verdi assimilated, in his mature work, much of the Wagnerian technique, without sacrificing the Italian virtues of vocal clarity and melody. This tradition was continued by Puccini. In French opera in the mid-19th century, represented by such composers as Delibes, Gounod, Saint-Saëns, and Massenet, the drama was subservient to the music. More serious artistic ideals were put into practice by Berlioz in *The Trojans* 1858, but the merits of his work were largely unrecognized in his own time.

Bizet's *Carmen* 1874 began a trend towards realism in opera; his lead was followed in Italy by Mascagni, Leoncavallo, and Puccini. Debussy's *Pelléas and Melisande* 1902 represented a reaction against the over-emphatic emotionalism of Wagnerian opera. National operatic styles were developed in Russia by Glinka, Rimsky-Korsakov, Mussorgsky, Borodin, and Tchaikovsky, and in Bohemia by Smetana. Several composers of light opera emerged, including Sullivan, Lehár, Offenbach, and Johann Strauss.

In the 20th century the Viennese school produced an outstanding opera in Berg's *Wozzeck* 1921, and the Romanticism of Wagner was revived by Richard Strauss in *Der Rosenkavalier* 1911. Other 20th-century composers of opera include Gershwin, Bernstein, and John Adams in the USA; Tippett, Britten, and Harrison Birtwistle in the UK; Henze in Germany; Petrassi in Italy; and the Soviet composers Prokofiev and Shostakovich.

opera buffa (Italian 'comic opera') type of humorous opera with characters taken from everyday life. The form began as a musical intermezzo in the 18th century and was then adopted in Italy and France for complete operas. An example is Rossini's *The Barber of Seville* 1816.

opéra comique (French 'comic opera') opera that includes text to be spoken, not sung; Bizet's *Carmen* 1874 is an example. Of the two Paris opera houses in the 18th and 19th centuries, the *Opéra* (which aimed at setting a grand style) allowed no spoken dialogue, whereas the *Opéra Comique* did.

opera seria (Italian 'serious opera') type of opera distinct from *opera buffa*, or humorous opera. Common in the 17th and 18th centuries, it tended to treat classical subjects in a formal style, with most of the singing being by solo voices. Examples include many of Handel's operas based on mythological subjects.

operetta light form of opera, with music, dance, and spoken dialogue. The story line is romantic and sentimental, often employing farce and parody. Its origins lie in the 19th-century opéra comique and is intended to amuse. Examples of operetta are Jacques Offenbach's *Orphée aux enfers/ Orpheus in the Underworld* 1858, Johann Strauss's *Die Fledermaus/The Flittermouse* 1874, and Gilbert and Sullivan's *Pirates of Penzance* 1879 and *The Mikado* 1885.

ophicleide an obsolete brass instrument of the bugle family. It was a development of the ▷serpent and was played with fingered keys. Although there were alto, bass, and double bass variants, only the bass model was used commonly, until superseded by the bass tuba. It was used in military bands and in the orchestral scores of composers including Berlioz, Verdi, and Wagner.

op. posth. abbreviation for ▷opus posthumous.

opus (Latin 'work') a term, used with a figure, to indicate the numbering of a composer's works, usually in chronological order.

opus posthumous a work of which the existence became known after the composer's death.

oratorio dramatic setting of religious texts, scored for orchestra, chorus, and solo voices, lacking the theatrical effects of props and costumes. Its origins lie in the *Laude spirituali* performed by St Philip Neri's Oratory in Rome in the 16th century, followed by the first definitive oratorio in the 17th century by Cavalieri. The form reached perfection in such works as J S Bach's *Christmas Oratorio* 1734, and Handel's *Messiah* 1742.

The term is sometimes applied to secular music drama in which there is little or no stage action, as in Stravinsky's *Oedipus Rex* 1927, and Messiaen's *St François d'Assise* 1983. In the earliest oratorios there was often an element of ritual and spatial dramatization, and Bach himself introduced audience participation with the chorales of his *St Matthew Passion* 1729. In 1993 Jonathan Miller reintroduced simple actions to a London performance of Bach's *St John Passion* 1724 with telling effect.

orchestra group of musicians playing together on different instruments. In Western music, an orchestra typically contains various bowed string instruments and sections of wind, brass, and percussion. The size and format may vary according to the needs of composers.

The term was originally used in Greek theatre for the semicircular space in front of the stage, and was adopted in 17th-century France to refer first to the space in front of the stage where musicians sat, and later to the musicians themselves.

The string section is commonly divided into two groups of violins (first and second), violas, cellos, and double basses. The woodwind section became standardized by the end of the 18th century, when it consisted of two each of flutes, oboes, clarinets, and bassoons, to which were later added piccolo, cor anglais, bass clarinet, and double bassoon. At that time, two timpani and two horns were also standard, and two trumpets were occasionally added. During the 19th century, the brass section was gradually expanded to include four horns, three trumpets, three trombones, and tuba. To the percussion section a third timpano was added, and from Turkey came the bass drum, side drum, cymbals, and triangle. One or more harps became common and, to maintain balance, the number of string instruments to a part also increased. Other instruments used in the orchestra may include xylophone, celesta, piano, and organ. The orchestra used to be conducted by means of a violin bow, but by Mendelssohn's time the baton was implemented.

The term may also be applied to non-Western ensembles such as the Indonesian gamelan orchestra, consisting solely of percussion instruments, mainly tuned gongs and bells.

orchestration the art of scoring a composition for an orchestra or band; or the choice of instruments in a score expanded for orchestra (often by another hand). A work may be written for piano, and then transferred to an orchestral score.

Orff Carl 1895–1982. German composer and educator. Most of his work is for the stage, including his most famous work, the cantata ◊*Carmina Burana* 1937, which is now usually performed as a concert piece. His style emphasizes rhythmic patterns, basic harmonies, and the relationship between melody and speech.

organ keyboard wind instrument of ancient origin, producing sound from pipes of various sizes and shapes. Apart from its continued use in serious compositions and for church music, the organ has been adapted for light entertainment. The pipes, either ◊flue pipes or reeds, each of which sounds only one note, are fed from a windchest that contains compressed air supplied by bellows. Every 'stop' (a button or lever at the console) controls a 'rank' (row of pipes) of different tone quality. When a key is depressed, a valve is opened allowing air to pass through the particular pipe. This may be achieved mechanically ('tracker' action), pneumatically, or electrically. The pedalboard and keyboards, consisting normally of up to four manuals (the great, swell, choir, and solo manuals), control different groups of ranks.

The organ developed from the panpipes and hydraulis (water organ), and is mentioned in writings as early as the 3rd century BC. Organs were imported to France from Byzantium in the 8th and 9th centuries, after which their manufacture in Europe began. Introduction of the key system dates from the 11th–13th centuries, the first chromatic keyboard from 1361.

The electric tone-wheel organ, which substitutes electric oscillators and amplifiers for pipes, was invented 1934 by the US engineer Laurens Hammond (1895–1973).

organum medieval ◊polyphony in which voices move in parallel fourths or fifths.

Ormandy Eugene 1899–1985. Hungarian-born US conductor. He was music director of the Philadelphia Orchestra 1936–80. Originally a violin virtuoso, he championed the composers Rachmaninov and Shostakovich.

ornamentation (also *graces*, *agréments*, *embellishment*) decorative filling-in of a melody, most common during the 17th and 18th centuries, or accentuation of a structural feature such as a cadential phrase, by rhetorical flourishes or cascades of notes, indicated by special notational signs. Examples of ornament are the turn (a form of melodic pirouette around a note), the trill (rapid oscillation between adjacent notes), the appoggiatura (upward or downward inflection), the arpeggio (spreading of a chord), and the mordent (a form of shortened trill).

oscillator an electrical generator used to convert electricity into sound. It produces an oscillating current that may be heard as sound when played at a frequency between 16 Hz and 20,000 Hz and attached to an amplifier and loudspeakers. Different types of tones produced by an oscillator include ◊sine waves and ◊saw-tooth waves.

ossia (Italian, from *'O sia'*, 'or else') indicating an alternative version of a given passage. It often appears during a technically difficult passage, providing a simpler version for less accomplished musicians.

ostinato (Italian 'obstinate') a persistently repeating melodic or rhythmic figure.

Ostinato plays an important role in Stravinsky's *The Rite of Spring* 1913 and also in the *Carmina Burana* 1937 of Carl Orff; ostinato-like structures are also characteristic of Balinese ◊gamelan music as transcribed by Colin McPhee. In the 1960s, ostinato in the form of a repeating electronic tape loop of melody and sound fragments provided a starting point for the minimalism of Terry Riley (1935–), Steve Reich, Philip Glass, and John Adams.

overblowing a technique of exciting higher harmonics in a wind instrument by increasing air pressure at the mouthpiece, causing it to sound an octave (second harmonic) or twelfth (third harmonic) higher.

The note in an ascending scale at which a player switches to overblowing is called the ***break point***.

overtones tones of the ◊harmonic series, excluding the first harmonic (fundamental), which determine the tone quality or ◊timbre of an instrument.

overture the opening piece of a ballet, opera or other large-scale work; also an independent, one-movement work (***concert overture***), often written for a specific time or place, such as Brahms's *Academic Festival Overture 1880*.

The use of an overture in opera began during the 17th century; the 'Italian' overture consisting of two quick movements separated by a slow one, and the 'French' of a quick movement between two in slower tempo.

P

p abbreviation for *piano* (Italian 'soft').

Pachelbel Johann 1653–1706. German organist and composer. Although his only well-known work today is the *Canon and Gigue* in D major for three violins and continuo, he was a leading progressive composer of keyboard and religious works, influencing J S Bach.

Paderewski Ignacy Jan 1860–1941. Polish pianist, composer, and politician. After his debut in Vienna 1887, he became celebrated in Europe and the USA as an interpreter of the piano music of Chopin and as composer of the nationalist *Polish Fantasy* 1893 for piano and orchestra and the *'Polonia' Symphony* 1909. In 1919 he became prime minister of the newly independent Poland, which he represented at the Peace Conference following World War I, but continuing opposition forced him to resign the same year. He resumed a musical career 1922, was made president of the Polish National Council in Paris 1940, and died in New York.

Paganini Niccolò 1782–1840. Italian violinist and composer. He was a concert soloist by the age of nine. Possibly the greatest violinist ever, he drew on folk and gipsy idioms to create the modern repertoire of virtuoso techniques. His dissolute appearance, wild love life, and amazing powers of expression, even on a single string, fostered rumours of his being in league with the devil. His compositions include six concertos and various sonatas and variations for violin and orchestra, sonatas for violin and guitar, and guitar quartets.

Palestrina Giovanni Pierluigi da 1525–1594. Italian composer. A writer of secular and sacred choral music, he was regarded as the most perfect exponent of Renaissance ♭counterpoint. Apart from motets and madrigals, he also wrote 105 masses, including *Missa Papae Marcelli*.

panpipes or *syrinx* set of unpierced pipes in cane, clay, or other material, graded by length to provide a scale of pitches. The pipes, each of which plays one note, are tied together in a row, and the player blows across one end to sound the instrument. Invented in ancient Greece (according to legend, by the god Pan), the pipes flourish in the folk music traditions of South America, Eastern Europe, and Japan. They produce a notably pure tone with a breathy onset.

pantonality alternative name for ◊atonality. The term was coined by Schoenberg, who wanted to convey a type of tonality which embraces all keys simultaneously, in preference to 'atonality', which he felt implies a negative tonality.

Panufnik Andrzei 1914–1991. Polish-born composer and conductor. His music is based on the dramatic interplay of small-scale motifs within an often clear formal framework. Though mostly tonal, his works have also involved microtonality (using divisions of the octave smaller than semitones).

He was a pupil of the Austrian composer and conductor Felix Weingartner (1863–1942). He came to Britain 1954, following political oppression, and became a British citizen 1961.

parlando singing in a half-speaking manner, often rapidly articulated, used in ◊recitative.

Parry Charles Hubert Hastings 1848–1918. English composer and teacher. He is most famous for his vocal works, including songs, motets, the setting of Milton's *Blest Pair of Sirens*, and especially Blake's *Jerusalem*. He held posts at the Royal College of Music and at Oxford University.

part or *voice* an independent line of a contrapuntal work, for example a fugue in four parts.

part the written music designated for each musician or group of musicians, for example the 'soprano part', in contrast to a ◊score, which provides all the parts on each page; or a large-scale section of a composition, for example Part I of Elgar's *Dream of Gerontius* 1900.

Parthenia (Greek 'Maidenhood') punning title of a collection published 1611 of pieces for the virginals composed by William Byrd, John Bull, and Orlando Gibbons, engraved in standard notation and aimed at a new market of domestic amateur keyboard musians.

partita a set of variations, originating in the late 16th century, as in works by Frescobaldi; or a suite of pieces, as in Bach's partitas from the Clavier-Übung 1731.

part-song technically, any song composed for a number of vocal parts, often used to describe ◊madrigals, but generally referring to songs of homophonic texture, that is where the melody is sung in the top voice and the other voices provide harmonic accompaniment. It is associated with 19th-century choral works by composers including Schumann, Parry, and Elgar.

part-writing in composition, the blending of each individual ◊voice (independent line) into a coherent whole; the successful application of ◊counterpoint to a composition.

passacaglia virtually indistinguishable from the chaconne, a form of construction over a ◊ground bass in triple (3/4), in which dramatic tension is created by the juxtaposition of developing melodies with an unchanging harmonic background. An example is Benjamin Britten's disturbing setting of Tennyson's poem *The Kraken* in *Nocturne* 1958.

The term was originally used in Spanish and Italian guitar music of the early 17th century to denote a variation form.

passage a non-technical term referring to a length of music of unfixed duration, but usually a short section, which is characterized by a single melodic or textural feature.

passage-work a type of musical texture characterized by fast running notes that are technically difficult, and in the case of the 19th-century repertory, often 'showy'.

passepied French dance in triple time, faster and less strict than a minuet, featured in French opera of the 17th century and suites by German composers including Bach's *English Suite* No. 5 *c.* 1725.

passing note a note which is dissonant in relation to the local harmony, which is placed between two notes consonant with the harmony. It usually occurs on weak part of the beat. For example, given a harmony of C major and a melody of E – D – C, D is a passing note.

pastorale a vocal or instrumental piece imitating the music of a shepherd's pipes, or evoking a rustic character. Often in moderate compound time (6/8 or 12/8) with a tonic ◊pedal point (static bass note) derived from the drone of a shepherd's pipes, the pastorale originated in Italy, where, as part of the Christmas tradition, shepherds came into the towns playing music. Examples include Bach's Pastorale from his *Christmas Oratorio* 1734 and Handel's Sinfonia pastorale from his *Messiah* 1742.

pastorale a stage performance developed during the 16th century, based on a legendary or pastoral subject. One of the ancestors of opera, this related genre became popular in the 17th and 18th centuries. An example is Handel's *Acis and Galatea* 1718.

Patti Adelina 1843–1919. Anglo-Italian soprano. Renowned for her performances of Lucia in Donizetti's *Lucia di Lammermoor* and Amina in Bellini's *La sonnambula*, at the age of 62 she was persuaded to come out of retirement to make a number of gramophone recordings, thus becoming one of the first opera singers to be recorded.

pavane or ***pavan*** stately dance of 16th-century Paduan origin, usually in slow ◊common time (4/4), the music of which is often coupled with a ◊galliard. Composers include Dowland and Byrd, and more recently Ravel, whose *Pavane pour une infante défunte/Pavane for a Dead Infant* 1899 for piano was orchestrated 1905.

Pavarotti Luciano 1935– . Italian tenor. A singer of impressive dynamic range, his operatic roles have included Rodolfo in *La Bohème/Bohemian Life*, Cavaradossi in *Tosca*, the Duke of Mantua in *Rigoletto*, and Nemorino in *L'Elisir d'amore*. He first performed the title role of *Otello* in Chicago 1991. He has done much to popularize opera, performing to wide audiences outside the opera houses including open-air concerts in New York and London city parks.

He collaborated with tenors José Carreras and Placido Domingo in a recording of operatic hits coinciding with the World Cup soccer series in Rome 1990.

Pears Peter 1910–1986. English tenor. He was the life companion of Benjamin Britten and with him co-founded the ◊Aldeburgh Festival. He inspired and collaborated with Britten in a rich catalogue of song cycles and operatic roles, exploiting a distinctively airy and luminous tone, from the title role in *Peter Grimes* 1947 to Aschenbach in *Death in Venice* 1973.

pedal point in organ music, a bass note played by the foot, of indefinite length, usually at the end of a piece, establishing the final key and over which a performer may improvise an elaborately decorated cadence. In other kinds of music, the term also applies to static bass notes over which the harmonies may change.

Penderecki Krzystof 1933– . Polish composer. His expressionist works, such as the *Threnody for the Victims of Hiroshima* 1961 for strings, employ imaginative textural combinations, ◊cluster and percussion effects. One of the first composers to experiment with 'utilitarian' sources of sound, such as typewriters and rustling papers, he later turned to religious subjects and a more orthodox style, as in the *Magnificat* 1974 and the *Polish Requiem* 1983. His opera *The Black Mask* 1986 uncovered a new vein of surreal humour.

pentatonic scale a scale of five notes, equivalent to the black notes of the piano and their transpositions. Found as early as 2000 BC, the pentatonic scale is common in folk music from America to the Celtic nations to China.

Pepusch Johann Christoph 1667–1752. German composer. He settled in England about 1700. He contributed to John Gay's ballad operas *The Beggar's Opera* and *Polly*. Interested in musicology and theory, he founded the *Academy of Ancient Music* 1726.

Perahia Murray 1947– . US pianist and conductor. He is noted for his well-balanced interpretations of the Classical repertory. He has recorded all of the Mozart piano concertos with the English Chamber Orchestra, conducting from the keyboard.

percussion instrument musical instrument played by being struck with the hand or a beater. Percussion instruments can be divided into those that can be tuned to produce a sound of definite pitch, such as the timpani, tubular bells, glockenspiel, and xylophone, and those of indefinite pitch, including bass drum, tambourine, triangle, cymbals, and castanets.

The *timpano* is a hemispherical bowl of metal with a membrane stretched across the rim, affixed and tuned by screwtaps; *tubular bells* are suspended on a frame; the *glockenspiel* is a small keyboard of aluminium alloy keys; the *xylophone* has hardwood rather than metal bars.

The *snare drum* is a shallow double-sided drum on the underside of which gut coils or metal springs are secured by a clamp and rattle against the underside when the drum is beaten, while the *bass drum* produces the lowest sound in the orchestra; the *tambourine* has a wooden hoop with a membrane stretched across it, and has metal discs suspended in the rim; a *triangle* is formed from a suspended triangular-shaped steel bar, played by striking it with a separate bar of steel – the sound produced can be clearly perceived even when played against a full orchestra; *cymbals* are two brass dishes struck together; *castanets* are two hollow shells of wood struck together; and the *gong* is a suspended disc of metal struck with a soft hammer.

perfect pitch alternative term for ♭absolute pitch.

performance practice the study of how music was performed in the age in which it was written. A discipline associated with the ♭authenticity movement, it was first applied to music written in the ♭Baroque period and earlier, and later also to that of the ♭Classical period, but recent academic interest in early recordings of the 20th century has led to the expansion of performance practice to embrace music of any period before the present day.

Peri Jacopo 1561–1633. Italian composer. He served the Medici family, the rulers of Florence. His experimental melodic opera *Euridice* 1600 established the opera form and influenced Monteverdi. His first opera, *Dafne* 1597, is now lost, as is much of his other music.

period in musical analysis, one of the basic structural units of melody, consisting of a pair of phrases, the first often ending with an 'imperfect cadence' ('half close'), the second often ending with a 'perfect cadence' ('full close').

Perlman Itzak 1945– . Israeli violinist. He is one of the great virtuosos in modern times, combining a brilliant technique and distinctive tone with concern for every detail. His repertory spans the works of the 19th and 20th centuries; perhaps his most notable interpretation is that of the Tchaikovsky Violin Concerto in D 1878.

Pérotin the Great (Perotinus Magnus) *c.*1160–*c.*1220. French composer. His church music has a timeless resonance and introduced new concepts of harmony and expression to traditional ♭organum (early medieval harmony).

perpetuum mobile (Latin 'perpetually in motion') a piece of music in which there is a rapid and repetitive figuration of notes, especially as part of the accompaniment. Similar to ◊motoric rhythm.

Philharmonic Society group of people organized for the advancement of music; the term is derived from Greek 'love of harmony'. The Royal Philharmonic Society was founded in London 1813 by the pianist Johann Baptist Cramer (1771–1858) for the purpose of improving musical standards by means of orchestral concerts organized on a subscription basis. Another Philharmonic Society was founded in New York 1842.

phrase one of the most basic structural units of melody, equivalent or similar in instrumental terms to the amount of music a singer would sing in one breath. There is no fixed length for a phrase, but many traditionally fall into four-bar units. In the 19th century some composers such as Beethoven, Chopin, Liszt, and Wagner also favoured much longer phrases. Phrases are usually indicated by ◊slur markings and are performed ◊legato (smoothly and continuously) unless otherwise directed.

piacevole Italian 'pleasing', 'agreeable'; similar to ◊dolce.

piano or *pianoforte* (originally *fortepiano*) stringed musical instrument played by hammers activated from a keyboard; it is capable of dynamic gradation between soft (piano) and loud (forte) tones, hence its name. The first piano was constructed 1704 and introduced 1709 by Bartolommeo Cristofori, a harpsichordmaker in Padua. It uses a clever mechanism to make the keyboard touch-sensitive. Extensively developed during the 18th century, the piano attracted admiration among many composers, although it was not until 1768 that Johann Christian Bach gave one of the first public recitals on the instrument.

By the end of the 18th century there were two basic types of piano. The Viennese piano, as exemplified by the Graf and Streicher firms, featured a sensitive shallow touch of dry tone. The English piano of John Broadwood had a heavier, less sensitive ◊action of more resonant tone. This evolved into the modern piano after further refinements in the action and the use of a metal frame to allow an increased tension of the strings and greater tone. Pianos exist today as vertically-strung uprights and horizontally-strung grands.

piano or *p* Italian 'soft'.

Pianola trademark for a type of ◊player piano (mechanical piano).

piccolo woodwind instrument, the small- piccolo
est member of the flute family, sounding an
octave above the concert flute. Vivaldi composed three concertos for piccolo. Used
adjectively, 'piccolo' is also an alternative
term for ◊sopranino.

Pierné (Henri Constant) Gabriel 1863–
1937. French composer and conductor. He
succeeded César Franck as organist to the
church of Ste Clothilde, Paris, and conducted the Colonne Orchestra from 1903.
His numerous ballets include *Cydalise et le
chèvre-pied/Cydalise and the Satyr* 1923,
containing the 'Entry of the Little Fauns'.

pipe generic term used to describe the hollow cylinder or cone of woodwind and brass instruments in which air vibrates to generate sound; or one
of many tubes which make up some musical instruments, as in an organ
pipe or panpipes.

pipe a small woodwind instrument popular in the 13th century. A
◊whistle flute played only by the left hand, it freed the right hand to play
its traditional accompanying drum, the tabor.

piston on a brass instrument, a valve which alters the length of tubing
through which air vibrates, changing the pitch. The first valve lowers the
pitch a whole tone, the second a semitone, the third three semitones. Most
orchestral brass instruments today employ three valves, but sometimes a
fourth is added.

Piston Walter (Hamor) 1894–1976. US composer and teacher. He wrote
a number of textbooks, including *Harmony* 1941 and *Orchestration* 1955.
His Neo-Classical works include eight symphonies, a number of concertos, chamber music, the orchestral suite *Three New England Sketches*
1959, and the ballet *The Incredible Flutist* 1938.

pitch The frequency of a sound wave, measured in hertz (Hz), represented in music by the name of a particular note A–G in the appropriate
◊register. In *concert pitch*, A above middle C (A4) is the reference tone to
which instruments are tuned. *Absolute pitch* (also called *perfect pitch*) is

an ability to name or reproduce any note heard or asked for; it does not necessarily imply high musical ability. In string instruments, pitch depends on the length, composition, and tension of the string in vibration, transmitted to a resonating soundbox. Tuned percussion instruments generate pitch by a combination of natural reverberation of the vibrating body, and the natural frequency of any associated resonator, such as the shell of a drum or the soundboard of a piano. The fundamental pitch of a wind instrument (excepting free reeds) depends on the period of oscillation of the travelling pressure wave within the tube, and is a function of the length of the tube. In organ terminology, pipes are classified in wavelength pitch as 4-foot, 8-foot, 16-foot, depending on their octave range.

più Italian 'more', as in *più mosso* ('more moved', 'faster') or *più lento* 'slower').

pizzicato (Italian 'pinched') an instruction to pluck a bowed stringed instrument (such as the violin) with the fingers. It is heard to advantage in the *Pizzicato Polka* 1870 by Johann Strauss II and Josef Strauss and in the 'Playful Pizzicato' of Benjamin Britten's *Simple Symphony* 1934.

plainsong ancient chant of the Christian church sung freely in unison and unaccompanied. It was first codified by Ambrose, bishop of Milan, (see ◊Ambrosian chant) and then by Pope Gregory in the 6th century (see ◊Gregorian chant).

player piano mechanical piano designed to reproduce key actions recorded on a perforated paper roll. Debussy, Mahler, Grainger, and Stravinsky recorded their own works on piano roll. The concert *Duo-Art* reproducing piano encoded more detailed information, to the extent that audiences were unable to distinguish a live performance from a reproduced performance.

plectrum a small piece of wood, ivory, horn, metal, or plastic used to pluck certain string instruments including the guitar or mandolin. The quills of a harpsichord fulfil the same function.

poco Italian 'little'; as in *poco crescendo* ('getting a little louder') or *crescendo poco a poco* ('getting louder little by little').

pointillism a term borrowed from 19th-century painting describing a form of 1950s ◊serialism in which melody and harmony are replaced by complexes of isolated tones. Pointillism was inspired by Webern and adopted by Messiaen, Boulez, Nono, Stockhausen, and Stravinsky.

Although not strictly serial, the music of Iannis Xenakis and John Cage at this time is also pointillist in texture.

polka a Bohemian dance originating in the 19th century which became popular thoughout Europe. In quick duple time, it was used in art music by Smetana (in *The Bartered Bride* 1866, *Bohemian Dances* 1878), Dvořák, and others.

polonaise Polish dance of characteristic rhythm, in stately triple time (3/4), that was common in 18th-century Europe. Of the many composers who have written polonaises, those by Chopin may be the finest, expressing his love for Poland.

polyphony music combining two or more 'voices' or parts, each with an independent melody. A strict form of polyphony is ◊counterpoint.

polytonality the simultaneous existence of two or more keys in a piece of music, associated in particular with composers such as Stravinsky, Ives, and Darius Milhaud, whose miniature *Serenade* for orchestra 1922 combines up to six major keys. Two keys superimposed is bitonality.

The effect is akin to multiplexing, allowing the ear to fasten on any one line at will, but the combination effect is less coherent.

pop abbreviation of 'popular', referring to 20th-century music of great diversity that appeals to a wide audience. Characterized by strong rhythms of African origin, simple harmonic structures often repeated to strophic melodies, and the use of electrically amplified instruments, pop music generically includes the areas of ◊jazz, rock, country and western, rhythm and blues, soul, and others.

portamento (Italian 'carrying') in singing and on string instruments, an expressive device in which one note is 'carried' to the next by a slide, without an interruption of tone production. It is sometimes indicated by a ◊slur connecting the two notes, but usually freely interpreted by a performer. It was used more frequently in the first half of the twentieth century and earlier.

portato a type of articulation midway between ◊staccato (detached) and ◊legato (tied). It is indicated by a ◊slur over the notes, each of which is marked by a staccato dot.

position on a stringed instrument, one of a few specific areas on the ◊fingerboard where the left hand is placed in order for the player to find a set of notes. On the trombone, 'position' refers to the placement of the slide for playing different notes.

In violin positions, first position is furthest away, nearest to the ◊scroll end of the fingerboard. Second and third position are closer in, nearer to the body of the instrument.

position in harmony, the spacing of a chord. For example, 'root-position' is a chord in which the ◊root of the chord is in the bass; 'open-position harmony' is a chord in which the notes are spread out, as opposed to 'closed-position harmony', in which every note of the harmony is filled within an octave.

post-modernist a style of composition in which the composer draws on the influence of a variety of musical periods and styles. Used specifically to describe the music of certain 20th-century composers, Stravinsky was the first great post-modernist, working in Neo-Classical and serial styles, as well as a more traditional, yet progressive Russian style. Post-modernism began to blossom after the vogue of ◊integral serialism in the 1950s, when composers reacted against the rigid restrictions imposed by that technique (of fixing the parameters of every compositional component: pitch, rhythm, dynamics, duration etc). Contemporary post-modernist composers include Peter Maxwell Davies, who writes in a wide range of styles, influenced by elements of music from 16th-century masters to the modern techniques of the ◊twelve-tone system.

Poulenc Francis (Jean Marcel) 1899–1963. French composer and pianist. A self-taught composer of witty and irreverent music, he was a member of the group of French composers known as 'Les Six'. Among his many works are the operas *Les Mamelles de Tirésias/The Breasts of Tiresias* 1947 and *Dialogues des Carmélites/Dialogues of the Carmelites* 1957, and the ballet *Les Biches/The Little Darlings* 1923. In later years the deliberately disconcerting humour of his work gave way to music of grace and melodic charm.

pp abbreviation of *pianissimo* ('very soft'); *ppp* is very, very soft.

prelude a composition intended as the preface to further music, especially preceding a ◊fugue in Baroque music, forming the opening piece of a ◊suite, or setting the mood for a stage work, as in Wagner's *Lohengrin* 1850. As used by Chopin, a prelude is a short self-contained piano work.

prepared piano a piano altered in such a way as to produce a different ◊timbre or special effects. It was introduced by Henry Cowell; John Cage developed and popularized the technique, producing novel sounds by placing objects on the strings (in, for example, *Bacchanale* 1940).

presto Italian 'quick'; faster than allegro. *Prestissimo* is of the greatest possible speed.

Previn André (George) 1929– . German-born US conductor and composer. Principal conductor of the Los Angeles Philharmonic 1986–89. His work on television and stage has helped popularize classical music. His compositions include film scores (for which he has won four Oscars), concertos for piano 1971 and guitar 1984; he has conducted Gershwin and Mozart concertos from the keyboard and recorded many US and British composers.

Price Leontyne 1927– . US opera singer. She played a leading singing role in Ira Gershwin's revival of his musical *Porgy and Bess*. Gaining a national reputation, she made her operatic debut in San Francisco 1957. Price appeared at La Scala in Milan 1959 and became a regular member of the Metropolitan Opera in New York 1961.

Price was born in Laurel, Mississippi, and educated at Central State College in Ohio. She was trained as a soprano at the Juilliard School of Music in New York.

prima donna (Italian 'first lady') strictly, the singer of the principal female role in an opera. By the 19th century the term had entered nonmusical vocabulary to describe an arrogant and hystrionic person, either male or female.

prima volta (Italian 'first time') passage at end of a section, before a repeat sign, to be substituted with the *seconda volta* ('second time') passage at the same point during the repeat.

principal subject the main, first theme of a piece in ◊sonata form or rondo form. It is usually the first important theme to appear, doing so in the ◊tonic key.

programme music music that interprets a story, depicts a scene or painting, such as Schumann's *Kinderszenen/Scenes from Childhood* 1838, or which illustrates a literary or philosophical idea, such as Richard Strauss's ◊symphonic poem *Don Juan* 1889. It became popular in the Romantic era, although earlier composers used it, such as Vivaldi in *Le quattro stagione/The Four Seasons c.* 1725.

Prokofiev Sergey (Sergeyevich) 1891–1953. Soviet composer and pianist. His music includes operas such as *The Love for Three Oranges* 1921; ballets for Sergey Diaghilev, including *Romeo and Juliet* 1935; seven symphonies including the *Classical Symphony* 1917; music for film, including Eisenstein's *Alexander Nevsky* 1939; piano and violin concertos; songs and cantatas (for example, that composed for the 30th anniversary of the October Revolution); and *Peter and the Wolf* 1936 for children, to his own libretto after a Russian folk tale.

Prokofiev was essentially a Neo-Classicist in his use of form, but his extensive and varied work demonstrates great lyricism, humour, and skill. He studied at St Petersburg under Rimsky-Korsakov and achieved fame as a pianist, leaving Russia 1918 after the Revolution, and living for some time in the USA and in Paris. He returned to the USSR in 1933, but most of his music was criticized by the authorities. During this period his output was considerably reduced.

prolation system of proportional timing in Renaissance music, relating shifts in tempo to harmonic ratios, for example 1:2, 2:3, and so on.

promenade concert originally a concert where the audience was free to promenade (walk about) while the music was playing, now in the UK the name of any one of an annual BBC series (the Proms) at the Royal Albert Hall, London, at which part of the audience stands. They were started by English conductor Henry Wood 1895.

psalm a song from the Old Testament Book of Psalms. It may be sung antiphonally in ◊plainsong or set by individual composers to music in a great variety of styles, from Josquin Desprez' *De profundis* to Stravinsky's *Symphony of Psalms* 1930.

Puccini Giacomo (Antonio Domenico Michele Secondo Maria) 1858–1924. Italian opera composer. His music shows a strong gift for romantic melody and dramatic effect and his operas combine exotic plots with elements of *verismo* (realism). They include *Manon Lescaut* 1893,

La Bohème/Bohemian Life 1896, *Tosca* 1900, *Madame Butterfly* 1904, and the unfinished *Turandot* 1926.

pulse a basic unit of rhythm and metre. See ◊beat.

punta Italian 'point', as in *a punta d'arco* ('at the point of the bow'), instructing a string player to use only the tip of the bow, as opposed to the heel (the end which is held by the player's hand).

Purcell Henry 1659–1695. English Baroque composer. He was celebrated during his lifetime and is today acknowledged to be one of the finest composers England has produced. His music balances high formality with melodic expression of controlled intensity, for example, the opera *Dido and Aeneas* 1689 and music for Dryden's *King Arthur* 1691 and for *The Fairy Queen* 1692. He wrote more than 500 works, ranging from secular operas and incidental music for plays to cantatas and church music.

quadrille square dance of 19th-century France for four, six, or eight couples; or the music for the dance, which consists of popular tunes, and alternates between compound duple time (6/8) and simple duple time (2/4).

quadruplet a group of four notes to be played in the time of three. It is indicated by a ◊slur over the four notes with the number '4' written above. It usually occurs in compound time.

Quantz Johann Joachim 1697–1773. German flautist and composer. He composed 300 flute concertos, but is best remembered for writing the treatise *On Playing the Transverse Flute* 1752. He improved the flute's adaptability by adding the second key and devising a sliding tuning mechanism.

quarter note US term for *crotchet*, a note value one quarter the duration of a ◊semibreve.

quarter tone an interval, half that of a ♭semitone. A kind of ♭microtone, it is the smallest interval commonly used in Western music, by 20th-century composers such as Boulez and Stockhausen.

quartet an ensemble of four musicians, or the music written for such a group. The most common type of quartet is the ♭string quartet.

quasi Italian 'as if'; as in *sonata quasi fantasia* ('sonata in the manner of a fantasia').

quaver (US *eighth note*) a note value one eighth the duration of a ♭semibreve. It is written by a filled black note-head with a stem and flag (tail).

Quilter Roger 1877–1953. English composer. He wrote song settings of Tennyson and Shakespeare, including 'Now Sleeps the Crimson Petal' 1904 and 'To Daisies' 1906, incidental music *A Children's Overture* 1920, and chamber music.

quintet an ensemble of five musicians, or the music written for such a group. A common type of quintet is the piano quintet, which often consists of a ♭string quartet and piano.

quintuplet a group of five notes to be played usually in the time of four. It is indicated by a slur over the five notes with the number '5' written above it.

R

Rachmaninov or *Rakhmaninov* Sergei (Vasilevich) 1873–1943. Russian composer, pianist, and conductor. After the 1917 Revolution he emigrated to the USA. His music is melodious and emotional and includes operas, such as *Francesca da Rimini* 1906, three symphonies, four piano concertos, piano pieces, and songs. Among his most famous works are the Prelude in C-Sharp Minor 1882 and *Rhapsody on a Theme of Paganini* 1934 for piano and orchestra. After leaving Russia he found it difficult to compose, but he went on to become one of the 20th-century's greatest pianists, making several early recordings.

rackett Renaissance double-reed woodwind musical instrument incorporating a ninefold straight tube packed into a 22 cm/9 in compact cylinder. It emits a strong, rasping tone (extending to F1 in double-bassoon range).

raga (Sanskrit *rāga* 'tone' or 'colour') in ◊Indian music, a scale of notes for music associated with a particular mood or time of day; the equivalent term in rhythm is tala. A choice of raga and tala forms the basis of improvised music; however, a written composition may also be based on (and called) a raga.

Rakhmaninov alternative spelling for ◊Rachmaninov.

rallentando or *rall.* (Italian 'slowing down') gradually reducing the speed of a passage; synonymous with ritardando.

Rameau Jean-Philippe 1683–1764. French composer, theorist, and organist. During his early years he worked as an organist, and published his *Treatise on Harmony* 1722 which established academic rules for harmonic progression. After composing varied works for keyboard, voice, and orchestra, he turned his attention to opera at age 50, writing over 20 in the genre, such as *Castor and Pollux* 1737. These works are noted for their striking harmonies, orchestration, and ◊recitative.

rasch German 'quick'.

Rattle Simon 1955– . English conductor. Principal conductor of the City of Birmingham Symphony Orchestra (CBSO) from 1979, he has built the CBSO into a world-class orchestra, with a core repertoire of early 20th-century music; he has also commissioned new works, and in recent years turned to the 19th-century repertory. A popular and dynamic conductor, he achieves a characteristically clear and precise sound.

rauschpfeife double-reed woodwind instrument similar to a ◊shawm, in soprano or sopranino range, of wide bore and having a powerful reedy tone, revived as a Renaissance broken consort or folk instrument.

Ravel (Joseph) Maurice 1875–1937. French composer and pianist. His work is characterized by its sensuousness, exotic harmonics, and dazzling orchestral effects. Labelled an Impressionist alongside Debussy, Ravel's work is in fact often quite different. It is contrapuntally more complex and draws more frequently on traditional forms, as in his first published work, *Menuet antique* 1899 for piano. His orchestral works sometimes seem less naturally suited to the medium than Debussy's; many originated as piano works, such as *Ma mère l'oye/Mother Goose* 1910. Other examples of his music include the piano pieces *Pavane pour une infante défunte/Pavane for a Dead Infanta* 1899, *Gaspard de la nuit* 1908, and the ballets *Daphnis et Chloë* 1912 and *Boléro* 1928.

Rawsthorne Alan 1905–1971. British composer. His *Theme and Variations* for two violins 1938 was followed by other tersely energetic works including *Symphonic Studies* 1939, the overture *Street Corner* 1944, *Concerto for Strings* 1950, and a vigorously inventive sonata for violin and piano, 1959.

RCA Mark II synthesizer pioneer digitally programmable analogue synthesizer developed 1959 by Harry Olsen and Herbert Belar and installed in the joint Columbia-Princeton electronic studio under the direction of US composers Otto Luening and Milton Babbitt, its best-known advocate. It was the first integrated device for preprogrammed synthesis and mixing of electronic and concrete sound materials, employing a punched card control system.

recapitulation the section of ◊sonata form following the development section, in which the themes are presented in a manner similar or identical to the exposition, except that any material which was originally presented in the ◊dominant or any other key, appears in the ◊tonic key. A 'false' recapitulation was used at times by Beethoven and 19th-century composers either to present an additional development of musical ideas or to present temporarily the main themes in a key other than the tonic, as in the first movement of Beethoven's Sonata No. 3 1795.

recitative in opera and oratorio, sung narration used to connect arias, partly modelled on the rhythms and inflections of speech. Often sung on a single note, with ascending or descending deviations based on the natural melody of spoken language, it is usually sparingly accompanied by harpsichord or organ.

recorder any of a widespread range of woodwind instruments of the ◊whistle type which flourished in ◊consort ensembles in the Renaissance and Baroque eras, along with viol consorts, as an instrumental medium for polyphonic music. A modern consort may include a sopranino, soprano (descant), alto (treble), tenor, bass, and great bass.

Early Renaissance recorders are of fairly wide bore and penetrating tone; late Renaissance and Baroque instruments are ◊fipple flutes of narrower bore and sweet to brilliant tone. The solo recorder remained a popular solo instrument into the 18th century, and the revival of popular interest in recorder playing after 1920, largely through the efforts of Arnold ◊Dolmetsch, led to its wide adoption as a musical instrument for schools.

reed instrument any of a class of wind instruments employing a single or double flexible reed, made of cane, metal, or plastic, which vibrates under pressure within an airtight enclosure (the mouth, ◊windcap, bellows, airbag) and acts as a valve admitting pulses of pressurized air into a tubular resonator. Single-reed instruments, where the reed vibrates against the material of the instrument, include clarinets and saxophones; double-reeds, where the reeds vibrate against each other, include oboes, shawms, bagpipes, and bassoons. See also ◊free-reed instrument.

Most reed instruments incorporate finger holes to alter the pitch, and can be overblown to sound at the octave or twelfth higher. They are more efficient than wind instruments of the flute variety in converting energy to sound in the tenor and bass registers.

regal portable reed organ powered by bellows, invented about 1460 in Germany and current in Europe until the 17th century. A modern version is used in Indian popular music.

Reger (Johann Baptist Joseph) Max(imilian) 1873–1916. German composer, organist, and pianist. An opponent of ◊programme music, his works embody a particular blend of contrapuntal ingenuity and Romantic sentimentality, and include organ works, *Four Symphonic Poems* 1913, sonatas, Romantic character pieces, and orchestral variations and fugues on themes by Beethoven, Mozart, and other less well-known composers.

register a set of organ pipes, controlled by one stop, used in ◊registration. Also, a certain vocal or instrumental range of pitches, often associated with a characteristic timbre. For example, the ◊chalumeau register of a clarinet or the ◊head voice register of a singer.

registration in organ and harpsichord playing, the selection of stops available (levers affecting the qualities and power of the instrument), either prescribed by a composer or left to the player's taste.

Reich Steve 1936– . US composer. His minimalist music, influenced in part by his studies of African drumming, employs simple patterns carefully superimposed and modified to highlight gradually changing melodies and rhythms; examples are *Phase Patterns* for four electronic organs 1970, *Music for Mallet Instruments, Voices, and Organ* 1973, and *Music for Percussion and Keyboards* 1984.

relative of the connection between major and minor keys which bear the same ◊key signature. The relative major's ◊tonic note is three semitones higher than that of the relative minor. For example, C major is the relative major of A minor, and B minor is the relative minor of D major.

répétiteur (French 'coach') a musician who coaches opera singers in learning their parts, and may also run rehearsals. Many conductors of opera first began their careers as *répétiteurs*.

reprise a repeat of previous material, usually following an intervening and contrasting section. In ◊sonata form the term has two meanings: usually it is synonymous with ◊recapitulation, but in early sonatas in which a double bar precedes the development it may refer to a repeat of the ◊exposition, as in sonatas by C P E Bach. In ◊rondo form the term denotes the recurring main theme. In the ◊binary form composition of 17th-century France, the term denotes the second section, as in dance-movements in the suites of Jean-Henri D'Anglebert (1635–1691).

requiem in the Roman Catholic church, a mass for the dead. It is taken from the opening Latin words: *Requiem aeternam dona eis, Domine* (Grant them eternal rest, Lord). Musical settings include those by Palestrina, Mozart, Berlioz, Verdi, Fauré, and Britten.

resolution a progression from a dissonant harmony to a less dissonant or consonant harmony. For example, in an ◊appoggiatura (a form of melodic ornament), the dissonant melodic note usually resolves by moving a step lower, thus creating a consonant harmony. Resolving dissonance by moving a step lower is the traditional method. During the 19th century composers used other kinds of resolution more frequently than before, such as moving a step higher or sometimes incorporating a leap. Composers of the 20th century often do not resolve dissonance at all.

Respighi Ottorino 1879–1936. Italian composer, conductor, violinist, and pianist. His works combine traditional forms with more exotic colours reminiscent of Rimsky-Korsakov, who was his teacher. His rich orchestrational technique is evident in the ◊symphonic poems *Fontane di Roma/The Fountains of Rome* 1917 and *Pini di Roma/The Pines of Rome* 1924 (incorporating the recorded song of a nightingale). Other works include operas and chamber music.

response a type of ◊antiphony used in the Anglican church, in which the congregation replies to the ◊plainsong chants of the priest; in Reformed churches, it refers to a short piece sung by the choir following a prayer. In this context the response often consists of a repeated 'amen'.

rest a silence, or the notation indicating a silence.

retrograde a process in which the order of notes is reversed. It is used as a basic technique in 20th-century ◊serialism, in addition to ◊inversion. However, it also occurs in music of the Middle Ages, as a form of musical ◊riddle, the first known example found in the 13th century. Haydn uses retrograde motion in the third movement of his Symphony No. 47 in G 1772, as does Beethoven in the final fugue of his piano sonata *Hammerklavier* 1818.

rf or *rfz* abbreviation of ◊rinforzando, a sudden accentuation of a note or short phrase.

R.H. abbreviation of 'right hand', directing a pianist to use the right hand, usually in order to facilitate a technically difficult passage, dividing the notes between both hands. It can also be notated in French or Italian as M.D. (abbreviation for *main droite* or *mano destra*, respectively). The opposite of L.H. ('left hand').

rhapsody instrumental ◊fantasia of the 19th and 20th centuries, often based on folk melodies, such as Lizst's *Hungarian Rhapsodies* 1854.

rhythm One of the basic components of music: a pattern deriving from the duration of notes, which themselves form part of a divisible bar and ◊metre. A rhythm may be based on classical verse or dance, bar and metre, repeat in the form of an ◊ostinato, or constantly change, as in much 20th-century music.

ricercare (Italian 'researched') an abstract composition, usually contrapuntal, and exhibiting 'learned' techniques, as in J S Bach's several examples from *The Musical Offering* 1740.

Richter Sviatoslav (Teofilovich) 1915– . Russian pianist. An outstanding virtuoso of keen intellect and emotional depth, he is recognized especially for his interpretations of Schubert, Schumann, and Rachmaninov. He has also given first performances of several sonatas by Prokofiev (the Ninth Sonata is dedicated to Richter).

rigaudon lively French country dance in duple time (2/4) or quadruple time (4/4), in four-bar phrases (like a square dance). It originated in the 17th century, appearing in operatic ballets by Lully and Rameau and was known also in England. A more modern example includes a rigaudon from Grieg's *Holberg Suite* 1884.

Rimsky-Korsakov Nikolay Andreyevich 1844–1908. Russian composer. A leading member of The ◊Five, he incorporated Russian folk tunes and legends into his music. His superb orchestration left its mark on future composers, notably his pupil Stravinsky. His operas include *The Maid of Pskov* 1873, *The Snow Maiden* 1882, *Mozart and Salieri* 1898, and *The Golden Cockerel* 1907, a satirical attack on despotism that was banned until 1909.

Other works include the symphonic poem *Sadko* 1867, the programme symphony *Antar* 1869, and the symphonic suite *Scheherazade* 1888. He also completed works by other composers, for example, Mussorgsky's *Boris Godunov*. He was also an author of an influential text on orchestration.

rinforzando or *rf* or *rfz* (Italian 'reinforcing') a sudden accent on a single note or short phrase or group of notes. It differs slightly from ◊sforzando, which applies to only one note per marking.

ripieno (Italian 'replenished', 'supplementary') in music of the 17th and 18th centuries, describing the full complement of players, as opposed to a ◊concertante (group of instrumental soloists). It is used especially in the context of the ◊concerto grosso, designating the full orchestra, but it may be used to describe other music which exploits the textural contrast of a different number of players, as in Bach's *St Matthew Passion* 1729.

rit. abbreviation of ◊ritardando (Italian 'slowing'); less commonly for ◊*ritenuto* (Italian 'held back').

ritardando or *rit.* (Italian 'slowing') gradually getting slower; synonymous with rallentando.

ritenuto or *riten.* or occasionally *rit.* (Italian 'held back') the immediate reduction of speed, as opposed to a gradual change as with ritardando and rallentando.

ritornello (Italian 'a little return') a repeating section: in the 14th and 15th centuries, it was the refrain at the end of each madrigal verse, the music being treated separately from the previous material, often including a change of metre; in 17th-century opera and song, it was an instrumental conclusion or refrain added to the end of an aria or song; in the Classical period (1750 to 1820) it was used in concerto composition, denoting the return of the full orchestra (or tutti) after a solo passage.

rococo a term borrowed from architecture, describing a highly florid and decorative style of music of the 18th century. It was first associated with the music of François Couperin and is applicable to much music until the period of Mozart, Haydn, and C P E Bach.

Rodrigo Joaquín 1901– . Spanish composer. His works are filled with Spanish folklore or ambience as in the famous *Concierto de Aranjuez* 1939 or the *Concerto heroico* 1943. He has always composed in a conservative, lucid Neo-Classical style that is less adventurous than ◊Falla but nevertheless as effective and colourful.

Romanticism a movement concerned with subjective emotion expressed primarily through melody, often involving the use of folk idioms, and a cult of the artist-musician as visionary and hero (virtuoso). Linked with a decline in the importance of Classical form and nationalistic feelings, the Romantic movement reached its height in the late 19th century, in the works of Wagner.

The reaction against 18th-century Classical values first appears as imagery of untamed natural forces, in the hero figure of Mozart's opera *Don Giovanni* 1787 and Haydn's *Stürm und Drang* realization of *The Creation* 1798. The essentially private emotional world of Schubert and Schumann lieder (songs) was rapidly transformed into the national mythic heroism of Wagner and Verdi, experienced in the flesh in such virtuoso figures as Paganini and Liszt. Towards the end of the 19th century, however, the heroic ideal was increasingly challenged by intimations of fallibility as in the anti-hero of Mussorgsky's *Boris Godunov* 1874, and by the cheerful cynicism of Richard Strauss's *Till Eulenspiegel* 1895. In Mahler, Elgar, and Sibelius Romanticism became expansive and elegiac. The decline of Romanticism is also associated with the crisis of harmony (concerning the emergence of ◊atonality) at the beginning of the 20th century. The social and political upheavals of this period were also incongruous with the Romantic style of music.

rondo or *rondeau* musical form in which verses alternate with a refrain. In instrumental terms, a recurring 'A' theme alternates with contrasting 'B' and 'C' themes, in the manner 'ABACA' etc. Often festive in character, it is a popular final movement of a sonata, concerto, or symphony.

root in a chord, the ◊tonic note from which the other notes are derived. For example, in a chord consisting of any spacing or arrangement of the notes C – E – G, C is always the root. A chord is considered in 'root-position' when the root is the lowest voice or part, usually in the bass.

rosin a resin, refined from distilled oil of turpentine, that is applied to the hairs of a bow of a string instrument. By adding friction, it helps the string to vibrate when the bow is drawn across them.

Rossini Gioacchino (Antonio) 1792–1868. Italian composer. His first success was the opera *Tancredi* 1813. In 1816 his ◊opera buffa (comic

opera) *Il barbiere di Siviglia/The Barber of Seville* was produced in
Rome. During 1815–23 he produced 20 operas, and created (with
Donizetti and Bellini) the 19th-century Italian operatic style. His comic
operas, for which he is most famous, are characterized by their grace, wit,
and fresh simplicity, perhaps reflected by the fact that some were written
in only two weeks.

After *Guillaume Tell/William Tell* 1829, Rossini gave up writing
opera and his later years were spent in Bologna and Paris. Among the
works of this period are the *Stabat Mater* 1842 and the piano music
arranged for ballet by Respighi as *La Boutique fantasque/The Fantastic
Toyshop* 1919.

Rostropovich Mstislav 1927–   . Russian cellist and conductor. One of
the greatest cellists this century, he became an exile 1978 because of his
sympathies with political dissidents. Prokofiev, Shostakovich,
Khachaturian, and Britten wrote pieces for him. Since 1977 he has
directed the National Symphony Orchestra, Washington, DC.

Rouget de Lisle Claude-Joseph 1760–1836. French army officer and
composer. He composed, while in Strasbourg 1792, the 'Marseillaise', the
French national anthem.

round an alternative name for a ◊canon, in which voices imitate each
other exactly.

Royal Academy of Music Music school and college in London,
founded 1822 by John Fane, Lord Burghesh, later 11th Earl of
Westmorland. It was granted a royal charter 1830. Based in Marylebone
Road, it provides a full-time complete musical education.

Royal College of Music British college providing full-time complete
musical education. Founded 1883, it is in Kensington, W London, near
the Royal Albert Hall.

Royal College of Organists an association founded in London 1864
to promote the composition and study of organ music, and raise the
standards of musicianship by issuing diplomas such as the A.R.C.O.
(Associate of the Royal College of Organists).

Royal Opera House Britain's leading opera house, sited at Covent
Garden, London. The original theatre opened 1732, was destroyed by fire

1808 and reopened 1809. It was again destroyed by fire 1856, and the third and present building dates from 1858. It has been the home of the Royal Opera and the Royal Ballet since 1946.

rubato (from *tempo rubato*, Italian 'robbed time') a subtle fluctuation of tempo for expressive purposes, practised to the greatest extent by pianists (who lack other expressive means, such as ♭vibrato). It may be applied to isolated notes in the form of an agogic accent (increasing the duration of a note) or to entire phrases. It is most typical of Romantic music, and traditionally consists of taking time from some notes and passing it to others.

Rubbra Edmund 1901–1986. British composer. He studied under Holst and Vaughan Williams, specializing in contrapuntal writing, as exemplified in his study *Counterpoint* 1960. His compositions include 11 symphonies, chamber music, and songs.

Rubinstein Anton Grigorievich 1829–1894. Russian pianist and composer. One of the great virtuosos of his day, he did not join the Russian nationalist movement of his contemporaries, The ♭Five. His music follows a more Western European style, but although solidly constructed it lacks the imaginative touch of genius.

Rubinstein Artur 1887–1982. Polish-born US pianist. Considered by many to be the greatest 20th-century piano virtuoso. His early encounters with Joseph Joachim and Eugène Ysaÿe link his interpretations of Beethoven, Mozart, and Chopin with the virtuoso Romantic tradition. He was also a noted interpreter of de Falla.

Ruckers family of Flemish harpsichordmakers founded by Hans Ruckers (c. 1545–1598) and continued by his sons *Iohannes* (1578–1643), *Andreas* (1579–?), and their descendants. The instruments were noted for their engineering precision and matchless tone, and were imitated widely. Over 100 still exist.

Ruggles Carl 1876–1971. American composer. He was an associate, during the 1920s and 1930s, of the experimentalist composers Ives, Varèse, and Cowell, trying to forge a new direction in music. His instrumental forms were, however, more conservative than those other composers, as in his most famous work *Sun-Treader* 1932 for orchestra, which, as is quite typical for Ruggles, uses elements of ♭serialism, but in a polyphonic texture.

S

Sacher Paul 1906– . Swiss conductor. In 1926 he founded the Basel Chamber Orchestra, for which he has commissioned a succession of works from contemporary composers including Bartók's *Divertimento* 1937, Stravinsky's Concerto in D 1946, and Boulez's *Messagesquisse* 1977. He also founded the Schola Cantorum Basiliensis 1933, concerned with research into original ◊performance practice and ◊early music.

Sachs Hans 1494–1576. German poet and composer. He composed 4,275 *Meisterlieder/Mastersongs*, and figures prominently in Wagner's opera *Die Meistersinger von Nürnberg/The Mastersingers of Nuremberg* 1868.

sackbut musical instrument of the brass family, a precursor of the trombone. It was common from the 14th century and has been revived in ◊early music performance. It has a narrower bell than the modern instrument. Its sound is dignified and mellow.

sackbut

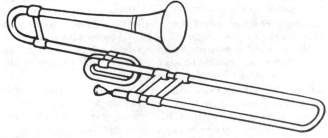

Sadler's Wells a theatre in London built in the 17th century. It was famous for the opera and ballet companies which resided there. In 1974 the opera company changed its venue and also its name to the English National Opera.

Saint-Saëns (Charles) Camille 1835–1921. French composer, pianist, and organist. His works are characterized by elegant form and knowledge of Viennese Classical models within a Romantic harmonic framework. He was a traditionalist, opposed to the music of Debussy, and outraged by Stravinsky's *Last Rite of Spring 1913*. Among his many lyrical Romantic pieces are concertos, the ◊symphonic poem *Danse macabre/Dance of Death* 1874, in which he introduced the xylophone to illustrate dancing skeletons, the opera *Samson et Dalila* 1877, and the orchestral *Le Carnaval des animaux/The Carnival of the Animals* 1886, a 'zoological fantasy' in 14 movements.

saite German 'string'; as in *mit einer Saite* ('with one string') instructing a pianist to use the *una corda* or ◊soft pedal.

Salieri Antonio 1750–1825. Italian composer. He taught Beethoven, Schubert, and Liszt, and was the musical rival of Mozart, whom it has been suggested, without proof, that he poisoned, at the emperor's court in Vienna, where he held the position of court composer. He was widely regarded by his contemporaries as one of the greatest composers of the day.

Salonen Esa-Pekka 1958– . Finnish conductor and composer. He studied French horn, and made his UK conducting debut 1983 as a short-notice replacement for Michael Tilson Thomas, leading to further engagements with the London Philharmonia Orchestra.

Salzburg Festival annual music festival held in the Austrian town where Mozart was born. Although the festival concentrates on the works of Mozart, other composers are also represented. It grew from the first eight Mozart festivals held between 1877 and 1910. The new theatre opened 1960 and has the largest stage in the world.

Salzedo Carlos 1885–1961. French-born harpist and composer. He studied in Paris and moved to New York, where he cofounded the International Composers' Guild. He did much to promote the harp as a concert instrument, and invented many unusual effects.

sampling a technique of computer synthesis involving the recording of a live source, conversion to digital code, storage, and subsequent manipulation of an acoustic signal.

The maximum duration of a sample is limited by the storage capacity of the sampling device, typically a memory chip. Certain electronic keyboards use sampling to copy the sound of ◊acoustic instruments.

Sándor György 1912–   . Hungarian- born US pianist. He is famous for his performances and recordings of works by Prokofiev and Bartók (who was his teacher). He has transcribed for piano *L'Apprenti sorcier/The Sorcerer's Apprentice* by Dukas.

sarabande English and French 17th-century court dance, originating in Spain and probably Mexico. In slow to moderate ◊triple time with a rhythmic emphasis on the second beat, it is found as a movement in the Baroque ◊suite, as in J S Bach's works.

Sargent (Harold) Malcolm (Watts) 1895–1967. English conductor. He was chief conductor of the BBC Symphony Orchestra 1950–57, conductor in chief of the annual Henry Wood ◊promenade concerts at the Royal Albert Hall from 1957, and musical director of numerous choral societies. He championed Vaughan Williams and Holst and conducted the first performances of Walton's oratorio *Belshazzar's Feast* 1931 and opera *Troilus and Cressida* 1954.

sarod Indian plucked or bowed lute with up to six melody strings and additional ◊sympathetic strings for added resonance. It is smaller than the ◊sitar and has two resonating chambers.

sarod

sarrusophone any of a family of double-reed wind instruments invented 1856 by a French bandmaster named Sarrus, of which the double bass instrument is heard in Stravinsky's sacred cantata *Theni* 1958. Made of brass, its tone is clear and unforced in the bass register.

Satie Erik (Alfred Leslie) 1866–1925. French composer. His aesthetic of ironic simplicity, as in the *Messe des pauvres/Poor People's Mass* 1895, acted as a nationalist antidote to the perceived excesses of German Romanticism. His piano pieces, such as the three *Gymnopédies* 1888, are precise and tinged with melancholy, and parody Romantic expression with surreal commentary.

Debussy, Varèse, and John Cage were among his admirers. Mentor of the group 'Les Six', he promoted the concept of *musique d'ameublement* (furniture music), anticipating the impact of radio. His *Parade* 1917 for orchestra includes a typewriter, and he invented a new style of film music for René Clair's *Entr'acte/Interval* 1924.

satz (German 'setting') a movement of a multi-movement work (for example *erster Satz*, 'first movement'); a theme (*Hauptsatz*, 'main theme'); or a style of composition (*Freier Satz*, 'free style').

saw-toothed wave an electronically-generated tone characterized by its abrasive ◊timbre. It is named after the jagged pattern of its sound wave.

saxhorn family of brass musical instruments related to the ◊bugle. They are played with valves instead of the usual keys, and were invented 1842–5 by the Belgian Adolphe Sax (1814–1894).

saxophone member of a hybrid brass instrument family of conical bore, with a single-reed woodwind mouthpiece and keyworks, invented by Belgian instrumentmaker Adolphe Sax (1814–1894) about 1840. Soprano, alto, tenor, and baritone forms remain current. The soprano saxophone is usually straight; the others are characteristically curved back at the mouthpiece and have an upturned bell (opening at opposite end to mouthpiece). Initially a concert instrument of suave tone, the saxophone was incorporated into dance bands of the 1930s and 1940s, and assumed its modern guise as an solo jazz instrument after 1945. It has a voicelike ability to bend a note.

It features in Hindemith's opera *Cardillac* 1926 as a symbol of decadence, and in Stravinsky's *Ebony Concerto* 1945, written for Woody Herman (1913–1987).

Scala, La or *Teatro alla Scala* greatest Italian opera house, established in Milan 1778. Many of Italy's finest opera composers have written for La Scala, including Puccini, Verdi, and Donizetti.

scale a sequence of pitches that establishes a key, and in some respects the character of a composition. A scale is defined by its starting note and may be major or minor depending on the order of intervals.

A *diatonic scale* has seven notes, an *octatonic scale* has eight, and a *pentatonic scale* has five. A *chromatic scale* is the full range of 12 notes:

it has no key because there is no fixed starting point. A ***whole-tone scale*** is a six-note scale and is also indeterminate in key: only two are possible.

Scarlatti (Pietro) Alessandro (Gaspare) 1660–1725. Italian Baroque composer. Based in Rome and Naples, he made several important innovations in the development of opera, including the introduction of the ◊da capo aria, which became a regular feature of opera, and use of the orchestral ◊ritornello. He composed more than 100 operas, including *Tigrane* 1715, as well as church music and oratorios.

Scarlatti (Giuseppe) Domenico 1685–1757. Italian composer and harpsichordist. He was the eldest son of *Alessandro Scarlatti* (1660–1725). He lived most of his life in Portugal and Spain in the service of the Queen of Spain. He wrote over 500 sonatas for harpsichord, short pieces in ◊binary form demonstrating the new freedoms of keyboard composition, and inspired by Spanish musical idioms. These works are highly inventive, involving crossing the hands and other technical devices, and experimenting with ◊sonata form. He also wrote masses, cantatas, and concertos.

Scherchen Hermann 1891–1966. German conductor. He collaborated with Schoenberg 1911–12, and in 1919 founded the journal *Melos* to promote contemporary music. He moved to Switzerland 1933, and was active as a conductor and teacher. He wrote two texts, *Handbook of Conducting* and *The Nature of Music*. During the 1950s he founded a music publishing house, Ars Viva Verlag, and an electronic studio at Gravesano.

scherzo (Italian 'joke') a lively piece, usually in rapid triple time (3/4); since Beethoven, often used for the third movement of a symphony, sonata, or quartet as a substitute for the statelier minuet or trio.

Schnabel Artur 1882–1951. Austrian pianist, teacher, and composer. He taught music at the Berlin State Academy 1925–30 before settling in the USA 1939 where, in addition to lecturing, he composed symphonies and piano works. He excelled at playing Beethoven, and published his own edition of Beethoven's 32 sonatas.

schnell German 'fast'.

Schnittke Alfred Garriyevich 1934– . Alternative translation of ◊*Shnitke*.

Schoenberg Arnold (Franz Walter) 1874–1951. Austro-Hungarian composer. After Romantic early works such as *Verklärte*

Nacht/Transfigured Night 1899 his works became harmonically more complex and chromatic until it became impossible to detect the presence of a key, as in *Three Pieces* 1909 for piano. During this atonal ◊expressionist period, highly unpredictable harmonic and rhythmic patterns appeared, as in *Ewartung* 1909. The problem of lack of structure in this music was resolved by Schoenberg's discovery of the ◊twelve-tone system. This technique was further developed by his pupils Alban Berg and Anton Webern.

Driven from Germany by the Nazis, he settled in the USA 1933, where he worked as a teacher. Later works include the unfinished opera *Moses und Aron* 1951.

Schubert Franz (Peter) 1797–1828. Austrian composer. His music is abundant with lyrical and inventive melodies, almost to the point of overshadowing its other merits, including a facility for imaginative modulation and progressive use of ◊cyclic forms. Despite ill-health and death at the age of only 31, his output was prodigious. His nine numbered symphonies include the incomplete Eighth in B minor (the 'Unfinished') 1822 and the Ninth in C major (the 'Great') 1828. He wrote chamber and piano music, including the *Forellenquintett/Trout Quintet* 1819, and over 600 lieder embodying the Romantic expression of emotion with pure melody. They include the cycles *Die schöne Müllerin/The Beautiful Maid of the Mill* 1823 and *Die Winterreise/The Winter Journey* 1827.

Schuman William Howard 1910– . US composer and teacher. His music is melodic, if sometimes tempered by ◊polytonality, and often emphasizes ◊motoric rhythm or other intense rhythms, as in *American Festival Overture* 1939. His large-scale conception suits the orchestral medium, for which he has written nine symphonies. He has also written chamber and vocal works.

Schumann Clara (Josephine) (born Wieck) 1819–1896. German pianist and composer. She married Robert Schumann 1840 (her father had been his piano teacher). During his life and after his death she was devoted to popularizing his work, appearing frequently in European concert halls. Remembered as a first-rate pianist, she was also a composer in her own right. Her compositions include Concerto in A Minor 1836 for piano and orchestra, a Piano Trio *c.*1846, and romances for piano. She also profoundly influenced Brahms and his music.

serenade evening music, traditionally played or sung in the open air (characteristically by a man beneath the window of a woman he is courting); specifically, an instrumental piece in several movements for chamber orchestra or wind instruments, originally conceived as informal evening entertainment, such as Mozart's *Eine kleine Nachtmusik/A Little Night Music*.

serialism a compositional technique in which musical elements are ordered in a row or ◊series. Forms of serialism include most commonly the ◊twelve-tone system, and at its most extreme, ◊integral serialism.

series or ***tone row*** or ***note row*** an order of pitches, or occasionally other musical elements (inluding dynamics and duration). Usually all twelve notes of the ◊chromatic scale are used as a basis for serial composition (see ◊twelve-tone system). The row may be used as a basis for melody or harmony, and in reverse (◊retrograde) and inverted forms as well as in its original order.

The US composer Milton Babbitt introduced a convention of numbering a series as intervals from zero to a maximum of 11 half-steps or semitones, in which zero equals the starting note, in order to simplify the mathematical operations associated with serial composition.

A diatonic row is used by Stravinsky in his *Cantata* 1952 and a thirteen-note row by Stockhausen in *Mantra* for two pianos and electronics 1970.

serpent

Serkin Rudolf 1903–1991. Austrian-born US pianist and teacher. Remembered for the quality and sonority of his energetic interpretations of works by J S Bach and Mozart, Beethoven, Schubert, and Brahms. He founded, with German violinist Adolf Busch (1891–1952), the Marlboro Festival for chamber music in Vermont, and served as its director from 1952 until his death.

serpent a keyed brass instrument of the cornett family originating in the 16th century. It has a distinctive S-shape (resembling a serpent, hence its name) and became popular as a church and military band instrument. It was superseded in the nineteenth century by the ◊ophicleide and tuba, but has seen a revival this century as a result of the ◊authenticity movement.

Sessions Roger (Huntington) 1896–1985. US composer. His international modernist style secured an American platform for serious German infuences, including Hindemith and Schoenberg, and offered an alternative to the lightweight, fashionable Modernism of Darius Milhaud and Alain Paris (1947–   ). An able symphonist, his works include *The Black Maskers* (incidental music) 1923, eight symphonies, and *Concerto for Orchestra* 1971.

seventh an ◊interval of seven diatonic notes. A seventh is an 'imperfect interval' (having 'major' and 'minor' variants). A major seventh consists of eleven semitones (for example, C – B natural). A minor seventh consists of ten semitones (C – B flat).

sextet an ensemble of six musicians, or music written for such a group. Brahms wrote several string sextets.

sextuplet a group of six notes of equal length, played in the time of (usually) four. It is indicated by a ◊slur over the six notes with the number '6' written above.

sforzando *sf* or *sfz* (Italian 'forcing') a sudden accent placed on a single note or chord. Its loudness depends on the surrounding dynamics. For example, if the dynamic marking prior to 'sforzando' is 'piano' (soft), then it is not accented as loudly as if the prior marking were 'forte' (loud).

shake an alternative name for ◊trill, in which two adjacent notes rapidly alternate.

Shankar Ravi 1920–   . Indian composer and musician. A virtuoso of the ◊sitar, he has, through his many recordings and recitals, increased awareness in the West of ◊Indian music. He has also composed two concertos for sitar and orchestra 1971 and 1981, and film music, including scores for Satyajit Ray's *Pather Panchali* 1956 and Richard Attenborough's *Gandhi* 1982, and founded music schools in Bombay and Los Angeles.

sharp a note or a key that is played higher in pitch than the written value, indicated by a flat sign or key signature. It can also refer to inaccurate into-nation by a player.

shawm member of a family of double-reed conical bore musical instru-ments of piercing tone, including the zorna (Turkey), shanai (India), sona (China), and tarogato (Hungary). The Renaissance shawm emerged around 1200 as a ◊consort instrument, the reed enclosed by a ◊windcap. It was a forerunner of the oboe.

Shnitke or *Schnittke* Alfred Garriyevich 1934–   . Russian composer. He has experimented with ◊integral serialism and unusual instrumental textures, which are characteristically rich with a prominent use of strings, often using quotations and parodies. Among his many works are ... *pianis-simo* ... 1969 for orchestra, *Sinfonia* 1972, the oratorio *Nagasaki* (1958), and *Minnesang/Lovesong* 1981 for 48 voices.

Shostakovich Dmitry (Dmitriyevich) 1906–1975. Russian composer. He achieved world fame at the age of 20 with his first symphony, written as a diploma for the St Petersburg Conservatory. His music, though tonal, ranges from dissonant and grotesque to lyrical. After a heart attack in 1969 his music embraced a darker quality. Throughout his work, a strong sense of orchestration and structure prevails. This may explain the widely-held view that he is the 20th-century's finest symphonist. He wrote 15 symphonies, chamber and film music, ballets, and operas, the latter including *Lady Macbeth of Mtsensk* 1934, which was suppressed by the Soviet authorities as 'too divorced from the proletariat', but revived as *Katerina Izmaylova* 1963.

Sibelius Jean (Christian) 1865–1957. Finnish composer. The most famous of Finnish composers, his style is characterized by long phrases built from short themes, which in orchestral works, appear expressively in the strings. Remembered especially for *Finlandia* 1900 and his seven symphonies, Sibelius strove for a musical logic, binding the ◊motives together. He also wrote choral music and a Violin Concerto 1904.

He studied the violin and composition at Helsinki and went on to Berlin and Vienna. In 1940 he abruptly ceased composing and spent the rest of his life as a recluse.

siciliano a dance of the 17th and 18th centuries which originated in Sicily. In a relaxed compound time (6/8 or 12/8), it is closely associated with the ◊pastorale. It appears as a slow movement in Baroque sonatas, for example in those by Bach, Handel, and Corelli.

side drum double-headed drum. See ◊snare drum.

Sills Beverly 1929– . US soprano. Her high-ranging ◊coloratura is allied to a subtle emotional control in French and Italian roles, notably as principal in Donizetti's *Lucia di Lammermoor* and Puccini's *Manon Lescaut*. She sang with touring companies and joined the New York City Opera 1955. In 1979 she became director of New York City Opera and retired from the stage 1980.

simile (Italian 'similar') directing the musician to continue performing a previously notated indication. For example, if the first few bars of a piece are marked ◊staccato (detached) a composer may simply write *simile* rather than continue to mark individual staccato dots.

simple time a metre in which each beat divides into two units. For example, 4/4 consists of four beats, each of two quavers.

Sinding Christian (August) 1856–1941. Norwegian composer. His Romantic-style works, influenced by Liszt and Wagner, include four symphonies, piano pieces (including *Rustle of Spring* from *Six Pieces* 1896), and songs. His brothers Otto (1842–1909) and Stephan (1846–1922) were, respectively, a painter and a sculptor.

sine wave an electronically-generated tone, considered to be 'pure' because of its lack of ◊overtones.

sinfonietta orchestral work that is of a shorter, lighter nature than a ◊symphony, for example Janáček's *Sinfonietta* 1926. It is also the name for a small-scale orchestra specializing in such works, for example the London Sinfonietta.

Singspiel (German 'sing play') term originally applied to all opera, later confined to opera with spoken dialogue rather than ◊recitative (sung narration). Mozart provided the greatest examples with *Die Entführung aus dem Serail/The Abduction from the Seraglio* 1782 and *Die Zauberflöte/The Magic Flute* 1791. During the 19th and 20th centuries *Singspiel* came to imply a comic or light opera of contemporary manners or ordinary life.

sitar Indian stringed instrument, of the lute family. It has a pear-shaped body and long neck supported by an additional gourd resonator. A

principal solo instrument, it has three to
seven strings extending over movable
frets, two concealed strings that provide a
continuous drone, and nine to thirteen
◊sympathetic strings. It is played with a
plectrum, producing a luminous and sup-
ple melody responsive to nuances of
pressure. Since the 1960s the sitar has
become known more widely in the West,
largely due to the work of Ravi Shankar.

sitar

Six, Les (French 'the six') a group of
French composers: Georges Auric, *Louis
Durey* (1888–1979), Arthur Honegger,
Darius, Milhaud Francis Poulenc, and
Germaine Tailleferre (1892–1983).
Formed 1917 the group had Jean Cocteau
(1889–1963) as its spokesman and
adopted Erik Satie as its guru; it was anti-
establishment, reflected contemporary
trends in music, and was dedicated to producing works free from foreign,
especially Wagnerian, influences. The group split up in the early 1920s.

sixteenth note US term for *semiquaver*, a note value 1/16th the duration of a ◊semibreve.

sixth an ◊interval of six diatonic notes. A sixth is an 'imperfect interval'
(having 'major' and 'minor' variants). A major sixth consists of nine
semitones (for example, C – A). A minor sixth consists of eight semitones
(C – A flat).

Skryabin or *Scriabin* Alexander (Nikolayevich) 1872–1915. Russian
composer and pianist. His early works were influenced by Chopin and
Liszt, but he moved towards a more complex and ambiguous harmonic
style, influenced by mystical philosophy, such as his emotional
◊symphonic poem *Prometheus* 1911, and symphonies such as *Divine
Poem* 1903. He wrote many piano works, including sonatas and études.

slur a curved line written above or below a group of notes, indicating that
all the associated notes are to be played or sung ◊legato (smoothly). If

staccato dots appear beneath the slur, then this indicates ◊portato, a form of detached articulation. A slur connecting two notes of the same pitch is called a ◊tie.

Smetana Bedřich 1824–1884. Bohemian composer and pianist. A nationalist, he took part in the Bohemian uprising of 1848. Although musically influenced by the Germanic tradition, his music has a strong Czech flavour, as in, for example, the operas *Prodaná Nevěsta/The Bartered Bride* 1866 and *Dalibor* 1868. Despite becoming deaf 1874, he continued to compose, including the famous symphonic suite *Má Vlast/ My Country* 1880. He conducted the National Theatre of Prague 1866–74.

smorzando (Italian 'dying') getting gradually softer, dying away. It can also imply some ritardando (slowing down).

Smyth Ethel (Mary) 1858–1944. English composer and author. Her studies in Leipzig reflect her musical style. Her works include *Mass in D* 1893 and operas *The Wreckers* 1906 and *The Boatswain's Mate* 1916. In 1911 she was imprisoned as an advocate of women's suffrage.

snare drum

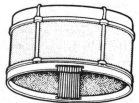

snare drum or *side drum* double-headed drum used in military bands and the orchestra, with skins at both upper and lower ends of the instrument. Cords or wires lying against the underside skin rattle when the upper skin is played, adding definition to each attack.

soft pedal or *una corda pedal* on the piano, the left pedal, which reduces volume. On a grand piano this is achieved by moving the position of the hammers so that fewer strings per note are struck. On an upright piano the hammers are moved closer to the strings.

solfeggio also *sol-fa* a method of teaching music, usually singing, originated by Guido d'Arezzo (*c*.991–?). In *tonic sol-fa*, systematized by *John Curwen* (1816–1880), the notes of a scale are named by syllables 'doh, ray, me, fah, soh, lah, te', in which 'doh' represents the ◊tonic note of the key. In *fixed sol-fa*, 'doh' always represents the note C.

solo (Italian 'alone') a piece or passage written for one performer. Sometimes this implies an accompaniment provided by another player or players; for instance, Bach's solo cello sonatas are written for unaccompanied cello, but his solo violin concertos are written for a single violinist with orchestral accompaniment.

solo organ fourth manual of an organ, characterized by pipes and stops of distinctive tone quality, (resembling individual instruments). Typically, one hand plays a 'solo' on this manual, while the other provides a softer accompaniment on another manual.

Solti Georg 1912– . Hungarian-born British conductor and pianist. He was music director at the Royal Opera House, Covent Garden, London, 1961–71, and became director of the Chicago Symphony Orchestra 1969. He is famous for his recordings of the 19th-century repertory, including Wagner, Strauss, and Mahler. His interpretations are both well-disciplined and passionate.

sonata (Italian 'sounded') essay in instrumental composition for a solo player or a small ensemble and consisting of a single movement or series of movements. The name signifies that the work is not beholden to a text or existing dance form, but is self-sufficient.

   The term originated in the 16th century to designate any music that was played rather than sung. During the 17th century it described compositions in five or more contrasting sections, to be played by an ensemble. The *Baroque sonata* evolved from this form, consisting of 3–6 movements. There were two varieties: the *sonata da camera* (chamber sonata), and a more serious *sonata da chiesa* (church sonata). During the 18th century sonatas were written more often for a solo instrument, especially a keyboard instrument. This was the period in which ◊sonata form developed. In the late 19th and 20th centuries, the term 'sonata' has often been used to describe any substantial solo work, not necessarily one conforming to a particular style or form.

sonata form the structure of a sonata first movement, typically divided into an ◊exposition section (where principal themes are clearly outlined), a ◊development section (reworking of ideas, or introduction of new ones, in another key or keys), and a ◊recapitulation section (repetition of material in the exposition). It also provides the framework for first movements in general, including symphonies, concertos, and string quartets.

It was developed during the 18th century, introducing the possibility of open and continuous development to music previously limited to closed dance routines. It exploits tension caused by moving between the tonic key and other related keys (especially the dominant). During the 19th century, when ◊chromaticism began to obscure these clear relationships, sonata form lost its paramount position as a musical form.

sonatina a small-scale sonata. Although usually light and relatively easy to play, some 20th-century composers such as Ravel and Darius Milhaud have written technically demanding works of this kind. Formally, sonatinas often differ from sonatas in having a reduced development (central) section.

song a setting of words to music for one or more singers, with or without instrumental accompaniment. Songs may be sacred, for example a psalm, motet, or cantata, or secular, for example a folk song or ballad.

In verse song, the text changes in mood while the music remains the same; in ◊lieder and other forms of art song, the music changes in response to the emotional development of the text, for example in the dissonant madrigals of Italian composer Don Carlo Gesualdo and the song cycles of Schubert and Wolf.

song cycle sequence of songs related in poetic and musical material, and sung as a single entity, used by Romantic composers such as Schubert, Schumann, and Wolf.

song form alternative name for ◊ABA form.

sopranino or *piccolo* an instrument of the highest range, above ◊soprano.

soprano female voice of the highest range (approximate range D4–A5); and usually the highest-pitched instrument of a family, for example soprano saxophone, soprano cornet.

Some operatic roles require the extended upper range of a ◊coloratura soprano (extending to approximately F6); Kiri Te Kanawa's voice extends into this range.

soprano clef C clef in which middle C (C4) is represented by the lowest line of a five-line stave.

sordino (Italian 'mute') or *sourdine* a ◊mute, usually of a violin, viola, or cello. In printed music the phrase *con sord* means 'with the mute in place' (on the bridge), while *senza sord* means 'take the mute off'.

sordune Renaissance double-reed musical instrument in tenor or bass register, of folded-back conical bore, an ancestor of the bassoon. The reed is enclosed in a ◊windcap.

sostenuto Italian 'sustained', similar to ◊legato ('tied'). It can also imply a slower speed than the overall tempo marking, similar to ◊ritenuto.

sostenuto pedal the middle pedal on a grand piano with three pedals (many have only two). When depressed while certain keys are held down, it prevents the dampers of those particular keys from returning to the string until the pedal is released. It allows the hands to play other notes while still sustaining the sound of a previous set of notes.

sotto voce (Italian 'under the voice') very soft playing or singing.

soundboard in a string keyboard instrument, the piece of wood over which the strings are stretched, which acts as a resonator, amplifying the sound.

soundbox or *resonator* an enclosed space in which the vibrations of a string are captured and naturally amplified (that is, without electronic amplification). On a member of the string family, it forms the body of the instrument. On a string keyboard instrument the ◊soundboard forms one surface of the soundbox.

sousaphone

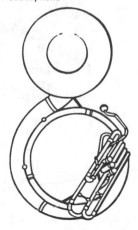

soundpost in a string instrument, a piece of wood inside the body of the instrument which connects the front and back surfaces of the ◊soundbox. It supports the weight of the bridge and helps to distribute vibrations throughout the instrument.

Sousa John Philip 1854–1932. US bandmaster and composer. A writer of marching music, such as 'The Stars and Stripes Forever!' 1897.

sousaphone large bass tuba designed to wrap round the player in a circle and having a forward-facing bell. It was designed by John Sousa, and the first model was made in 1898. Today they are largely fabricated in lightweight fibreglass.

space-time notation a form of ♭graph notation pioneered by US composer Earle Brown in which notes are represented visually by horizontal lines, longer notes receiving relatively longer lines than shorter notes. It involves the performer 'reading time' instead of counting beats, and is useful where musical time is measured chronometrically, as in Stockhausen's instrumental score for the electronic composition *Kontakte/Contacts* 1960.

It originates with piano-roll music, which is cut from an original paper roll representing pitches and durations by pencilled lines (see ♭player piano).

spinet 17th-century laterally tapered domestic keyboard instrument of up to a three-and-a-half octave range, having a plucking action and single strings; it was the precursor of the harpsichord.

spinet

Spohr Ludwig (Louis) 1784–1859. German violinist, composer, and conductor. He travelled throughout Europe as a soloist and leader of orchestras, playing with the London Philharmonic Society 1820. His music reflects his career as a violinist, including 15 violin concertos, chamber music, and 9 symphonies. He was one of the first conductors to use a ◊baton.

sprechgesang (German 'speech-song') a type of vocal technique, a hybrid of pure song and speech. It consists of recitation on approximate pitches, notated usually by cross-shaped symbols instead of usual notes. Although the pitches are approximate, the rhythm tends to be notated by traditional means. It was first introduced in ◊Humperdinck's melodrama *Königskinder* 1897. Schoenberg used it in several works, including *Pierrot Lunaire* 1912, as did Berg in his operas *Wozzeck* 1920 and *Lulu* 1935.

staccato (Italian 'detached') indicating a style of playing or singing music in which every note is shortened from its full value and separately articulated rather than phrased continuously as in legato ('tied').

   The sign for staccato is a dot above or below the note head; for an emphatic staccatissimo ('extremely staccato') the dot is arrow-shaped, while for a more gentle effect, mezzo staccato or ◊portato, a line or slur is drawn over the dot.

staff alternative name for ◊stave.

Stainer John 1840–1901. English organist and composer. He became organist of St Paul's 1872. His religious choral works include *The Crucifixion* 1887, an oratorio, and *The Daughter of Jairus* 1878, a cantata.

Stanford Charles Villiers 1852–1924. Irish-born British composer and teacher. A leading figure in the 19th-century renaissance of British music, his many works include operas such as *Shamus O'Brien* 1896, seven symphonies, chamber music, and church music. Among his pupils were Vaughan Williams, Holst, and Frank Bridge.

Stanley John 1713–1786. English composer and organist. His works, which include organ ◊voluntaries (solos) and concertos for strings, influenced Handel. He succeeded William Boyce as ◊Master of the King's Musick 1779.

stave or *staff* the five-line grid, reading from left to right, on which music is notated. The pitch range of stave notation is indicated by a ◊clef.

Steinway and Sons a company of piano manufacturers founded in New York 1853 by German-born Heinrich Steinweg (later Henry Steinway) (1797–1871). Steinway transformed the 19th-century piano to the modern instrument, introducing 'overstringing' (where the bass strings pass on an angle above some of the higher-pitched strings, thereby enriching the tone quality), larger metal frames that allowed the inclusion of strings of higher tension and better tone quality, and various improvements in the ◊action. Since Russian pianist and composer Anton Rubinstein represented the company in the 1870s, most concert artists have preferred the brilliant tone and superior control of Steinway instruments.

Stern Isaac 1920– . Russian-born US violinist. Both a fine concert soloist and chamber music player, his tone is warm and his style impeccable. He has premiered works by William Schuman and Leonard Bernstein.

stochastic of a compositional procedure based on probability theory, where the work's inner details are left to chance (a random sequence of chosen notes), the main outline having been fixed by the composer. Iannis Xenakis introduced this technique to 20th-century composition, relying on computers to generate specific notes, having written a program determining the overall parameters.

Stockhausen Karlheinz 1928– . German composer. A leading member of the avant-garde, he has continued to explore new musical sounds and compositional techniques since the 1950s. One of the first composers to serialize dynamics and duration as well as pitch (◊integral serialism), he has also used written ◊aleatory music, as in *Klavierstücke XI/Keyboard Piece XI* 1956. He is one of the greatest composers working in the electronic medium. His major works include *Gesang der Jünglinge/Song of the Youths* 1956, which combines a boy's voice (altered electronically) with synthesized sounds, *Kontakte/Contacts* 1960, and *Sirius* 1977. Since 1977 all his works have been part of *LICHT/LIGHT*, a cycle of seven musical ceremonies intended for performance on the evenings of a week. He has completed *Donnerstag/Thursday* 1980, *Samstag/Saturday* 1984, *Montag/Monday* 1988, and *Dienstag/Tuesday* 1992. Earlier works include *Klavierstücke I–XIV/Keyboard Pieces I–XIV* 1953–1985, *Momente* 1964, and *Mikrophonie I* 1964.

Stokowski Leopold 1882–1977. English-born US conductor. An outstanding innovator, he promoted contemporary music with enthusiasm, was an ardent popularist, and introduced changes in orchestral seating. He cooperated with Bell Telephone Laboratories in early stereophonic recording experiments in the mid-1930s, and was a major collaborator with Walt Disney in the programming and development of 'Fantasound' optical surround-sound recording technology for the animated film *Fantasia* 1940.

stop a knob which controls a ◊register on an organ or a manual on some harpsichords, enabling the player to alter the instrument's tone quality in various ways. See also ◊registration.

stopping an action affecting pitch: on a string instrument, the shortening of the vibrating length of the string (raising pitch), by pressing the finger onto the string, bringing the string into contact with the fingerboard; on a horn (especially a valveless natural horn), the alteration of pitch and timbre by blocking the bell to varying degrees, with the hand; in an organ, the blocking of one end of a pipe, lowering pitch by one octave.

Stradivari Antonio (Latin form *Stradivarius*) 1644–1737. Italian stringed-instrumentmaker, generally considered the greatest of all violinmakers. He was born in Cremona and studied there with Niccolò ◊Amati. He produced more than 1,100 instruments from his family workshops, over 600 of which survive. The secret of his skill is said to be in the varnish but is probably a combination of fine proportioning and ageing.

Straus Oscar 1870–1954. Austrian composer. A pupil of Max Bruch, he was chief conductor and composer at the Überbrettl cabaret, becoming a master of light satirical stage pieces. He is remembered for the operetta *The Chocolate Soldier* 1908.

Strauss Johann (Baptist) 1825–1899. Austrian conductor and composer. He was the son of composer *Johann Strauss* (1804–1849) and brother of composer Josef Strauss (1827–1870). In 1872 he gave up conducting and wrote operettas, such as *Die Fledermaus/The Bat* 1874, and numerous waltzes, such as *The Blue Danube* and *Tales from the Vienna Woods*, which gained him the title 'the Waltz King'.

Strauss Richard (Georg) 1864–1949. German composer and conductor. He followed the German Romantic tradition left by Wagner, but had a strongly personal style, characterized by his bold, colourful orchestration. He first wrote ◊symphonic poems such as *Don Juan* 1889, *Till Eulenspiegels lustige Streiche/Till Eulenspiegel's Merry Pranks* 1895, and *Also sprach Zarathustra/Thus Spake Zoroaster* 1896. He then moved on to opera with *Salome* 1905 and *Elektra* 1909, both of which have elements of ◊polytonality. He reverted to a more traditional style with *Der Rosenkavalier/The Knight of the Rose* 1911. He recorded some of his own works as a conductor during the first decade of the 20th century, for example *Tod und Verklärung/Death and Transfiguration* 1889.

Stravinsky Igor 1882–1971. Russian composer. He studied under Rimsky-Korsakov and won international acclaim as composer of the scores for the Diaghilev ballets *The Firebird* 1910, *Petrushka* 1911, and *The Rite of Spring* 1913, though the intense, irregular rhythms and complicated harmonies (sometimes involving ◊polytonality) proved highly controversial at the time. After leaving Russia permanently, Stravinsky turned to 17th- and 18th-century models for his pieces, though always injecting fresh ideas (especially of harmony and rhythm) into his work. His versatile work of this Neo-Classical period ranges from his ballet *Pulcinella* 1920 to the choral-orchestral *Symphony of Psalms* 1930. In the early 1950s Stravinsky began experimenting with ◊serialism, but not always entirely strictly: vestiges of ◊tonality are often present in works of this period, which include *Canticum Sacrum* 1955 and the ballet *Agon* 1957.

stretto (Italian 'drawn together') in a ◊fugue, the imitative entry of the subject in different voices, so that each voice begins before the previous statement of the subject has finished. The result is an intensification, appropriate to the close of a fugue; alternatively, indicating the acceleration or intensification of a passage, such as the end of the last movement of Beethoven's Fifth Symphony.

stringendo (Italian 'tightening') increase in the tension of a passage by intensifying the tempo, in a manner similar to an ◊accelerando ('quickening').

string instrument musical instrument that produces a sound when a stretched string is made to vibrate. Today the strings are made of gut, metal, and Pearlon (a plastic). Types of string instruments include: *bowed* (violin family, viol family); *plucked* (guitar, ukelele, lute, sitar, harp, banjo, lyre); *plucked mechanically* (harpsichord); *struck mechanically* (piano, clavichord); and *hammered* (dulcimer).

string quartet ◊chamber music ensemble consisting of first and second violins, viola, and cello, or music written for such a group. Important composers for the string quartet include Haydn (more than 80 string quartets), Mozart (27), Schubert (20), Beethoven (17), Dvořák (8), and Bartók (6). String-quartet music evolved in the 18th century from the decorative but essentially vocal style of viol music into a vigorously instrumental style exploiting the instruments' full expressive potential. The older hierarchy of solo and accompanying voices also changed to a ◊concertante style offering solo opportunities for each player.

subdominant the fourth note (or degree) of the diatonic scale. For example, F in the C major scale; the chord of the subdominant is a ◊triad built upon the subdominant note.

subito Italian 'sudden'; as in *subito piano* ('suddenly soft') playing softly immediately, without any gradual dynamic change (unlike decrescendo).

subject a principal melody of a work, similar to a ◊theme. The term is used specifically to describe the main musical ideas of a sonata-form movement, as in first and second subjects. It is also used to describe the opening melody of a ◊fugue, which appears in imitation in all the voices. A fugue has only one subject, except in double and triple fugues.

submediant the sixth note (or degree) of the diatonic scale, for example A in the C major scale; the chord of the submediant is a ◊triad built upon the submediant note.

suite in Baroque music, a set of contrasting instrumental pieces based on dance forms, known by their French names as allemande, courante, sarabande, gigue, minuet, gavotte, passepied, bourrée, musette, rigaudon, and so on. The term refers in more recent usage to a concert arrangement of set dance pieces from an extended ballet or stage composition, such as Tchaikovsky's *Nutcracker Suite* 1892. Stravinsky's suite from *The Soldier's Tale* 1920 incorporates a tango, waltz, and ragtime.

supertonic the second note (or degree) of the diatonic scale, for example D in the C major scale; the chord of the supertonic is a ◊triad built upon the supertonic note.

Sullivan Arthur (Seymour) 1842–1900. English composer. He wrote operettas in collaboration with W S Gilbert, including *HMS Pinafore* 1878, *The Pirates of Penzance* 1879, and *The Mikado* 1885. Their partnership broke down 1896. Sullivan also composed serious instrumental, choral, and operatic works – for example, the opera *Ivanhoe* 1890 – which he valued more highly than the operettas.

Other Gilbert and Sullivan operettas include *Patience* (which ridiculed the Aesthetic movement) 1881, *The Yeomen of the Guard* 1888, and *The Gondoliers* 1889.

surbahar Indian bass lute, a relative of the ◊sitar.

suspension a progression of chords in which one note of a chord is tied over to the next chord, while the other voices move to a new harmony, thereby causing ◊dissonance with the tied note. The dissonance is traditionally resolved by the tied note moving a step lower, to a note consonant with the local harmony.

sustaining pedal or *damper pedal* or *loud pedal* on a piano, the pedal on the right which, when depressed, lifts all the dampers. This allows the notes to continue vibrating after the fingers release the keys. In addition to prolonging the tone of notes played by the fingers, it also enriches the tone quality by allowing other strings to vibrate by means of ◊sympathetic resonance. Used sparingly in 18th-century music, in the 19th century the sustaining pedal was used increasingly to create impressionistic effects.

Sutherland Joan 1926–   . Australian soprano. A singer of commanding range and impeccable technique, she made her debut 1952 in England in *The Magic Flute*; later roles included *Lucia di Lammermoor*, Donna Anna in *Don Giovanni*, and Desdemona in *Otello*. She retired from the stage 1990.

Svendsen Johan 1840–1911. Norwegian composer, violinist, and conductor. After a career as a virtuoso violinist, he took up composing. He was a friend of Grieg, who admired his orchestrational technique. His style, though Romantic, shows elements of Norwegian folk music. He wrote two symphonies and other orchestral works, as well as chamber and vocal works. He was the greatest Scandinavian conductor of his period.

Sweelinck Jan 1562–1621. Dutch composer, organist, harpsichordist, and teacher. He was the first composer to write an independent part for the pedal keyboard (pedalboard) in organ works, a technique which reached its peak in J S Bach's organ compositions. He taught many of the next generation's organists of the German school.

swell organ second manual (keyboard) of an organ, characterized by a 'swell' mechanism which can vary the volume given any combination of stops. The swell organ sometimes has the greatest number of stops and pipes, ranging from a wide variety of flues to a selection of reeds.

sympathetic resonance the physical phenomenon whereby a vibrating string can induce another, intitially unmoving, string to vibrate also, without any physical contact. Only strings which are related to others within the ◊harmonic series are subject to sympathetic resonance. For example, a string will cause another, an octave higher, to vibrate by sympathetic resonance because the latter is the first ◊overtone of the former.

sympathetic string a string which is not plucked, bowed, or hit by a hammer, but sounded by means of ◊sympathetic resonance. Instruments employing sympathetic strings in order to enrich the timbre include the viola d'amore and certain pianos.

symphonic poem a term coined by Franz Liszt for his 13 one-movement orchestral works that interpret an idea or a story from literature or history, also used by many other composers. Richard Strauss preferred the title 'tone poem'.

symphony composition for orchestra, traditionally in four separate but often closely related movements. During the 17th and 18th centuries the term had additional meanings: an overture (of usually three contrasting sections) to an opera, or an orchestral piece played between sections of a vocal work, as in Handel's *Messiah* 1742. The symphony as we know it today developed in the 18th century from the Italian ◊overture and dance ◊suite, incorporating ◊sonata form in at least one movement.

Haydn and Mozart established the mature form of the symphony, in four movements, which usually follows the pattern (movement to movement): 1. fast (in ◊sonata form); 2. slow; 3. moderate (◊minuet) or lively

(◊scherzo); 4. fast (often in ◊rondo form or ◊sonata form). Beethoven (who replaced the minuet with the scherzo) expanded the form (with his *Eroica* symphony 1803), which has since been modified and sometimes dramatized as quasi-programme music by Tchaikovsky, Bruckner, Dvořák, Mahler, Sibelius, Vaughan Williams, Walter Piston, Prokofiev, Carl Nielsen, Shostakovich, and Aaron Copland.

syncopation the deliberate upsetting of rhythm by shifting the accent to a beat that is normally unaccented.

synthesizer musical device designed to generate sound or alter existing sounds, usually by electronic means.

Modern electrical synthesizers date from the Telharmonium 1904 of US inventor Thaddeus Cahill, incorporating the tone wheel, a sound generator subsequently used in the ◊Hammond organ. Later synthesizers include the analogue ◊trautonium, ◊ondes Martenot, ◊RCA Mark II Synthesizer, ◊Moog, ◊ARP, and ◊Synthi 100; and digital Fairlight, Synclavier, Roland, Oberheim, and Yamaha keyboards, and the ◊IRCAM 4X series synthesizer.

Synthi 100 computer-controlled analogue synthesizer developed 1972-75 by Peter Zinovieff (1934–) from his successful EMS briefcase synthesizer.

Compositions using the Synthi 100 include Henze's *Tristan* 1973 for piano, orchestra, and tape music and Stockhausen's *Sirius* 1977 for soloists and tape music.

Szymanowski Karol (Maliej) 1882–1937. Polish composer. He is regarded as the father of Polish 20th-century composition, combining modern harmonies in his later works with traditional Polish form and melody. He wrote, most notably, works for piano, violin, orchestral works, and operas. He was director of the Conservatoire in Warsaw from 1926.

T

tabla pair of Indian tuned drums, one cylindrical, one bowl-shaped, played with the fingers and used to accompany other instruments, such as the ♭sitar. They produce a clear, rich sound and are responsible for maintaining the music's *tala* (rhythmic identity).

tabla

tablature an old form of music notation, indicating finger positions on a graph representing fingerboard and strings, and therefore specific only to the instrument to which it applies, for example, the lute, guitar, or ukelele.

Prior to 1700, tablature protected the status of court lutenists, as the notation could not be interpreted by other instruments, but with the introduction of a universal standard ♭notation, for example in the *Parthenia* 1611, a collection of pieces for virginals by Byrd, Bull, and Gibbons, the way was open for amateur instrumentalists to perform music at a level of virtuosity of the professional lutenist.

tacet (Latin 'be silent') score indication signifying that during a complete movement or a specific section of a movement, an instrument is not required to play.

tafelmusik (German 'table music') music for voices or instruments performed around a table, often as relaxation after a meal. A group or society of singers is called a *Liedertafel*. There are examples of it in works by Telemann, and in Strauss' *Der Rosenkavalier* 1911 (played by an offstage band).

tail pin or *end pin* adjustable metal rod protruding from the bottom of a cello or double bass, used to stabilize the instrument on the floor at a height comfortable to the player.

Takemitsu Toru 1930– . Japanese composer. He was mainly self-taught and was initially influenced by Schoenberg, Messiaen, and ◊musique concrète. Like other composers of his generation (such as Ligeti) he is interested in the treatment of texture. His use of the electronic medium is well exemplified in *Relief statique* 1955.

Takt German 'time'; as in *im Takt*, 'in time'. It can also mean 'beat' or 'bar'.

Tallis Thomas c. 1505–1585. English composer. He was a master of ◊counterpoint. His works include *Tallis's Canon* ('Glory to thee my God this night') 1567, the antiphonal *Spem in alium non habui c.*1573 for 40 voices, and a collection of 34 motets, *Cantiones sacrae* 1575 (of which 16 are by Tallis and 18 by Byrd). He was joint organist (with his pupil William Byrd) of the ◊Chapel Royal from 1572. In 1575 Elizabeth I granted Tallis and Byrd the monopoly for printing music paper in England.

tambourine ancient percussion instrument, held by one hand, and shaken or beaten with the other. It is almost unchanged since Roman times, consisting of a shallow drum with a single skin and loosely set jingles in the rim that accentuate the beat.

tambourine

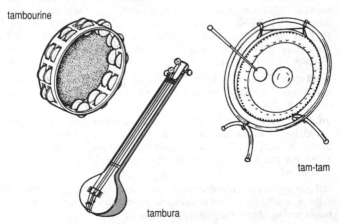

tam-tam

tambura

tambura Indian plucked drone instrument with four strings, tuned by a movable bridge, which provides accompaniment, often for the ◊sitar. The south-Indian version, the *mayuri*, can also be played with a bow.

tam-tam a large gong, originating in China. It has been used in Western music since the 19th century by composers including Puccini, Stravinsky, and Stockhausen.

tango a dance developed in Argentina during the early 20th century. It is in moderately slow duple time (2/4) and employs syncopated rhythms. Similar to the ◊habanera, from which it evolved, the tango consists of two balanced sections, the second usually in the ◊dominant key or the ◊relative minor of the first section. William Walton uses a tango in his suite *Façade* 1926.

tape music music composed onto magnetic tape and reproducible only with the aid of audio equipment. It may include acoustic, concrete (as in ◊*musique concrète*), or synthesized elements. Tape music may be intended to be played by itself or with a live player's accompaniment, as in Stockhausen's Kontakte 1960.

tarantella a southern Italian dance in very fast compound time (6/8). Although commonly believed to be named after the tarantula spider, it is more likely named after the southern Italian town of Taranto. It became popular during the 19th century, several composers writing tarantellas employing a ◊*perpetuum mobile* in order to generate intense energy. Examples include those by Chopin, Liszt, and Weber.

Tartini Giuseppe 1692–1770. Italian composer, violinist, and educator. In 1728 he founded a school of violin playing in Padua. A leading exponent of violin technique, he composed numerous sonatas and concertos for strings, including the celebrated sonata *Devil's Trill c.*1714. He also wrote several treatises, invented a new violin bow, and studied acoustics.

Tate Phyllis (Margaret) 1911–1987. British composer. Her works include *Concerto for Saxophone and Strings* 1944, the opera *The Lodger* 1960, based on the story of Jack the Ripper, and *Serenade to Christmas* 1972 for soprano, chorus, and orchestra.

Tavener John (Kenneth) 1944– . English composer. A writer of austere vocal works including the dramatic cantata *The Whale* 1968 and the opera *Thérèse* 1979. *The Protecting Veil* 1987 for cello and strings alone, became a best-selling classical recording in the early 1990s. Tavener draws on Eastern European idioms and Orthodox Christian traditions; he joined the Russian Orthodox Church 1978 and has composed music for the church. He described his chamber opera *Mary of Egypt* 1991, premiered at Aldeburgh 1992, as a 'moving icon'.

Taverner John 1495–1545. English organist and composer. He wrote masses and motets in polyphonic style, showing great contrapuntal skill, but as a Protestant renounced his art. He was imprisoned 1528 for heresy, and, as an agent of Thomas Cromwell, assisted in the dissolution of the monasteries.

Tchaikovsky Pyotr Il'yich 1840–1893. Russian composer. His strong sense of melody, personal expression (sometimes reflecting his violent mood swings), as well as brilliant orchestration, are clear throughout his works, which are grounded in the Romantic tradition. His music has, to an extent, an affinity with Saint-Saëns and Bizet, and the delicacy of Mozart. He was the first Russian composer to establish a firm reputation with Western audiences. His works include six symphonies, three piano concertos, a violin concerto, operas (for example, *Eugene Onegin* 1879), ballets (for example, *The Nutcracker* 1892), orchestral fantasies (for example, *Romeo and Juliet* 1870), and chamber and vocal music.

Professor of harmony at Moscow 1865, he later met Balakirev. Tchaikovsky was interested in the Russian nationalist movement in music, but did not become as heavily involved in it as some of his contemporaries, such as The ◊Five.

Te Deum a hymn based on the text 'Te Deum laudamus' (Latin 'We praise Thee, O God'), originating possibly in the writings of St Ambrose or Bishop Nicetius of Remesiana. In the Roman Catholic liturgy it is sung at ◊matins on feast days and on Sundays. In addition to its ◊plainsong variant, composers including Palestrina, Handel, and Berlioz have set the 'Te Deum'.

Te Kanawa Kiri 1944–   . New Zealand soprano. Te Kanawa's first major role was that of the Countess in Mozart's *The Marriage of Figaro* at Covent Garden, London, 1971. Her voice combines the purity and intensity of the upper range with an extended lower range of great richness and resonance.

Telemann Georg Philipp 1681–1767. German Baroque composer, organist, and conductor. One of the most prolific composers of all time, his output of concertos for both new and old instruments (including violin, viola da gamba, recorder, flute, oboe, trumpet, horn, and bassoon) represents a methodical and fastidious investigation into the tonal resources and structure of the new Baroque orchestra. Compared to his contemporary J S Bach, Telemann's music more closely approaches the easy charm of the Italian style. His works include 25 operas, 1,800 church cantatas, hundreds of other vocal works, and 600 instrumental works.

temperament a system of tuning ('tempering') the pitches of a mode or scale whereby intervals are lessened or enlarged, away from the 'natural'; in Western music this is done to allow a measure of freedom in changing key. J S Bach composed *The Well-Tempered Clavier* 1742, a sequence of 48 preludes and fugues in every key of the ◊chromatic scale, to demonstrate the superior versatility of tempered tuning.

In *equal temperament* (used today), every semitone is an equal distance apart, in terms of pitch. Other forms, including *mean-tone temperament*, favour the intonation of some keys at the expense of others by minutely increasing or decreasing the distance between certain semitones.

tempo (Italian 'time') the speed at which a piece should sound. Objectively, tempo corresponds to the repetition rate of an underlying beat, as established by the metronome. Subjectively, and in practice, tempo involves a balance of the mechanical beat value against the expressive demands of melody and rhythm.

Tempo indications in Renaissance music may refer to a notional value, for example ◊alla breve (indicating two minim beats in a bar). Classical tempo may indicate a style of movement, such as adagio (leisurely) or moderato (moderately fast); Romantic music tends increasingly towards emotional indications, for example agitato (agitated) or teneramente (tenderly).

Tennstedt Klaus 1926– . German conductor. He was musical director of the London Philharmonic Orchestra 1983–87, and a noted interpreter of Mozart, Beethoven, Bruckner, and Mahler.

tenor the highest range of adult male voice when not using ◊falsetto (approximate range C3–A5). The name is also applied to certain instruments playing at a lower register than the alto instrument of the same family (tenor saxophone, for example).

The tenor is the preferred voice for operatic heroic roles. Exponents include Luciano Pavarotti, Placido Domingo, and José Carreras.

tenor clef C clef in which middle C (C4) is represented by the second highest line of the five-line ♭stave. It was used by musicians and singers until the 18th century, but is now used mainly by instruments which read bass clef, except in their higher registers, such as the cello and bassoon.

tenuto (Italian 'held') holding a note for its full value. In music since the late 18th century, it often also implies that the note should be held beyond its notated value, causing an expressive effect, similar to an ♭agogic accent.

ternary form in musical analysis, a compositional structure in three sections, of which the outer sections form a near-symmetrical pair separated by a contrasting middle section. An example is the ♭minuet and trio; Late 18th-century ♭sonata form is a sophisticated ternary form with an extended middle (♭development) section.

tessitura (Italian 'texture') the average register of a part (high, middle, low) within the total range of the voice or instrument concerned. It is used specifically to refer to the voice and brass instruments before the invention of valves, when players often specialized in high or low tessituras.

thalumeau short thickset double-reed wind instrument, ancestor of the clarinet. It is also the term used to describe the dark lowest register of clarinet tone.

theme a basic melody or musical figure, which often occurs throughout a composition. It may be repeated literally, developed continuously and thereby transformed, or it may occur as a variation.

Theodorakis Mikis 1925–   . Greek composer. He was imprisoned 1967–70 for attempting to overthrow the military regime of Greece.

theorbo bass lute developed around 1500 and incorporating dual sets of strings, a set of freely vibrating bass strings for plucking with the thumb in addition to five to seven ♭courses over a fretted fingerboard. It survived to form part of the Italian Baroque orchestra about 1700.

Its close relative, the ♭chitarrone, has a longer neck.

theremin early electronic musical instrument invented 1920 by *Leon*

Theremin (1896–   ). It has the appearance of a radio and is played by
moving a hand in the vicinity of the aerial. Its sound is voicelike in the
soprano register, and trombonelike at a lower pitch, and it is capable of
producing only one tone at a time.

Edgard Varèse incorporated two theremins in *Ecuatorial* 1933; it has
also featured in film scores such as Bernard Herrmann's music for *The
Day the Earth Stood Still* 1951.

thesis (Greek 'lowering') in musical analysis, term borrowed from
Greek poetry, denoting a stressed beat (◊downbeat), usually in comparison with or reference to an ◊*arsis*, or unstressed beat (upbeat). In German
usage, *arsis* and *thesis* have opposite meanings to the original Greek and
English words.

third an ◊interval of three diatonic notes. A third is an 'imperfect interval'
(having 'major' and 'minor' variants). A major third consists of four semitones (for example, C – E). A minor third consists of three semitones (C –
E flat).

thirty-second note US term for *demisemiquaver*, a note value 1/32nd
the duration of a ◊semibreve.

Thomas Michael Tilson 1944–   . US conductor and pianist. He has been
principal conductor of the London Symphony Orchestra since 1988. An
enthusiastic proponent of 'authentic' restorations of modern repertoire, he
has championed US composers. He has made first recordings of Steve
Reich's *The Desert Music* 1983, the complete symphonies of Charles Ives,
and a reconstruction of George Gershwin's original *Rhapsody in Blue* featuring the composer on piano in a Duo-Art piano roll recording.

His career was launched 1969 when he took over from an unwell
William Steinberg (1899–1979) in the middle of a Boston Symphony
Orchestra Concert, subsequently becoming principal guest conductor for
the orchestra 1969–74.

Thomson Virgil 1896–1989. US composer and critic. He studied in
France with Nadia Boulanger 1921–22 and returned to Paris 1925–40,
where he was influenced by the many contemporary trends, particularly
Satie's philosophy of clarity and irony in music. He is best known for his
opera *Four Saints in Three Acts* 1933 to a libretto by Gertrude Stein
(1874–1946), and the film scores *The Plow That Broke the Plains* 1936

and *Louisiana Story* 1948. His music is notable for a refined absence of expression, his criticism for trenchant matter-of-factness, both at odds with the prevailing US musical culture.

thorough bass an alternative term for ◊*continuo*. 'Thorough' in this case is derived from the old spelling for 'through', meaning the technique is carried out continuously throughout a piece.

tie a ◊slur or curved line connecting two notes of the same pitch (or a group of such notes in a chord), usually over a bar line. It indicates that the second note is not to be reiterated, but played continuously as one long note.

Tilson Thomas Michael 1944– . US conductor. See ◊Thomas, Michael Tilson.

timbre the tone colour, or quality of tone, characteristic of a particular instrument or voice, determined by the balance and strength of harmonics present.

The study of timbre is one of the oldest sciences, dating back to Pythagoras whose experiments with the ◊monochord established the existence of harmonics. Organ design and music from about 1400 enabled different timbres to be compared and new timbres to be synthesized. French scientists Marin Mersenne and Joseph Sauveur investigated the physical and perceptual principles of timbre and Sauveur's *Système général des intervalles de son/General System of Sound Intervals* 1707 influenced Rameau's theory of harmony and provided a rational basis for the distinctively harmonic orientation of French music, for example Messiaen. In 1807 Jean-Baptiste Fourier established the mathematical principles of waveform reconstruction from harmonics of varying amplitudes. Development of the phonautograph by Léon Scott 1854 revealed the characteristic waveforms of voice and instrument timbres. Publication of Helmholtz's *On the Sensations of Tone* 1863 established the science of timbre synthesis, followed by the invention by Thaddeus Cahill of electric-powered sounding staves 1897 allowing the regulation of harmonics above a fundamental tone and thus the transformation of one timbre into another. See also ◊synthesizer.

time an alternative word for ◊metre or ◊tempo.

time signature a numerical sign placed after the clef and key signature indicating the metre of the music. Consisting usually of two numbers, the upper number represents the number of beats in a bar, the lower number the type of beat, expressed as a fraction of a unit (♭semibreve). Hence 3/4 is three crotchet beats to the bar and 6/8 is two beats each of three quavers; alla breve represents 2/2, or two ♭minim beats to a bar; C (common time) represents 4/4, four crotchet beats to a bar.

timpani or *kettledrums* tuned drums derived from medieval nakers (from Arabic *naqqara*), each consisting of a single skin stretched over a bowl resonator that tunes and focuses the sound.

timpani

Originally used in pairs tuned to the ♭tonic and ♭dominant key, their numbers were increased and mechanisms introduced during the 19th century to allow pitch changes during a performance. The modern instrument is tunable by pedal and by the traditional screws around the rim of the drum. A normal symphony orchestra will have up to five timpani (ranging in pitch from about B1 to G3).

Tippett Michael (Kemp) 1905– . English composer. His works include the operas *The Midsummer Marriage* 1952, *The Knot Garden* 1970, and *New Year* 1989; four symphonies; *Songs for Ariel* 1962; and choral music including *The Mask of Time* 1982.

His work ranges from the dissonant and dense to the lyrical and expansive. He first made his name during World War II with his oratorio *A Child of Our Time* 1944, and was briefly imprisoned as a conscientious objector 1943.

toccata (Italian 'touched') a display piece for keyboard instruments, such as the organ. The word 'toccata' refers to the finger technique being emphasized. In the Baroque period it was often a virtuosic prelude preceding a ♭fugue, but the term has also been used by several 20th-century composers to denote a type of orchestral piece, such as the 4th movement of Vaughan Williams's Eighth Symphony 1955.

tonality a sense of key orientation in relation to form, for example the step pattern of a dance as expressed by corresponding changes of direction from a tonic or 'home' key to a related key. Most popular and folk music worldwide recognizes an underlying tonality or reference pitch against which the movement of a melody can be clearly heard. The opposite of tonality is ◊atonality.

tone or *whole tone* US for *note*, an interval consisting of two semitones, for example the interval of C – D.

tone the quality of sound; for instance, different strings of a violin may be able to sound the same note (pitch) given certain fingerings, but each string has a different tone.

tone a ◊plainsong melody.

tone poem an alternative name for ◊symphonic poem.

tone row alternative term for ◊series.

tonguing on a woodwind or brass instrument, the technique used to separate and articulate notes. The flow of wind is interrupted by subtle movements of the tongue, as if pronouncing the letter 't'. In fast passages *double tonguing* ('t-k') or *triple tonguing* ('t-t-k') is possible on certain instruments, especially the flute and brass instruments. *Fluttertonguing*, introduced by Richard Strauss for a trilling effect, consists of an extended rolled 'r'.

tonic the first degree or 'key note' of a scale (for example, the note C in the scale of C major), or the 'home key' in a composition (for example, the chord of C major is the tonic in a composition in the same key).

Tortelier Paul 1914–1990. French cellist. His powerfully intuitive style brought him widespread fame as a soloist from 1947. Romantic in temperament, he specialized in the standard 19th-century repertoire of Elgar, Walton, and Kodály, as well as Bach's solo suites.

From 1956 Tortelier taught at the Paris Conservatoire, where his pupils included English cellist Jacqueline Du Pré.

Toscanini Arturo 1867–1957. Italian conductor. He made his mark in opera as three-times musical director of La Scala, Milan, 1898–1903, 1906–08, and 1921–29, and subsequently as conductor 1937–54 of the NBC (National Broadcasting Company) Symphony Orchestra which was established for him by NBC Radio. His wide-ranging repertoire included

Debussy and Respighi, and he imparted an Italianate simplicity to Mozart and Beethoven when exaggerated solemnity was the trend in Germany.

transcription the arrangement by a composer of a piece by another composer for a different combination of instruments. Liszt and Rachmaninov were famous for their transcriptions for piano, the playing of which required virtuousic skill.

transition a passage connecting two sections of a piece. For example, in a sonata-form movement a transition often connects the first and second subjects (principal melodies). The *retransition* is the transition connecting the development and the recapitulation. Transition is also an alternative name for ◊modulation, especially if the change of keys is abrupt.

transposing instrument musical instrument that sounds at a different pitch from that of the written notes. For example an instrument in B flat such as a clarinet sounds a whole tone lower, one in D sounds a tone higher, while a basset horn or French horn in F sounds a fifth lower than written (all non-transposing instruments such as orchestral strings and piano are considered as being 'in C'.

transposition performance in a different key from that indicated in the printed music, or the appearance of a theme or motif in a different key from that of its first appearance.   A passage of music in which a phrase is repeatedly transposed is a sequence.

trautonium polyphonic keyboard synthesizer invented 1928 by German acoustician Friedrich Trautwein (1888–1956) and subsequently developed by Oskar Sala as the *Mixtur-trautonium*. A Neo-Classical *Concerto for Trautonium and Strings* was composed by Hindemith 1931, and Richard Strauss included the instrument in his *Japanese Festival Music* 1940. The instrument remained popular with Hollywood composers until the 1950s.

treble the highest register of a boy's voice (approximately equivalent in range to the ◊soprano voice of a woman; about F4–C6) or the highest-pitched member of a family of instruments, for example the treble viol; the term is also used to refer to the right hand of a piano piece.

treble clef G clef in which the G above middle C (G4) is represented by the second-lowest line of a five- line stave. Most instruments with a range above middle C use treble clef, including violin, clarinet, trumpet, and piano (right hand).

tremolo a rapidly pulsating tremor on one note or sometimes between two or more notes, created by rapid movement of the bow on a stringed instrument, or a rapid shake of the voice. A buzzing tremolo produced by brass instruments is called *flatterzunge* ('flutter-tongue').

The effect is exploited to picturesque effect in Rimsky-Korsakov's 'Flight of the Bumble-Bee' interlude from the opera *The Legend of Tsar Saltan* 1900.

triad a chord of three notes consisting of a ◊root, ◊third, and ◊fifth. There are four types of triad: major (for example C – E – G), minor (C – E flat – G), augmented (C – E – G sharp), and diminished (C – E flat – G flat).

triangle small percussion instrument consisting of a thin metal bar bent into the shape
of a triangle. Hit by a metal rod, it produces
a tinkling tone of high, indefinite pitch.
Compositions which call for a prominent triangle part include Liszt's Piano Concerto in
E flat 1849 (revised 1853, 1856) and the
third movement of Brahms's Fourth
Symphony 1885.

triangle

trill a rapid oscillation between adjacent notes, also called a *shake*, exploited both for impressionistic effect, as in the opening bars of Bartók's Piano Concerto No 2 1931, or to create dramatic tension and ambiguity, as at end of a solo ◊cadenza in a concerto.

trio in general terms, an ensemble of three instruments; or, an abbreviation of *piano trio*, an ensemble of violin, cello, and piano. Also the name for an interlude between repeats of a ◊minuet or ◊scherzo, for a trio of players.

trio sonata the most important genre of Baroque chamber music, usually written for two violins (or viols) and cello (or bass viol), with a keyboard continuo. At the end of the 17th century it developed into the *sonata da chiesa* and the *sonata da camera* (see ◊sonata). Notable examples include those by Couperin, Handel, Vivaldi, Corelli, and Purcell.

triplet a group of three notes of equal length, played in the time of two. It is indicated by a slur over the three notes with the number '3' written above.

triple time a metre in which the bar may be divided into three beats, as in 3/4 and 9/8.

tritone the interval of both the diminished fifth and augmented fourth, exactly half the octave, and considered in the Middle Ages to be the moral antithesis of the octave's perfect ◊consonance, or *diabolus in musica* (devil in music). Its prominence during the late 19th and early 20th century helped to undermine the remaining foundations of ◊tonality, as in Debussy's *Prélude à l'après-midi d'un faune* 1894.

trombone

trombone brass wind instrument of mainly cylindrical bore, incorporating a movable slide which allows a continuous ◊glissando (slide) in pitch over a span of half an octave. The tenor and bass trombones are staple instruments of the orchestra and brass band, also Dixieland and jazz bands, either separately or as a tenor-bass hybrid in B flat/F.

A descendant of the Renaissance ◊sackbut which flourished about 1400–1700, the Baroque trombone has a shallow cup mouthpiece and modestly flared bell giving a firm, noble tone to which the modern wide bell adds a brassy sheen. The smaller alto trombone, which is heard less often, features in the 'Praeludium' of Alban Berg's *Three Orchestra Pieces* 1915 (revised 1929). The contrabass trombone requires an extension handle to control the slide; valve versions are also found.

troubadour class of poet musicians in Provence and S France in the 12th–13th centuries, which included both nobles and wandering minstrels. The troubadours originated a type of lyric poetry devoted to themes of courtly love and the idealization of women and to glorifying the deeds of their patrons, reflecting the chivalric ideals of the period. Little is known of their music, which was passed down orally.

The troubadour tradition spread to other parts of Europe, including northern France (the trouvères) and Germany (the ◊Minnesingers).

trumpet member of an ancient family of lip-reed instruments existing worldwide in a variety of forms and materials, and forming part of the brass section in a modern orchestra. Its distinguishing features are a generally cylindrical bore and

trumpet

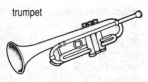

straight or coiled shape, producing a penetrating tone of stable pitch for signalling and ceremonial use. Valve trumpets were introduced around 1820, giving access to the full range of chromatic pitches. The virtuoso repertory of the Baroque period's valveless trumpet could only be played at high pitch, where the harmonics are closer together.

Today's orchestral trumpet is valued for its clearly focused, brilliant tone, and variants of the normal C4 trumpet in current use include the soprano, piccolo (clarino) trumpet, and bass trumpet, an addition suggested by Wagner. In brass bands the B flat soprano instrument is normally used.

tuba any of a family of brass, valved, lip-reed instruments of wide conical bore and deep, mellow tone, introduced around 1830 as bass members of the orchestra brass section and the brass band. The tuba is surprisingly agile and delicate for its size and pitch, qualities exploited by Berlioz, Ravel, and Vaughan Williams.

tuba

The tuba family includes an E flat tenor, B flat baritone (US 'tenor'), E flat bass or bombardon, an orchestral bass in F, and a B flat contrabass. Different shapes of tuba exist, including oval, upright with forward-facing bell, and the circular or helicon ♭sousaphone which wraps around the player. The Wagner tuba is a horn variant.

tubular bells percussion instrument (approximate range C2–F3), consisting of 18 tuned metal tubes of different lengths, which hang in a frame. They are struck at the top end with a rawhide mallet, and the resonance can be muted with a foot-operated damper. They produce bell effects, used both in orchestral works and opera music.

Tuckwell Barry (Emmanuel) 1931– . Australian-born British horn player. He is the greatest virtuoso of his generation, appearing to play technically formidable passages effortlessly. He has appeared both as a soloist and as a member of the Tuckwell Wind Quintet.

tuning the adjusting of pitch in instruments to the correct intonation, in order to avoid dissonance. For example, orchestral instruments tune to ◊concert pitch (A4). Keyboard instruments are more difficult to adjust, often requiring a professional tuner.

tuning fork a device for providing a reference pitch. It is made from hardened metal and consists of parallel bars about 10 cm/3–4 in long joined at one end and terminating in a blunt point. When the fork is struck and the point placed on a wooden surface, a pure tone is heard. It was invented 1711 by the English trumpeter John Shore (*c.* 1662–1752).

There are tuning forks for each musical pitch. A is known as 'concert pitch', since the instruments of the orchestra are tuned to A above middle C.

tutti (Italian 'all') in instrumental works, especially concertos, passages in which the orchestra plays, as opposed to the soloist.

twelve-tone system or *twelve-note system* system of musical composition, a kind of ◊serialism, invented by Arnold Schoenberg about 1921 in which all 12 notes of the chromatic scale must appear before the same note is played again. Such an arrangement is called a ◊series or 'tone row' (also 'note row'). A work using the system consists of restatements of the series, either in its original 'prime' series, or in permutations involving its ◊inversion, ◊retrograde and ◊transposition.

Invention of the method offered composers of ◊atonal music a discipline equivalent to the traditional tonal system, emphasizing skills of ◊counterpoint as an alternative to ◊harmony. The system was adapted in different ways by Schoenberg's pupils Berg and Webern. Twelve-tone composition is restricted in organization to pitch and interval; the later extension of the method to include organized scales of dynamics and durations is called ◊integral serialism.

U

ukelele small four-stringed Hawaiian guitar (patented in Hawaii 1917), of Portuguese origin. An easy instrument to play, its music is written in a form of ◊tablature, showing finger positions on a chart of the fingerboard.

unison of music in which all musicians play or sing the same notes without harmony. Strictly, unison implies that all musicians sound the same pitch in the same octave, but it is also used for the same pitch doubled at the octave.

upbeat or *anucrusis* or *arsis* at the beginning of certain pieces, one or several notes preceding the first full bar of music; also, the last or the weak beat of a bar, analogous to the upstroke of a conductor's hand. The opposite of downbeat.

urtext (German 'original text') an edition of music which tries to capture the original intentions of the composer, minimizing editorial interpretation as much as possible. Urtext editions are usually based upon the composer's sketches and manuscripts, as well as original and early editions of the works.

V

valse French spelling of ◊waltz.

valve a mechanism for diverting the air flow in a brass wind instrument through an extension loop, to vary the length and thus the pitch of the instrument. Most valve instruments are of the piston type, but older French horns have rotary valves operated by levers.

Varèse Edgard 1885–1965. French composer. He left Paris for New York 1916 where he cofounded the New Symphony Orchestra 1919 with the French-born US harpist Carlos Salzédo (1885–1961) to promote modern and pre-classical music. Renouncing the values of tonality, he discovered new resources of musical expression in the percussion sonorities of *Ionisation* 1931, the swooping sound of two ◊theremins in *Hyperprism* 1934, and the combination of taped and live instrumental sounds in *Déserts* 1954.

His *Poème Electronique* 1958, composed for the Brussels World Fair, employed multichannel sound projection in a tent-shaped pavilion designed for Philips by the French architect Le Corbusier (1887–1965) and Greek composer and architect, Iannis Xenakis.

variation a compositional form based on constant repetition of a simple theme, each new version being elaborated or treated in a different manner. The theme is easily recognizable; it may be a popular tune or – as a gesture of respect – the work of a fellow composer; for example, Brahms's *Variations on a Theme by Haydn* 1873, based on a theme known as the 'St Antony Chorale'. The principle of variations has been adopted in larger-scale and orchestral works by modern composers, for example Elgar's *Enigma Variations* 1899.

J S Bach, Mozart, Haydn, and Beethoven in his *Variations for Piano on a Theme of Diabelli* 1823 developed the 18th-century art from brilliant extemporization to compositions of symphonic elaboration. Wagner and Richard Strauss used motivic variation to illustrate character development in opera and ◊symphonic poems, a development carried forward by early film music. In Ravel's hands the theme and variation structure of *La Valse/The Waltz* 1921 is transformed into a symphonic poem on a theme of emotional decline into madness.

Vaughan Williams Ralph 1872–1958. English composer. His style was tonal and often evocative of the English countryside through the use of folk themes. Among his works are the orchestral *Fantasia on a Theme by Thomas Tallis* 1910; the opera *Sir John in Love* 1929, featuring the Elizabethan song Greensleeves; and nine symphonies 1909–58.

He studied at Cambridge, the Royal College of Music, with Max Bruch in Berlin, and Ravel in Paris. His choral poems include *Toward the Unknown Region* (Whitman) 1907 and *On Wenlock Edge* (Housman) 1909, *A Sea*

Symphony 1910, and *A London Symphony* 1914. Later works include *Sinfonia Antartica* 1953, developed from his film score for *Scott of the Antarctic* 1948, and the Ninth Symphony 1958. He also wrote *A Pastoral Symphony* 1922, sacred music for unaccompanied choir, the ballad opera *Hugh the Drover* 1924, and the operatic morality play *The Pilgrim's Progress* 1951. He also studied Renaissance ◊polyphony and compiled the *English Hymnal*, providing many new arrangements of hymns.

Venite music based on the text of *Psalm 95*, '*Venite*, *exultemus Domino* (Latin 'O come let us sing unto the Lord'). It is sung at Anglican ◊matins, either in ◊plainsong or to a composed setting. It is used as a prelude to the psalms.

Verdi Giuseppe (Fortunino Francesco) 1813–1901. Italian composer. One of the 19th century's greatest composers of opera, his traits of immediacy and grandeur remained constant throughout his career. His first major success was in 1842, with the opera *Nabucco*, followed by *Ernani* 1843 and *Rigoletto* 1851. Other works include *Il trovatore/The Troubadour* 1952 and *La traviata/The Woman Gone Astray* 1853, *Aïda* 1870, and the masterpieces of his old age, *Otello* 1886 and *Falstaff* 1893. Throughout his life his technical command grew, as did his conception of the orchestra's importance in relation to the vocal element.

During the mid-1800s, Verdi became a symbol of Italy's fight for independence from Austria, frequently finding himself in conflict with the Austrian authorities, who felt that his operas encouraged Italian nationalism.

verismo (Italian 'realism') referring to opera of 'extravagant realism', particularly Italian late Romantic opera of Leoncavallo, Puccini, and others, which depicts average people honestly, rather than concentrating on mythological events and heroes, as was the case in most opera up until this time.

vespers the seventh Roman Catholic office (or non-Eucharistic service) of the day. It is also used by the Anglican church to refer to ◊evensong. Monteverdi and Mozart have composed notable settings for this service.

vibraphone electrically amplified musical percussion instrument resembling a ◊xylophone but with metal keys. Spinning discs within resonating tubes under each key add a tremulant effect that can be controlled in speed with a foot pedal.

vibrato a rapid fluctuation of pitch for dynamic and expressive effect. It is distinct from a tremolo, which is a fluctuation in intensity of the same note.

On the violin or guitar it is produced by a wrist tremor influencing the finger position on the string; on a clavichord (◊bebung) it arises from a fluctuation of pressure on the key, causing the string to waver in tension and thus in pitch. Wind players achieve a coarse vibrato by finger action on a valve or key, trombones by a shake of the slide. These effects are not approved by orchestral musicians, who employ a chest or throat vibrato which is not a true vibrato but rather a tremolo.

Vibrato has been widespread since the 19th century but, since the rise of the ◊authenticity movement this century, is used more cautiously in 18th-century performance and only rarely in music before 1700.

Vickers Jon(athan Stewart) 1926–   . Canadian tenor. He has sung in all the major opera houses. With a ringing tone, clear enunciation, and deep involvement in his characterizations he has proved outstanding playing lead roles in Wagner's *Tristan und Isolde*, Britten's *Peter Grimes*, and Verdi's *Otello*.

Vienna State Opera greatest Austrian opera house and company, originally known as the Vienna Court Opera. There have been various theatres associated with the company, from the Theater bei der Hofburg 1748 to the most recent theatre, rebuilt in 1955. The company reached its height in the 1890s when Mahler was conductor.

Villa-Lobos Heitor 1887–1959. Brazilian composer and conductor who absorbed Russian and French influences in the 1920s to create Neo-Baroque works in Brazilian style, using native colours and rhythms. His gift for melody is displayed in the 'Chôros' 1929 (serenades) series for various ensembles, and the series of nine *Bachianas Brasileiras* 1945, treated in the manner of Bach. His other works include guitar and piano solos, chamber music, choral works, film scores, operas, and 12 symphonies.

vina Indian plucked string instrument in a variety of forms, including the ◊sitar, combining features of a zither and lute and consisting of a fretted or unfretted fingerboard overlaying dual resonant chambers. It has ◊sympathetic strings, giving a shimmering tone.

viol (from Italian *viola da gamba* (leg viol') member of a family of bowed six-stringed instruments with flat backs and narrow shoulders, which flourished particularly in England about 1540–1700, before its role was taken by members of the violin family. The suffix 'da gamba' distinguished the instrument from violins, played 'da braccio' (on the arm). Viols normally performed in ◊consort (ensemble), the early repertory deriving from sacred and secular vocal music but rapidly expanding to include dance music, ◊fantasias, and other genuinely instrumental forms.

viol

The three principal instruments are the treble, tenor, and bass (the latter known popularly today as the 'viola da gamba'). They are played upright, resting on the player's leg, have frets to aid ◊intonation, and are played without vibrato, producing a transparent, harmonious sound. The smaller instruments are rested against the knees. Tuning is largely in fourths, like a guitar. The double bass viol or *violone*, used in Baroque orchestras as ◊continuo support to the harpsichord or organ, became the model for the present-day ◊double bass. Composers include Byrd, Purcell, and John Jenkins (1592–1678).

viola

Viol-playing has been revived this century, due in large part to the efforts of the ◊Dolmetsch family.

viola bowed, stringed musical instrument, alto member of the ◊violin family. With its dark, vibrant tone it is suitable for music of reflective character, as in Stravinsky's *Elegy* 1944. Its principal function is supportive in string quartets and orchestras.

It plays a leading role in Berlioz's *Harold in Italy* 1834 and concertos by Walton 1929, revised 1961 (first performed by Hindemith), and Bartók 1945 (completed by Tíbor Serly (1901–1978)).

viola d'amore (Italian 'love viol') a member of the ◊viol family, though without frets and not *da gamba* ('of the leg') but played under the chin. More substantial than the modern viola, it has seven bowed strings as well as seven ◊sympathetic strings. It was most popular during the Baroque period, but was used occasionally by 19th-century composers, including Giacomo Meyerbeer and Berlioz. It has been revived in the context of the 20th-century ◊authenticity movement.

violin bowed, four-stringed musical instrument, the smallest and highest pitched (treble) of the ◊violin family. The strings are tuned in fifths (G, D, A, and E), with G as the lowest, tuned below middle C. Designed in the 16th–17th centuries without frets and with a complex body curvature to radiate sound, its voicelike tone and extended range established a new humanistic aesthetic of solo instrumental expression, and together with viol and cello, laid the foundation of the modern orchestra.

violin

Developed gradually during the 16th century from a variety of fiddle types, including the medieval rebec and *lira da braccio*, the violin was perfected in Italy by a group of makers including Nicolò ◊Amati, Antonio ◊Stradivari, and Giuseppe del Gesù ◊Guarneri, working in Cremona around 1670–1710.

Today's violin has not changed in form since that time, but in the late 18th-century aspects of the design were modified to produce a bigger sound and greater projection for the concert hall and to allow for evolving virtuoso expression. These include a lengthened fingerboard, an angled neck, and larger-sized basebar and soundpost.

The repertoire for solo violin exceeds most other instruments. Composers include Vivaldi, Tartini, J S Bach, Mozart, Beethoven, Brahms, Mendelssohn, Paganini, Elgar, Berg, Bartók, and Carter.

violin family family of bowed fretless stringed instruments developed in Italy during the 17th century, which eventually superseded the viols and formed the basis of the modern orchestra. There are three instruments: *violin*, *viola*, and *cello* (or *violoncello*); the double bass is descended from the bass viol (or violone).

violoncello full name of the ♭*cello*, tenor member of the violin family.

virginal a small type of harpsichord dating from the 16th century in which the strings run parallel to the keyboard. In the 16th century the term was used generally to describe any type of harpsichord.

virtuoso a performer of unusual interpretive and technical skill. In Romanticism, the virtuoso was seen as an artist-musician, a visionary and hero; Paganini and Liszt were virtuosos.

Vitry Philippe de 1291–1361. French composer, poet, and theorist. One of the masters of ♭*ars nova*, his works are characterized by contrapuntal intricacy. He wrote four treatises on ars nova and some of his motets survive today.

vivace Italian 'lively'; as in *allegro vivace* ('fast and lively').

Vivaldi Antonio (Lucio) 1678–1741. Italian composer, violinist, and conductor. One of the greatest masters of the Italian Baroque, his reputation spread to his contemporaries (including J S Bach, who transcribed ten of Vivaldi's concertos). He wrote 23 symphonies; 75 sonatas; over 400 concertos, including *Le quattro stagione/The Four Seasons c.* 1725 for violin and orchestra; over 40 operas; and much sacred music.

Born in Venice, he entered the church and was ordained as a priest 1703. He spent much time teaching music at a girl's orphanage in Venice and wrote for them and for himself. He was known as *il prete rosso* (Italian 'the red priest'), because of his red hair. He travelled widely in Europe and was much admired during his lifetime. By the end of his life, however, his music had declined in popularity, and he died in relative obscurity and poverty in Vienna. His work was largely neglected until the mid-19th century.

vocalize a piece for voice without words, sung on one or more vowels, usually 'ah', which is sustainable over the widest range and allows an open tone. Concert works include Ravel's *Vocalise en forme d'habanera*

1907, Rachmaninov's *Vocalise for Soprano and Orchestra* 1912 (revised 1915), Schoenberg's unfinished oratorio *Die Jakobsleiter/Jacob's Ladder* 1922, and Villa-Lobos's *Bachianas Brasileiras No 5* 1945.

voce Italian 'voice'; as in *colla voce* ('with the voice') directing an accompanist to follow carefully a singer's changes of tempo.

voice in human beings, the sound produced by a flow of air passing over the vocal cords, causing them to vibrate. The voice behaves like a ◊free-reed instrument, driven by air in the lungs pressurized by contraction of the diaphragm, and using the vocal folds, flanges of tissue in the larynx, as a flexible valve controlling the escape of air as a series of pulses. The larynx can be relaxed or tensed at will to vary the pitch. The timbre of the voice is created by the resonances of the mouth and nasal cavities.

The art of singing consists largely of training the voice to develop a pure and powerful tone. Formerly, theorists divided the voice into different registers, known as ◊chest voice and ◊head voice, based on what was believed to be the physiological source of voice production. Modern vocal registers are concerned primarily with the vocal range: soprano, mezzo-soprano, contralto (or simply alto) for women; tenor, baritone, bass for men; treble and alto for boys.

voice the independent parts of a contrapuntal work, whether played or sung.

voluntary a generic term for a quasi-improvisatory composition of the 16th century, but more specifically a piece for solo organ played at the beginning or the end of a church service. As the name suggests, the organ voluntary is often free in style, and may be improvised. During the 16th century voluntaries were usually short contrapuntal pieces, without a ◊cantus firmus ('fixed melody'). In the 17th and 18th centuries they developed a more secular style, incorporating elements of the suite, sonata, toccata, and even operatic aria. Composers of voluntaries include Purcell, John Blow, and Samuel Wesley.

von Karajan Herbert 1908–1989. Austrian conductor; see ◊Karajan, Herbert von.

W

Wagner Richard 1813–1883. German composer and conductor. His influence was immense. He was the symbolic leader of composers opposed to the conservative camp of Brahms, which continued to espouse Classical form. He foreshadowed the arrival of atonality with the unresolving 'Tristan chord'. He revolutionized the 19th-century conception of opera, envisaging it as a wholly new art form, called 'music drama', in which musical, poetic, and scenic elements should be unified through such devices as the ♦leitmotiv. His operas include *Tannhäuser* 1845, *Lohengrin* 1850, and *Tristan und Isolde* 1865. In 1872 he founded the Festival Theatre in Bayreuth; his masterpiece *Der Ring des Nibelungen/ The Ring of the Nibelung* 1876, a sequence of four operas (*Das Rheingold/ The Rhinegold* 1869, *Die Walküre/The Valkyrie* 1870, *Siegfried* 1876, and *Götterdämmerung/Twilight of the Gods*), was first performed there 1876. His last work, *Parsifal* 1882, was produced 1882. In addition to his music he was a prolific writer, expressing his philosophy and composing an autobiography.

Wagner's early career was as director of the Magdeburg Theatre, where he unsuccessfully produced his first opera *Das Liebesverbot/Forbidden Love* 1836. He lived in Paris 1839–42 and conducted the Dresden Opera House 1842–48. He fled Germany to escape arrest for his part in the 1848 revolution, but in 1861 he was allowed to return. He won the favour of Ludwig II of Bavaria 1864 and was thus able to set up the Festival Theatre in Bayreuth. The Bayreuth tradition was continued by his wife Cosima (Liszt's daughter, whom he married after her divorce from Hans von ♦Bülow); by his son Siegfried Wagner (1869–1930), a composer of operas such as *Der Bärenhäuter*; and by later descendants.

Walton William (Turner) 1902–1983. English composer. His early influences included jazz, but later his style came to represent a mixture of 19th and 20th century characteristics, with sharp rhythms and often dissonant harmonies, disguising a Romantic face. Among his works are *Façade*

1923, a series of instrumental pieces designed to be played in conjunction with the recitation of surrealist poems by *Edith Sitwell* (1887–1964); the oratorio *Belshazzar's Feast* 1931; and *Variations on a Theme by Hindemith* 1963.

He also composed a viola concerto 1929, two symphonies 1935, a violin concerto 1939, and a sonata for violin and pianoforte 1950.

waltz a dance in moderate triple time (3/4) that developed in Germany and Austria during the late 18th century. The waltz, associated particularly closely with Vienna, has remained popular up to the present day and has inspired composers including Chopin, Brahms, Johann and Richard Strauss, and Ravel.

Warlock Peter. Pen name of Philip Heseltine 1894–1930. English composer and writer. His style was influenced by the music of the Elizabethan age and by that of Delius. His works include the orchestral suite *Capriol* 1926 based on 16th-century dances, and the song cycle *The Curlew* 1922. His works of musical theory and criticism were published under his real name.

Webber Andrew Lloyd 1948–   . English composer of musicals; see ◊Lloyd Webber, Andrew.

Weber Carl Maria Friedrich Ernst von 1786–1826. German composer. He established the German Romantic school of opera with *Der Freischütz/The Marksman* 1821 and *Euryanthe* 1823, freeing it from the Italian tradition by modelling his own German themes on the form of French opera. He greatly influenced later operatic composers, including Wagner. He was ◊kapellmeister (chapel master) at Breslau 1804–06, Prague 1813–16, and Dresden 1816. He died during a visit to London where he produced his opera *Oberon* 1826, written for the Covent Garden theatre.

Webern Anton (Friedrich Wilhelm von) 1883–1945. Austrian composer. He wrote spare, enigmatic miniatures combining a pastoral poetic with severe structural rigour. A Renaissance musical scholar, he became a pupil of Schoenberg, whose ◊twelve-tone system he reinterpreted as abstract design in works such as the *Concerto for Nine Instruments* 1934 and the *Second Cantata* 1943. His constructivist aesthetic influenced the postwar generation of composers using ◊serialism, including Boulez and Stockhausen.

Weill Kurt (Julian) 1900–1950. German composer. He wrote chamber and orchestral music and collaborated with Bertolt Brecht on operas such as *Die Dreigroschenoper/The Threepenny Opera* 1928 and *Aufsteig und Fall der Stadt Mahagonny/The Rise and Fall of the City of Mahagonny* 1930, all attacking social corruption (*Mahagonny* caused a riot at its premiere in Leipzig). He tried to evolve a new form of ◊music theatre, using subjects with a contemporary relevance and the simplest musical means. In 1935 he left Germany for the USA where he wrote a number of successful Broadway scores.

Wellesz Egon (Joseph) 1885–1974. Austrian composer and musicologist. He taught at Vienna University 1913–38, specializing in the history of Byzantine, Renaissance, and modern music. He moved to England 1938 and lectured at Oxford from 1943. His compositions include operas such as *Alkestis* 1924; symphonies, notably the Fifth 1957; ballet music; and a series of string quartets.

Wesley Samuel 1766–1837. English organist and composer. Son of the famous composer of hymns Charles Wesley, he was regarded as the best organist of his day. In 1787 a fall left him with a recurrent illness, ending his career. He wrote many masses, motets, anthems (including *In exitu Israel*), and also secular music.

Wheatstone Charles 1802–1875. English physicist and inventor. Originally an instrumentmaker, he invented the harmonica and the concertina.

whistle any of a class of wind instruments including recorders, flutes, organ pipes, and panpipes, that uses a rigid edge to split the air flow and generate vibrations. Among the most ancient and widespread of musical instruments, whistles produce a relatively pure tone.

Most whistles relying on human breath are soprano or higher in pitch range; those of lower pitch such as organ pipes are usually powered by bellows. Some whistles are of single pitch, others have finger holes to vary the pitch and may be overblown to sound an octave or twelfth higher.

whole note US term for *semibreve*, a note value four times the duration of a crotchet.

whole tone an interval consisting of two semitones, for example the interval of C – D.

whole-tone scale a scale consisting of six whole tones per octave. There are only two possible variants: the scale including the notes C – D – E – F sharp – G sharp – A sharp, and the scale including the notes D flat – E flat – F – G – A – B. In Western music the whole-tone scale became popular with impressionist composers, including Debussy.

Widor Charles Marie 1844–1937. French composer and organist. He created the solo organ symphony, which in effect treats the instrument itself as an orchestra of variously coloured pipes and ◊stops. He wrote ten such symphonies, of which his famous *Toccata c.*1880 is the finale of his Fifth. Influenced to an extent by César Franck, Widor succeeded him as professor at the Paris Conservatoire. Among his other works are operas, ballets, and a treatise on orchestration.

Williams John (Christopher) 1942– . Australian guitarist. After studying with Segovia, he made his formal debut 1958. His extensive repertoire includes contemporary music and jazz; he has recorded the Rodrigo *Concerto de Aranjuez* 1939 three times.

Williamson Malcolm (Benjamin Graham Christopher) 1931– . Australian composer, pianist, and organist. His works include operas such as *Our Man in Havana* 1963, symphonies, and chamber music.

He settled in Britain 1953, and became Master of the Queen's Musick 1975.

windcap a cylindrical cover protecting the double reed of a woodwind instrument, such as the ◊crumhorn or ◊shawm. It keeps the player's lips from making direct contact with the reeds and forms a secure airtight container, ensuring consistency of air pressure and tone. In omitting the windcap, Baroque instruments introduced a new aesthetic of controlled variability of tone for expressive effect.

wind instrument musical instrument that is sounded by the performer's breath, making a column of air vibrate within a vented tubular resonator, sometimes activating a reed or reeds. The pitch of the note is controlled by the length of the column. Major types are of wind instrument are the ◊voice; ◊whistles, including the recorder and flute; ◊reed instruments, including most other woodwinds; ◊brass instruments, including horns; and ◊free-reed instruments such as the mouth organ.

Wittgenstein Paul 1887–1961. Austrian pianist. He was a brother of the philosopher Ludwig Wittgenstein (1889–1951). Despite losing his right arm in World War I he continued a career as a pianist, cultivating a virtuoso left-arm technique. He commissioned Ravel's *Concerto for the Left Hand* 1930, Prokofiev's Concerto No 4 in B Flat 1931, and concert works from Richard Strauss, Benjamin Britten, and others.

Wolf Hugo (Filipp Jakob) 1860–1903. Austrian composer. His outstanding lieder, of which there are more than 250, included the *Mörike-Lieder/Mörike Songs* 1888 and the two-volume *Italienisches Liederbuch/Italian Songbook* 1891, 1896. He brought a new concentration and tragic eloquence to the art of lieder. A subtle interaction between the voice and piano is also involved, the piano acting as more than an accompaniment to the singer. Among his other works are the opera *Der Corregidor/The Magistrate* 1895 and orchestral works, such as *Italian Serenade* 1892.

Wood Haydn 1882–1959. British composer. A violinist, he wrote a violin concerto among other works, and is known for his songs, which include 'Roses of Picardy', associated with World War I.

Wood Henry (Joseph) 1869–1944. English conductor. The London ◊Promenade Concerts (the Proms), of which he was conductor 1895–1944, are now named after him. He promoted a national interest in music and encouraged many young composers.

He studied at the Royal Academy of Music and became an organist and operatic conductor. As a composer he is remembered for the *Fantasia on British Sea Songs* 1905, which ends each Promenade season.

wood chimes musical instrument of the native Tay people of central Vietnam (Nguyen) and now common throughout Vietnam. It consists of differing lengths of hanging bamboo that are struck with a handheld stick.

woodwind musical instrument from which sound is produced by blowing into a tube, causing the air within to vibrate. Woodwind instruments include those, like the flute, originally made of wood but now more commonly of metal. The oboe, bassoon, flute, and clarinet make up the normal woodwind section of an orchestra. The saxophone, made of metal, is an honorary woodwind because it is related to the clarinet.

Woodwind instruments fall into two categories: ***reed instruments***, in which air passes through an aperture controlled by a vibrating flexible reed or pair of reeds; and those ***without a reed*** where air is simply blown into or across a tube. In both cases, different notes are obtained by effectively changing the length of the tube by covering holes along it. Reed instruments include clarinet, oboe, cor anglais, saxophone, and bassoon. In the recorder, flute, and piccolo, the function of a reed is achieved by the design of the mouthpiece.

Xenakis Iannis 1922–   . Romanian-born Greek composer. He studied music in Paris 1947–51 while practising as an engineering draughtsman for French architect Le Corbusier (1887–1965). Compositions such as *Metastaseis/After Change* 1954 for 61 players apply ◊stochastic principles (involving random components generated by computers) to the composition of densely-textured effects. Later works, including a setting of the *Oresteia* 1966 for choir and ensemble, draw on Greek legend.

xylophone musical percussion instrument of African and Indonesian origin, consisting of a series of resonant hardwood bars, each with its own distinct pitch, arranged in sequence and played with hard sticks. It first appeared as an orchestral instrument in Saint-Saëns's *Danse macabre/Dance of Death* 1874, illustrating dancing skeletons.

Since then, it has taken its place in the Western gamelan (percussion orchestra) of keyboard percussion instruments associated with modern French composers, for example Messian's *Oiseaux exotiques/Exotic Birds* 1956.

The 19th-century instrument has a limited range and no resonators, and produces a click tone of high intensity. The modern instrument has a greater range and more focused tone with tubular metal resonators, and can be played with hard or soft sticks. The marimba, a deeper-toned Latin American derivative, has wooden resonators.

Y

Ysaÿe Eugène-Auguste 1858–1931. Belgian violinist, conductor, and composer. One of the greatest and most individual virtuosos of his day, he toured as a soloist and conductor throughout Europe and America. Although he never studied composition formally, he mastered writing in a Romantic style. Today he is remembered especially for his solo violin sonatas and six violin concertos.

Z

Zabaleta Nicanor 1907–   . Spanish harpist. He enlarged the repertoire of original harp music by commissioning new works from, among others, Darius Milhaud and Joaquin Rodrigo, and by reviving interest in Classical harp music of the 15th and 16th centuries in Spain and Portugal.

zarzuela (from La Zarzuela, royal country house where it was first developed) Spanish musical theatre form combining song, dance, and speech. It originated as an amusement for royalty in the 17th century and found an early exponent in the playwright Calderón de la Barca (1600–1681). Often satirical, zarzuela gained renewed popularity in the 20th century with the works of *Frederico Moreno Tórroba* (1891–1982).

Zelenka Jan Dismas 1679–1745. Bohemian composer. He wrote lightweight orchestral works, trio sonatas, and solemn religious works including Magnificats in D 1725 and C 1727. He worked at the court of Dresden and became director of church music 1729. His compositions were rediscovered in the 1970s.

zither member of a family of musical instruments consisting of one or more strings stretched over a resonating frame. Simple stick and board zithers are widespread in Africa; in India the ◊vina represents a developed form of stick zither, while in Indonesia and the Far East versions of the *long zither* prevail. Tuning is by movable bridges and the long zither is played with a plectrum, producing an intense tone of sharp attack.

The modern concert zither, immortalized by Anton Karas in Carol Reed's film *The Third Man* 1949, has up to 45 strings of which five, passing over frets, are plucked with a plectrum for melody while the remainder are plucked with the fingers for harmonic accompaniment.

zither

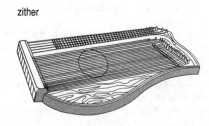

Chronology of Western music

AD 590   St Gregory the Great was elected pope. Under his rule, music attained new heights, initiating Gregorian chant.

1026   The Italian monk Guido d'Arezzo completed his treatise *Micrologus*. He founded modern notation and tonic sol-fa.

1207   Minnesingers (poet-musicians) Walther von der Vogelweide, Tannhauser, and Wolfram von Eschenbach competed in a song contest at Wartburg Castle, later celebrated in Wagner's opera *Die Meistersinger von Nürnberg*.

1240   The earliest known canon, *Sumer is Icumen In*, was composed around this year.

1280   *Carmina Burana*, a collection of students' songs, was compiled in Benediktbuern, Bavaria; Carl Orff was later inspired by their subject matter.

1288   France's greatest troubadour, Adam de la Halle, died in Naples.

1320   *Ars nova*, a tract by Philippe de Vitry, gave its name to a new, more graceful era in music.

1364   The early large-scale masterpiece, *Notre Dame Mass* of Guillaume de Machaut, was performed in Reims to celebrate the coronation of Charles V of France.

1453   John Dunstable, England's first composer of significance, died in London.

1473   The earliest known printed music, the *Collectorium super Magnificat* by Johannes Gerson, was published in Esslingen, near Stuttgart.

1521   Josquin Desprez, the leading musician of his time, died in Condé-sur-Escaut, Burgundy.

1550s   Production of violins began at the workshop of Andrea Amati in Cremona.

1575   Thomas Tallis and William Byrd jointly published their *Cantiones sacrae*, a collection of 34 motets.

1576   Hans Sachs, the most famous of the Meistersinger (mastersinger) poets and composers, died in Nuremberg.

1597   The first opera, *La Dafne* by Jacopo Peri, was staged privately at the Corsi Palazzo in Florence.

1610   Monteverdi's *Vespers* was published in Venice.

1637   The world's first opera house opened in Venice.

1644   Antonio Stradivari was born. More than 600 of his violins, made in Cremona, survived into the 20th century.

1672   The violinist John Banister inaugurated the first season of public concerts in London.

1709   Bartolemmeo Cristofori unveiled the first fortepiano in Florence.

1721   Bach completed his six *Brandenburg Concertos* for Baroque orchestra.

1722   Jean-Philippe Rameau's book *Traité de l'harmonie* was published, founding modern harmonic theory.

1725   Vivaldi's orchestral suite *The Four Seasons* was published in Amsterdam.

1732   Covent Garden Theatre opened in London.

1742   Handel's *Messiah* received its world premiere in Dublin.

1757   Johann Stamitz died in Mannheim, where he had made important contributions to the development of the symphony and raised the status of the orchestra.

1761   Haydn took up liveried service as vice kapellmeister with the aristocratic Esterházy family, to whom he was connected until his death 1809.

1788   Mozart completed his last three symphonies, numbers 39–41, in six weeks.

1798   The *Allgemeine Musikalische Zeitung*, a journal of music criticism, was first published in Leipzig.

1805   Beethoven's 'Eroica' Symphony was first performed; it vastly expanded the horizons of orchestral music.

1815   Schubert's output for this year included two symphonies, two masses, 20 waltzes, and 145 songs.

1816   Maelzel patents the metronome.

1821   Weber's *Der Freischütz/The Marksman* introduced heroic German Romanticism to opera.

1828   The limits of instrumental virtuosity were redefined by violinist Paganini's Vienna debut.

1830   Berlioz's dazzlingly avant-garde and programmatic *Symphonie fantastique* startled Paris concertgoers.

1831   Grand opera was inaugurated with *Robert le diable* by Giacomo Meyerbeer.

1851   Jenny Lind, a singer managed by P T Barnum, earned $176,675 from nine months' concerts in the USA.

1842   The Vienna Philharmonic Orchestra gave its first concerts.

1854   In Weimar, Liszt conducted the premieres of his first symphonic poems.

1855   Like most orchestras around this date, the New York Philharmonic for the first time sat down while playing (cellists were already seated).

1865   Wagner's opera *Tristan and Isolde* scaled new heights of expressiveness using unprecedented chromaticism. Schubert's *Unfinished Symphony* (1822) was premiered in Vienna.

1875   The first of a series of collaborations between Arthur Sullivan and the librettist W S Gilbert, *Trial by Jury*, was given its premiere.

1876   Wagner's *The Ring of the Nibelung* was produced in Bayreuth. Brahms' *First Symphony* was performed in Karlsruhe.

1877   Edison invented the cylindrical tin-foil phonograph.

1883   The Metropolitan Opera House opened in New York with a production of Gounod's *Faust*.

1885   Liszt composed Bagatelle without Tonality (his *Faust Symphony* of 1857 opened with a 12-note row).

1894   Debussy's *Prélude à l'après-midi d'un faune* anticipated 20th-century composition with its unusual harmonic and textural structure.

1895   Henry Wood conducted the first Promenade Concert at the Queen's Hall in London.

1899   Scott Joplin's *Maple Leaf Rag* was published in Sedalia, Missouri.

1902   Caruso recorded ten arias in a hotel room in Milan, the success of which established the popularity of the phonograph. By the time of his death 1921 he had earned $2 million from sales of his recordings.

1908   Saint-Saëns became the first leading composer to write a film score, for *L'Assassinat du duc de Guise*.

1912   Schoenberg's atonal *Pierrot lunaire*, for reciter and chamber ensemble, foreshadowed many similar small-scale quasi-theatrical works.

1913   Stravinsky's ballet *The Rite of Spring* precipitated a riot at its premiere in Paris.

1919   Schoenberg, who was experimenting with serial technique, set up the Society for Private Musical Performances in Vienna, which lasted until 1921.

1922   Alessandro Moreschi, last of the castrati, died in Rome.

1927   Jerome Kern's *Show Boat*, with libretto by Oscar Hammerstein II, laid the foundations of the US musical.

1930   The BBC Symphony Orchestra was founded in London under Sir Adrian Boult.

1937   Arturo Toscanini, one of the greatest conductors in the history of music, began his 17-year association with the NBC Symphony Orchestra.

1938   Prokofiev's score for Eisenstein's *Alexander Nevsky* raised film music to new levels. Big-band music became popular.

1939   Elisabeth Lutyens was one of the first English composers to use 12-note composition in her *Chamber Concerto No 1* for nine instruments.

1940   Walt Disney's *Fantasia* introduced classical music, conducted by Leopold Stokowski, to a worldwide audience of filmgoers.

1941   The 'Proms' moved to the Royal Albert Hall.

1942   In Chicago, John Cage conducted the premiere of his *Imaginary Landscape No 3*, scored for marimbula, gongs, tin cans, buzzers, plucked coil, electric oscillator, and generator.

1954   Stockhausen's *Electronic Studies* for magnetic tape were broadcast in Cologne. Edgard Varèse's *Déserts*, the first work to combine instruments and prerecorded magnetic tape, was performed in Paris.

1955   Pierre Boulez's *Le Marteau sans maître*, for contralto and chamber ensemble, was performed in Baden-Baden. Its formidable serial technique and exotic orchestration was acclaimed by the avant-garde.

1956   The first annual Warsaw Autumn festival of contemporary music was held. This became important for the promotion of Polish composers such as Lutoslawski and Penderecki.

1957   Leonard Bernstein's *West Side Story* was premiered in New York. A computer, programmed at the University of Illinois by

Lejaren Hiller and Leonard Isaacson, composed the *Illiac Suite* for string quartet.

1963 Shostakovich's opera *Lady Macbeth of Mezensk*, earlier banned and condemned in the Soviet newspaper *Pravda* 1936, was produced in a revised version as *Katerina Ismaylova*.

1965 Robert Moog produced a synthesizer that considerably widened the scope of electronic music.

1969 Peter Maxwell Davies' theatre piece *Eight Songs for a Mad King*, for vocalist and six instruments, was premiered under his direction in London by the Pierrot Players, later to become the Fires of London ensemble.

1976 Philip Glass' opera *Einstein on the Beach*, using the repetitive techniques of minimalism, was given its first performance in Paris.

1977 The Institute for Research and Coordination of Acoustics and Music (IRCAM) was founded in Paris under the direction of Pierre Boulez, for visiting composers to make use of advanced electronic equipment.

1983 Messiaen's only opera, *Saint François d'Assise*, was given its first performance in Paris. Lutoslawski's *Third Symphony* was premiered to worldwide acclaim by the Chicago Symphony Orchestra under Georg Solti. Compact discs were launched in the West.

1990 Many record chain stores ceased to stock seven-inch singles, accelerating the decline of vinyl records' share of the market.

1992 DCC (Digital Compact Cassettes) and MiniDisc (MD), two new audio formats, were launched by Philips and Sony, respectively. Classic FM radio station was launched in the UK, to bring classical music to as wide an audience as possible.

1993 A major gap in Haydn's compositions was filled by the discovery in Germany of six missing keyboard sonatas. In the UK, 21 previously unknown keyboard pieces by Purcell were discovered.

Key signatures

Both the major and minor keys are shown in this diagram. The white note represents the major key and the black note the minor.

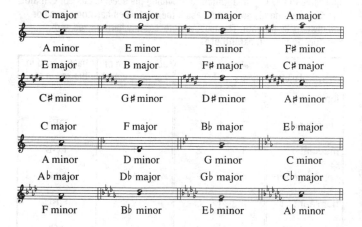

Note names and harmonies

The terms 'tonic ... leading note' may describe either a single note or a
chord. The diagram lists both scale degrees and chord abbreviations
applicable to any key, in addition to providing the specific case of C major.
The roman numerals are upper case if the associated harmony is major
and lower case if minor. The leading note is rarely harmonized and
therefore appears in parentheses.

analytical name	scale degree	note in key of C	abbreviation of harmony chord	basic chord in the key of C
tonic	1	C	I	CEG
supertonic	2	D	ii	DFA
mediant	3	E	iii	EGB
subdominant	4	F	IV	FAC
dominant	5	G	V	GBD
submediant	6	A	vi	ACE
leading note	7	B	(vii)	(BDF)

Notes and rests

name		note	rest
semibreve	(whole note)	𝅝	▬
minim	(half note)	𝅗𝅥	▬
crotchet	(quarter note)	♩	𝄽 or ⌐
quaver	(eighth note)	♪	𝄾
semiquaver	(16th note)	♬	𝄿
demisemiquaver	(32nd note)	♬	𝅀
hemidemisemi-quaver	(64th note)	♬	𝅁

Symbols

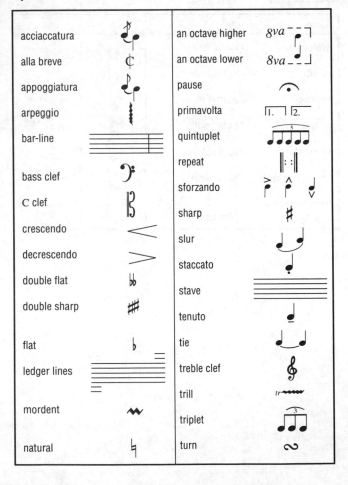

acciaccatura	
alla breve	
appoggiatura	
arpeggio	
bar-line	
bass clef	
C clef	
crescendo	
decrescendo	
double flat	
double sharp	
flat	
ledger lines	
mordent	
natural	
an octave higher	8va
an octave lower	8va
pause	
primavolta	1. 2.
quintuplet	
repeat	
sforzando	
sharp	
slur	
staccato	
stave	
tenuto	
tie	
treble clef	
trill	tr
triplet	
turn	

Time signatures

simple time			number of beats to each bar	compound time		
note-value of each beat				note-value of each beat		
𝅗𝅥	𝅘𝅥	𝅘𝅥𝅮		𝅗𝅥.	𝅘𝅥.	𝅘𝅥𝅮.
$\frac{2}{2}$ or ¢	$\frac{2}{4}$	$\frac{2}{8}$	2	$\frac{6}{4}$	$\frac{6}{8}$	$\frac{6}{16}$
$\frac{3}{2}$	$\frac{3}{4}$	$\frac{3}{8}$	3	$\frac{9}{4}$	$\frac{9}{8}$	$\frac{9}{16}$
$\frac{4}{2}$	$\frac{4}{4}$ or C	$\frac{4}{8}$	4	$\frac{12}{4}$	$\frac{12}{8}$	$\frac{12}{16}$

Orchestra setting

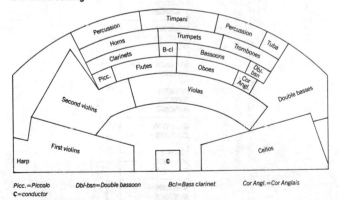

Picc.=Piccolo   Dbl-bsn=Double bassoon   Bcl=Bass clarinet   Cor Angl.=Cor Anglais
C=conductor

Orchestra: Setting most usual today. It is unbalanced — the bass instruments tend to the right, treble instruments to the left.

Pitch-naming system

In this book, pitches are specified using the system A0 to C8. For example, concert tuning pitch is A4, in which 'A' is the name of the note and '4' describes the particular register (in this case the fourth octave from the bottom note of the keyboard).

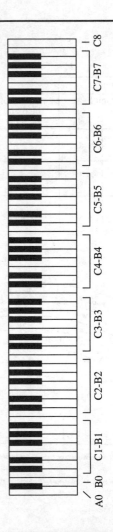